Grammar Practice in Context

English grammar practice exercises

covering the 100 most important

grammar topics and structures

by David Bolton & Noel Goodey

Richmond PUBLISHING

Richmond Publishing
19 Berghem Mews
Blythe Road
London W14 OHN
UK

ISBN: 84-294-4846-2
Depósito legal: M. 19.014-1997
Printed in Spain by Huertas S. A.

Design and layout Mike Cryer, eMC Design
Cover design   La Pot

Illustrations
Philip Bannister, Kathy Baxendale, Greg Becker,
Peter Cornwall, Stephen Dew, Mark Duffin, Richard Duszczak,
Debbie Ryder, Clyde Pearson, Kath Walker

Contents

Quick reference

We use the present simple to talk about:

- habits or regular activities and situations.
  *I usually **get up** at 7.15.   She **likes** white wine.*
- things that are generally or always true.
  *Water **boils** at 100°C.   It **rains** a lot in Wales.*
- In the third person singular affirmative the verb has a final *-s*.
  *The manager arrives first.   He start**s** work before 8.*
- We form the negative with *don't* (*doesn't* in the third person singular).
  *I **don't** smoke.   She **doesn't** smoke.*
  Note that we don't add *-s* to the verb that follows *doesn't*. (NOT She doesn't smokes.)
- We form questions with *Do ...?* (*Does ...?* in the third person singular).
  ***Do** you smoke?   **Does** he smoke?*
  Note that we don't use *Do/Does* to form questions with the verb *be*.
  ***Are you** English?* (NOT Do you be English?)
- Short answers:
  ***Are** you English? - Yes, I **am**.   **Do** you speak English? - Yes, I **do**.*
  ***Do** they live in London? - Yes, they **do**.   **Does** it rain a lot? - Yes, it **does**.*
  ***Does** this radio work? - No, it **doesn't**.*

1 Form true sentences using the verbs in the box.

brush	not read	drink	have (x2)	not wash	go (x2)	get up	live	watch	weigh

Example: *The average British man **sleeps** 8 hours 10 minutes a night.*

1 22% of British families .... to Spain for their holiday.

2 The average British woman .... 62 kilos.

3 British teenagers .... much, but they .... television for over 19 hours a week.

4 The average British teenager .... at 7.20.

5 A typical British man .... a bath twice a week, but he .... his hair each time.

6 British people .... , on average, six cups of tea a day.

7 The average British person .... his or her teeth for only 20 seconds.

8 Over 6 million British families .... a dog.

9 The average British person .... to the dentist twice a year.

10 British women .... , on average, 76 years.

2 Look at the table and complete the sentences, using the verb *speak*.

	English	Spanish	French	German	Arabic
Alain	✓	✓	✓	X	X
Marta	✓	✓	X	X	X
Anna	X	✓	X	X	X
Ahmed	X	X	✓	X	✓

1 Alain .... Spanish.   2 He .... German or Arabic.

3 Marta and Anna .... French or German.   4 But they .... Spanish.

5 Ahmed .... English or Spanish.   6 He .... French and Arabic.

3 Complete the questions and answers using the information in the timetable.

London (Paddington)	08.40	09.15	10.15	10.30	14.15	18.35	20.15
Reading	09.15	09.49	10.51	11.05	14.50	19.10	20.45
Bristol	-	10.06	12.02	-	15.45	-	21.50
Taunton	11.01	-	-	-	-	20.38	-
Exeter	11.27	12.08	13.05	13.20	17.01	21.08	23.15
Plymouth	12.40	13.15	14.08	14.23	18.06	22.18	00.22

1 What time .... the first train leave London? It .... London at ....

2 .... it stop in Bristol? ....

3 What time .... it *alcause* reach Exeter? It ....

4 .... the 09.15 and 10.15 trains both stop at Bristol? ....

5 .... they stop at Taunton? ....

6 .... the 10.30 train stop at Taunton? ....

7 .... the 14.15 train from London stop at Exeter? ....

8 What time .... the last train .... London? It ....

9 What time .... Plymouth? It ....

4 A young man is being interviewed outside a supermarket. Write the questions for his answers.

1 .... married? Yes, I am.

2 How often .... ? I go shopping about twice a week.

3 When .... ? I usually go in the evening, after work.

4 How often .... wife .... shopping? She goes about once a week.

5 How much .... ? I spend about £20.

6 .... about the same? No, she usually spends more.

7 How .... ? I pay by credit card.

8 .... different supermarkets? No, I don't. I always go to this one.

9 .... to this supermarket? No, she doesn't. She goes to one near her office.

Quick reference

We form the present continuous with the present tense of the verb *be + -ing*.

Affirmative	**Negative**	**Questions**
I'm listening	*I'm not listening*	*Am I listening?*
You're listening	*You aren't listening*	*Are you listening?*
He's listening	*He isn't listening*	*Is he listening?* Etc.

We use the present continuous:

- for something that's in progress now, at this moment. *Look! It's raining*.
- for a temporary activity or situation (which may not be in progress at the moment). *I'm going out with a boy called Gary. He's studying engineering at college.*
- for arrangements we've made for the future. *I'm having a party next Saturday.*
- with *always* to complain or express surprise/irritation about something that happens frequently. *She doesn't get on well with her parents. They're always criticising her.*
- BUT some verbs are <u>almost</u> never used in the present continuous. The most common are: *agree, be, believe, belong, care, forget, hate, hear, know, like, love, mean, mind, <u>notice</u>, own, remember, seem, suppose, understand, want, wish.*

    I love you. (NOT I'm loving you.) *What does this word mean?* (NOT What is this word meaning?)

---

1 **Two friends have just met each other in the street. Complete the dialogue.**

JAKE: Hi! *What/you/do* in town? (1) .... ?

ADAM: *I/take* these letters to the post office. Then *I/go* to the bank.

(2) ....

JAKE: *What/you/do* these days? (3) .... ?

ADAM: Well, *I/not/enjoy* my job at the moment. So *I/think of* changing it. *I/apply for* jobs in <u>advertising</u>.

(4) ....

.... What about you?

JAKE: *I/get <u>ready</u>* to go on holiday. (5) ....

ADAM: *You/always/go* on holiday! *Where/you/go* this time?

(6) ....

JAKE: *We/go* to Greece. *Alison/come* with me. *I/really/look forward* to it. (7) ....

ADAM: How long *you/go* for? (8) .... ?

JAKE: *We/not stay* for very long, only a week. (9) ....

ADAM: *What/Alison/do* these days? (10) .... ?

JAKE: She's still at college. *She/train* to be a teacher. (11) ....

ADAM: Well, *it/get* late. (12) .... I'd better go.

JAKE: Yes, me too. Bye!

2 Read this holiday postcard and write in the word that fits each space. Write only *one* word in each space. Use parts of the following verbs:

like sit have (x2) know seem stay be (x2) drink wish play belong

Dear Kate,
We (1) .... here on Skiathos and we´re (2) .... a marvellous time. We´re (3) .... in a villa which (4) .... to a rich British businessman.
    We really (5) .... Greek food. We already (6) .... several good restaurants near the harbour. We (7) .... lucky, because everybody here (8) .... to be able to speak English.
    At the moment I´m (9) .... in a beach taverna on Vromolimnos beach and I (10) .... drinking an iced coffee. Mike´s (11) .... a swim and the children (12) .... playing volleyball.
I (13) .... you were here with us.
Love,
Emma.

3 Put the verbs in brackets into the present continuous where possible.

FATHER: What (1 do) .... in there?

DAUGHTER: I (2 have) .... a bath.

FATHER: I (3 not believe) .... it! It (4 be) .... 7.45, two other people

(5 wait) .... to use the bathroom and you (6 have) .... a bath!

DAUGHTER: OK, I (7 be) .... as quick as I can.

FATHER: But I (8 want) .... to shave. You (9 know) I

(10 hate) .... being late for work.

DAUGHTER: OK, OK. I (11 dry) .... myself now.

FATHER: I (12 not care) .... what you (13 do) .... I just

(14 want) .... you to hurry up!

4 Put the verbs into the present continuous where possible.

Dear Prime Minister,
    I (1 write) .... to you because I (2 become) .... more and more worried about the policies of the present government. I (3 remember) .... the promises you made when you came to power. But what (4 happen) .... now?
Prices (5 go up) ...., unemployment (6 rise) ...., crime (7 get) .... worse and worse and you (8 do) .... nothing about it!
    I (9 know) .... that other countries in Europe have got similar problems and I (10 suppose) .... some things are outside your control. But you (11 say) .... always .... it (12 not be) .... your fault. You .... always (13 make) .... excuses and I particularly (14 hate) .... that. I (15 be) .... tired of hearing excuses. I (16 want) .... action.
Yours sincerely,
Charles Fortescue-Smyth

3 The present continuous OR the present simple? *He's smoking* OR *He smokes*?

Quick reference

We use the present continuous:

- for things that are in progress at the moment of speaking.
  Look! It's raining. Be quiet! The film's starting.
  You aren't listening to me. You're reading the paper.
- for a present activity or situation that may not be in progress at the moment of speaking.
  I'm not happy at work. I'm looking for a new job. He's studying maths at college.
- for future plans or arrangements.ᵃʳʳᵉᵍˡᵒ, ᵈⁱˢᵖᵒˢⁱᶜⁱᵒⁿ
  We're meeting at 8.30 this evening. The President is visiting China next month.

We use the present simple:

- for repeated actions and regular situations. We often use the words *always, often, usually, every week, never*, etc. with the present simple.
  He smokes. They often come late. He sells second-hand cars.
- for general facts and permanent situations.
  The sun rises in the east. They live in London.
- with verbs which describe a state (a situation which stays the same) and not an action.
  The most common verbs are: *believe, belong, contain, exist, forget, hate, hear, know, like, love, mean, need, own, prefer, realise, remember, seem, suppose, understand, want.*
  I want a drink. He doesn't like her. I love you.
- Some verbs (*think, have, be, see, smell, taste*) can describe a state or an action.
  When the verb describes a state, we use the present simple.
  She thinks she's beautiful. This egg is bad. This car has a sun-roof.
  When the verb is an action, we use the present continuous.
  What are you thinking about? You're being very silly. She's having a shower.

---

1 Match the five examples on the left with the various uses of the present simple and the present continuous on the right.

1 I smoke 20 cigarettes a day.

2 Smoking damages your health.

3 I'm smoking a lot nowadays.

4 I'm smoking.

5 I'm giving up smoking next week.

Present continuous

a) Present action

b) Present situation that may not be happening
   at the moment of speaking

c) Future plan/intention

Present simple

d) Facts

e) Habits/repeated actions

1 ....   2 ....   3 ....   4 ....   5 ....

2 **An English teacher in London is talking to her students. Match her questions with their answers.**

1 What are you reading, Adriana?
2 What do you read?

a) Books about ancient history.
b) A book about the Classical period of Greek history.

3 What do you do, Carlos?
4 What are you doing?

a) I'm an engineer.
b) I'm finishing this exercise.

5 Where do you live, Christos?
6 Where are you living?

a) In Athens.
b) With friends in a house in Kensington.

7 Yvette and Helene, what are you talking about?
8 What do you talk about?

a) What we're going to do after the class.
b) Lots of things, but usually boys.

9 Is it raining, Fabio?
10 Does it rain?

a) Only in the wet season.
b) Not at the moment.

11 What do you eat, Maria?
12 What are you eating, Maria?

a) Vegetarian food.
b) Some chocolate.

13 What language are you speaking, Marco and Dieter?
14 What language do you speak?

a) English, of course.
b) I speak Italian and Dieter speaks German.

1	4	7	10	13 ....
2	5	8	11	14 ....
3	6	9	12	

3 **A man is phoning the police. Put the verbs in brackets into the present simple or the present continuous.**

Hello. (1 Be) .... that the police? I (2 ring) .... to complain about the noise which (3 come) .... from the flat above me. They (4 have) .... a party and they (5 play) .... music - very loudly. The man who (6 live) .... there (7 have) .... a party every weekend. And every weekend I (8 ask) .... him to turn the music down but he (9 not take) .... any notice. And they (10 not leave) .... until 2 or 3 in the morning. I (11 not complain) .... very often. But tonight the noise is <u>awful</u> and it (12 keep) .... me <u>awake.</u> Oh good, you (13 send) .... a police car round. Where I (14 live) ....? Oh, 36 Philbeach Gardens, London W8.

4 Answer the questions about the boy in the picture.

a) Write eight sentences about Matthew. Look at the picture and write down four things *he is doing* and four things *he does*. Use these verbs.

wear (x2) watch work play (x2) ride use read listen

Examples: *He´s wearing a T shirt. He watches TV.*

1 ....

2 ....

3 ....

4 ....

5 ....

6 ....

7 ....

8 ....

b) Are the following statements about Matthew true or false?

1 a) He's watching TV.   b) He watches TV.   1 a) ....   b) ....

2 a) He plays tennis.   b) He's playing tennis.   2 a) ....   b) ....

3 a) He's using a   b) He uses a computer.   3 a) ....   b) ....
      computer.

4 a) He rides a   b) He's riding a   4 a) ....   b) ....
      motorbike.   motorbike.

12

5 A boy and a girl are getting to know each other at a party. Match the questions on the left with the answers on the right.

1 What do you do?	a) Yes, I am.
2 What are you studying?	b) I'm from Manchester.
3 What's that you're drinking?	c) I'm a student.
4 Are you enjoying the party?	d) I'm walking.
5 Where do you come from?	e) Yes, OK.
6 Where are you living at the moment?	f) Psychology.
7 How are you getting home?	g) I don't know what it's called.
8 Do you want to dance?	h) In a student hostel.

1 ....   2 ....   3 ....   4 ....   5 ....   6 ....   7 ....   8 ....

6 It is Tessa's first day at work. It is lunch time and Abby, a girl she works with, is telling her about the other people in the dining room. Look carefully at the text. Some of the lines are correct and some have a mistake. If a line is correct, put a tick (✓) after it. If a line has a mistake in it, underline the mistake and write the correction in the brackets.

The girl over there works in the accounts department. At the moment   (1 ....)

she <u>goes</u> out with that boy who's waiting to use the phone. He   (2 ....)

<u>works</u> in the accounts department this week but normally he works   (3 ....)

in the marketing department. The man over there who's putting on   (4 ....)

his jacket is the sales manager. <u>He's travelling</u> a lot so we don't see   (5 ....)

him very often. The woman who <u>sits</u> opposite him is his secretary.   (6 ....)

Some people <u>are thinking</u> they're having an affair but I don't believe   (7 ....)

it. Then there's Emma Harrison, the marketing manager. She <u>stands</u>   (8 ....)

by the door. She <u>start</u> work at 7.30 and doesn't leave till 8.00 in the   (9 ....)

evening. The man at the next table is Neil Wilson. He smokes 60   (10 ....)

cigarettes a day. Apparently, he <u>thinks</u> of giving it up, but I don't think   (11 ....)

he will. He's getting married next month and he <u>has</u> his honeymoon in   (12 ....)

the Seychelles. He's the chief accountant. <u>He's having</u> his own space in   (13 ....)

the car park. <u>He want</u> to become managing director.   (14 ....)

7 a) Write down three things you are doing now and three you are not doing.
b) Then write three things you normally do and three you do not normally do.
Check your answers with a teacher.

Examples: *I'm writing in English. I'm not watching television.*
          I get up at 7.30. I don't go to church.

The present continuous and the present simple with future meaning

Quick reference

- We use the present continuous to talk about things we've already arranged for the future.
  What **are you doing** this evening? - **I'm playing** tennis with Andy at 7.30.
  (NOT What do you do? I play tennis with Andy.) _horario_
  quie, horario _horario o_
- We use the present simple to talk about a timetable, schedule or programme of future events.
  I've got the details from the travel agent. We **check in** at the airport at 7.00. The plane **leaves** at
  8.15, and we **arrive** in Barcelona at 10.30.

1 **The Prime Minister will be in Torquay tomorrow. These are the arrangements that have been made for his visit.**

7.30	Arrival at Torquay station	12.15	Lunch with a local family
8.00	Breakfast with local party officials	14.00	Open the new shopping centre
9.00	Visit to Technicom electronics factory	16.30	Helicopter leaves Imperial Hotel
11.15	Town hall. Meet the mayor		

Complete the questions and answers about the Prime Minister's visit.

1 How/travel/to Torquay? ....

   He ....

2 What/do/at 8.00? ....

   He ....

3 he/do/anything at 9.15? ....

   Yes, he ....

4 Where/he/meet/the mayor? ....

   He ....

5 Who/he/have/lunch with? ....

   He ....

6 he/be/free/at 14.00? ....

   No, he ....

7 How/return to London? ....

   He ....

2 **Match the questions about holiday arrangements on the left with the answers on the right.**

1 Are you going on holiday this summer?   a) I'm renting an apartment near Naples.

2 Where are you going?   b) London Gatwick.

3 How long are you going for?   c) I'm going on my own.

4 Who are you going with?   d) By train.

5 Where are you staying?   e) Alitalia.

6 Where are you flying from?   f) To the south of Italy.

7 Which airline are you flying with?   g) Yes, I am.

8 How are you getting to Gatwick?   h) For two weeks.

1 ....   2 ....   3 ....   4 ....   5 ....   6 ....   7 ....   8 ....

3 **A friend is going to a rock concert on Saturday. You want to know something about it. Complete the second sentence so that it has a similar meaning to the first sentence, using the word(s) in brackets.**

Example: I want to know when the concert starts. (*when?*) *When does the concert start?*

1 I want to know where the concert is. (*where?*) .... the concert?

2 I want to know which bands are playing. (*which?*) .... bands ....?

3 I want to know how much tickets cost. (*how much?*) .... tickets ....?

4 I want to know how you're getting there. (*how?*) .... there?

5 I want to know when the concert finishes. (*what time?*) .... the concert ....?

4 **Put in the correct forms of the verbs. Use either the present continuous or the present simple.**

James Dent (1 go) .... to a football match in London tomorrow. England (2 play) .... Colombia. He (3 go) .... with his friend Richard. They (4 not go) .... by coach because James (5 not like) .... travelling by coach. They (6 go) .... by train. The train (7 leave) .... Bristol at 12.15. It (8 be) .... a fast train and (9 not stop) .... anywhere. It (10 arrive) .... in London at 13.45. James and Richard (11 take) .... enough money with them to buy lunch on the train. The match (12 start) .... at 15.00 and it (13 finish) .... at about 16.45. Their train home (14 leave) .... London at 18.00. They (15 arrive) .... back in Bristol at 19.45.

5 **Write down three things you are doing next week and one you are not doing.**

Examples: *I'm playing tennis on Tuesday.*
          I'm not going out on Friday evening.

Check your answers with a teacher

5 The past simple: *He was late for work. He arrived at 9.15*

Quick reference

- We use the past simple of the verb *be* (*was/were*) to talk about a past situation.
  *It **was** cold yesterday.   The shops **were** closed.*

Affirmative	Negative	Question
He was	*He wasn't*	*Was he?*
They were	*They weren't*	*Were they?*

- We use the past simple of regular and irregular verbs to talk about something that happened and finished at a particular moment in the past, a completed action. We usually say or know *when* the action happened.
  *I **left** school in 1995.   He **died** on Friday.   The programme **started** ten minutes ago.*

- Often we don't say when something happened. It is understood.
  *Amy went to a party yesterday. She **met** Tim, and Rick **was** there too. She **danced** with him all night.*

We also use the past simple to describe:

- something that happened regularly or continually in the past.
  *He **caught** the bus every morning at 8.10.   She **smoked** 20 cigarettes a day.*

- a situation that existed in the past over a period of time, not just at one fixed moment.
  *They **lived** in an old farm house.   She **had** four children.*

- The forms of the past simple:

	Affirmative	Negative	Questions
Regular verbs	*He lived*	*He didn't live*	*Did he live?*
Irregular verbs	*He went*	*He didn't go*	*Did he go?*

Note the short answers. *Did he go? – No he didn't.*

1 Odd records. Complete the sentences with verbs in the past simple. Choose from:

get on   eat   speak   ride   have   sit

1 A Russian woman, Feodor Vassiina (1707-1782) .... 69 children.

2 In 1993 Steve Meltzer of Brooklyn, New York .... 96 sausages in 6 minutes.

3 In 1982-83 Timothy Roy .... in a tree in California for 431 days non-stop.

4 University lecturer Kapila Kumarasinghe .... non-stop about Buddhism for 159 hours.

5 16 people .... the same bicycle and .... it for 50 metres in Tokyo in 1979.

2 Ann Miller went on a business trip to Canada last week. Complete the questions and her answers.

Example: weather/good? Yes   *Was the weather good? Yes, it was.*

1 flight/OK? .... Yes, ...

2 weather/hot? .... No, ...

3 meetings/useful? .... Yes, ...

4 food/good? .... Yes, ...

5 things/expensive? .... No, ...

6 the trip/successful? .... Yes, ...

16

3 Complete this newspaper story with verbs in the past simple. Choose from these verbs:

| not know   lose   ring   steal   make   go   be (x2)   get   understand   say   take   have |

On Tuesday last week Mrs Hilary Fox (1) .... her <u>purse</u> while on a shopping trip.

When she (2) .... home the telephone (3) .... The man at the other end

(4) .... he (5) .... the <u>manager</u> of a local supermarket and he (6) ....

her purse. She immediately (7) .... back to the supermarket. But the manager

(8) .... anything about her purse. But half an hour later she (9) .... the reason -

the same thief who (10) .... her purse (11) .... the phone call. Then, while she

(12) .... at the supermarket, he (13) .... the opportunity <u>to steal</u> everything in

her flat as well as her purse.

4 The mother of a teenage boy is <u>complaining</u> about her son. Complete what she says.

1 He loses a lot of things. Last week he .... his watch and a jacket.

2 He does very little homework. Last night he .... any.

3 He sleeps most of the day. Last Sunday morning he .... till midday.

4 He spends all his money on clothes. Last month he .... over £100.

5 He goes out a lot. Last week he .... out every evening.

6 And he always comes home late. Last Saturday night he .... till 3 a.m.

7 He leaves his room in a terrible mess. Yesterday he .... all his clothes on the floor.

8 He eats a lot. Yesterday he .... a whole loaf of bread when he came home.

5 Rob Howell lived for a year in Spain. Complete the questions for his answers.

1 When .... ? - I went in August.

2 Where .... ? - I lived in Barcelona.

3 .... ? - Yes, I got a job as an English teacher.

4 How .... ? - I found it through a friend.

5 Who .... ? - I taught groups of teenagers.

6 .... ? - No, it wasn't well paid.

6 Read this newspaper story. Look carefully at each line. Some of the lines are correct and some have a mistake. If a line is correct put a tick (✓) after it. If a line has a mistake in it, underline the mistake and write the correction in the brackets.

Carl Harris was in Brixton prison, London. He works in the prison kitchen.   (1 ....)

One morning he saw a chance to escape. A truck full of potatoes come into   (2 ....)

The prison yard. He took half the sacks of potatoes into the kitchen. The   (3 ....)

driver tells him to leave the rest in the truck. Harris then hid among the   (4 ....)

Sacks of potatoes which was still on the truck. The truck then left the prison.   (5 ....)

After half an hour the truck stopped and the driver gets out. Harris now   (6 ....)

thinks it was safe to come out. He couldn't believe it - he wasn't free,   (7 ....)

it is another prison yard! The other sacks of potatoes were for the   (8 ....)

prison in Wandsworth Prison, London!

6

The past continuous OR the past simple?
I was waiting for the bus OR I waited for the bus?

Quick reference

- We use the past continuous to talk about an action that was already in progress at a certain time in the past.

  *At 8.00 yesterday evening I **was having** a drink with a friend.*   *ultimo termino*
  fondo

- We often use the past continuous to describe a situation, to give the <u>background</u> to a scene that happened in the past.

  *I had a terrible morning. It **was raining**. The neighbours **were shouting** at each other. My head **was aching**. The radio **wasn't working**, and I **was feeling** depressed.*

- We use the past continuous to talk about an action or a situation that was in progress. We use the past simple to talk about a *completed* action in the past.

  *I **was doing** the washing-up when the phone **rang**.*

  *I **was doing** the washing-up (past continuous)*
  ....
  The phone
  rang. *(past simple)*

- Some verbs are almost never used in the past continuous. The most common are: *agree, be, believe, belong, care, forget, hate, have (possession), hear, know, like, love, mean, mind, notice, own, remember, seem, suppose, understand, want, wish.*

  *I **knew** the answer.* (NOT I was knowing the answer.)
  *I **didn't understand** him.* (NOT I wasn't understanding him.)

---

1 This is what Matthew did yesterday evening.

7.15 Left home	8.15 Came out of pub
7.25 Got to bus stop	8.25 Arrived at cinema
7.30 Bus came	10.20 Came out of cinema
7.45 Arrived in city centre	10.30 Went into pizza restaurant
7.55 Met Andrea	11.45 Got home
8.00 Went into pub	

What was Matthew doing, or what were Matthew and Andrea doing, at the following times? Choose verbs from the box.

wait (x2)   have   watch   walk   go   eat

Example: *At 7.20 he was walking to the bus-stop.*

1 At 7.27 .... for the bus.

2 At 7.40 he .... by bus to the city centre.

3 At 7.50 he .... for Andrea.

4 At 8.10 they .... a drink in a pub.

5 At 9.00 they .... a film.

6 At 10.40 they .... a pizza.

2 Sam had a party last night. His parents arrived home in the middle of the party. Describe what they found. Put in the correct form of the verbs.

There (1 be) .... a lot of noise. Sam and his friends (2 play) .... very loud

music. A lot of people (3 dance) .... Some people (4 not listen) ....

to the music. They (5 be) .... in the kitchen. They (6 eat) .... chips and ice

cream. One girl (7 lie) .... on the piano. A boy (8 be) .... asleep on the

sofa. He (9 not wear) .... his shirt, and he (10 have) .... a rose

between his teeth. The dog (11 hide) .... under the stairs.

3 Justin is telling a friend how he met his wife. Read the text carefully. Some of the lines are correct, and some have a mistake in them. If a line is correct, put a tick (✓) after it. If a line has a mistake in it, underline the mistake and write the correction in the brackets.

Example: 1 I <u>lived</u> in Paris when I first met her. (*was living*)

2 She was working at the Louvre and she was having a flat by the river.   (.....................................)

3 We were meeting at a café where we were sitting at separate tables.   (.....................................)

4 It was a beautiful spring day, and the sun shone.   (.....................................)

5 I went to the toilet when I bumped into her table and spilt her drink.   (.....................................)

6 I apologised to her and bought her another drink.   (.....................................)

7 While I was having my coffee, she came over and sat at my table.   (.....................................)

8 While we were talking, the waiter was coming with our bill.   (.....................................)

9 But we didn't see him because we looked lovingly at each other.   (.....................................)

4 Describe a series of events that happened to you recently. Use your imagination, if necessary. Use the past simple and the past continuous.

Example: *When I **got up**, it **was raining**. While I **was getting** dressed, the phone **rang**. While I **was talking** on the phone, the toast **caught fire.** Etc.*

Check your answers with a teacher

Quick reference

- The present perfect connects the past and the present. It refers to a past action, but we're more interested in the *present* results or effects of the past action.

  *I've **lost** my keys.* (I haven't got my keys now.)

  *The rain **has stopped**.* (It isn't raining now.)

- We form the present perfect with forms of the verb *have* + a past participle.

Affirmative	Negative	Questions
I've (I have) started	*I haven't started*	*Have I started?*
You've started	*You haven't started*	*Have you started?*
He's (He has) started	*He hasn't started*	*Has he started?*
She's started	*She hasn't started*	*Has she started?*
It's started	*It hasn't started*	*Has it started?*
We've started	*We haven't started*	*Have we started?*
You've started	*You haven't started*	*Have you started?*
They've started	*They haven't started*	*Have they started?*

Short answers

Have you started? – Yes, I have./No, I haven't.

Has the rain stopped? – Yes, it has./No, it hasn't.

1 **Helen's husband has left her. She is talking on the phone to a friend, Kate. Read the dialogue and decide which answer, A, B, or C best fits each space.**

KATE: What's the matter? What (1) ....

HELEN: John (2) .... me.

KATE: Where (3) ....?

HELEN: I don't know. He (4) .... an address or a telephone number. I (5) .... his office but they (6) .... from him so maybe he (7) .... his job.

KATE: (8) .... a note?

HELEN: No, he (9) ....

KATE: What (10) .... with him?

HELEN: He (11) .... much. Just a few clothes.

KATE: (12) .... the police?

HELEN: No, I (13) .... . I don't want to find him. I (14) .... enough of him!

1	A 's happened?	B happens?	C did happen?
2	A left	B 's left	C leaves
3	A did he go?	B has he go?	C has he gone?
4	A hasn't left	B haven't left	C hasn't leave
5	A 've ring	B 've rung	C 've rang
6	A not have heard	B haven't heard	C haven't hear
7	A 's lost	B 've lost	C 's lose
8	A Have he left	B Has he left	C He has left
9	A hasn't leave	B hasn't left	C hasn't
10	A he has taken	B 's he take	C 's he taken
11	A hasn't taken	B not has taken	C hasn't take
12	A Have you phoned	B You have phoned	C Has you phoned
13	A haven't phoned	B haven't	C not have
14	A 've have	B 's had	C 've had

2 Look at the picture and write sentences about what the student has or has not done, using the verbs and nouns in the box.

		do	have	clean	empty	forget	switch off	break
glass	breakfast	keys	the washing up	shoes	the lights	waste paper basket

1 .... 2 ....

3 .... 4 ....

5 .... 6 ....

7 ....

invitado huesped de hotel

3 A number of hotel guests are talking to a receptionist. Write the correct form of the verbs in brackets, using the present perfect. Then match the sentences on the left with those on the right.

1 I (lose) my umbrella. .... a) Can I have some more?

2 I (use) all the shampoo in my room. .... b) but I only want to stay for two.

3 I (leave) my key in my room, ... c) Have they been handed in?

4 I (put) my glasses down somewhere. .... d) Can you lend me one?

5 I (pay) for three nights, ... e) but it hasn't come.

6 I (forget) my room number. .... f) Can you tell me what it is?

7 I (have) a headache all day. .... g) so now I can't get in.

8 I (ring) for a taxi, ... h) Have you got an aspirin?

9 I (find) this key, ... i) Can you call a doctor?

10 I think I (break) my leg. .... j) and it doesn't belong to me.

1 .... 2 .... 3 .... 4 .... 5 .... 6 .... 7 .... 8 .... 9 .... 10 ....

4 a) Imagine you are feeling unhappy. Write three sentences with the present perfect explaining why.

Example: *I'm feeling unhappy because I've lost my job.*

b) Then imagine you are feeling happy and explain why.

Check your sentences with a teacher.

Quick reference

- The present perfect connects the past and the present. We use it to talk about what has or hasn't happened in the period up to this moment.
  *I'm painting the flat at the moment. I've **done** the kitchen and the living room, but I **haven't finished** the bedroom.*

- We use *already* to emphasise that the action has happened *before* the moment of speaking.
  *Why don't you phone Dave? - I've **already** phoned him.*

- We use *yet* in questions and negative sentences to say that something hasn't happened up to now, but that we expect it to happen some time in the future. We usually put *yet* at the end of the sentence. *Has the train left **yet**? - No, it hasn't left **yet**.*

- We often use *just* (= a very short time ago) with the present perfect. It goes in mid-position, between *have/has* and the main verb.
  *Why are you so happy? - I've **just** passed my driving test.*

- We often use *ever* with the present perfect to ask if something has happened at any time up to the present. *Ever* and *never* go in mid-position.
  *Have you **ever** won the lottery? - No, I've **never** won a penny.*

- We often use *before* (= before now) with the present perfect. We usually put it at the end of the sentence. *I'm sure I've heard that song **before**.*

- We sometimes use *never* and *before* in the same sentence.
  *I've **never** eaten caviar **before**.*

α **1** The Trent family are very happy today. Some exciting things have happened.
Look at the pictures and make sentences, using *just* and these verbs: **buy, start, pass, win.**

2 Beth ....
.... all her exams.

1 They ....
....
in the National Lottery.

3 Gillian Trent ....
.... new job.

4 George Trent ....
.... new car.

2 Harry's mother will not let him go out this evening until he has done certain things. So far he has done the washing up, he has made his bed, he has finished his homework and he has had a bath. But he has not tidied his room, he has not fed the dog, he has not shaved and he has not found his front door key. His mother is talking to him. Write Harry's replies, using *already* and *yet*.

1 Before you go out, you must make your bed. - I ....

2 Is your room tidy? - No, I ....

3 You must do the washing up. - I ....

4 And you must finish your homework. - I ....

5 I want you to have a bath. - I ....

6 And what about the dog? - I ....

7 And you need a shave too. - I know. I ....

8 Have you got your front door key? - No, I ....

3 Jessica Dale is having an interview for a new job with a travel company. Write the interviewer's questions, using *ever*.

1 .... abroad?
    Yes, I've been to Spain, Italy, the USA and Australia.

2 .... for a travel company?
    No, but I've worked as a tourist guide in London.

3 .... German or Spanish?
    I've never learnt German, but I learnt Spanish at school.

4 .... seriously ill?
    No, I've never been ill for more than a week.

5 .... a computer?
    Yes, I use a computer all the time at home.

4 Complete the text, using *already, yet, just, ever, never, before*.

Ryan Briggs is very excited. He's (1) .... met a beautiful girl called Lauren. She was at the

party he went to last night. He's (2) .... had a girlfriend (3) .... Girls

(4) .... seem to be interested in him. At the party Lauren asked him 'Have you

(5) .... been out with a girl (6) .... ?' Ryan told her a lie and said, 'Yes, but I've

(7) .... been out with a girl like you.' He's (8) .... phoned her three times today,

but he hasn't been able to contact her (9) .... So he's (10) .... driven round to

her house. Lauren has (11) .... seen him arrive. She's (12) .... decided she

doesn't want to see him, but she hasn't decided how to tell him (13) ....

5 **What things in your life have you not done? (But you hope to do them in the future.) Write three sentences, using *yet*.**
Example: *I haven't been to the USA yet.*
What things in your life have you never done? Write three sentences.
Example: *I've never ridden a motorbike.*
What things in your life do you not want to do because you have done them once? Write three sentences, using *already*.
Example: *I've already been to Eurodisney.*

Check your answers with a teacher.

9 The present perfect (other uses)

Quick reference

- We often use the present perfect with *today, this morning, this week, this year*, etc. when these periods aren't completed at the moment of speaking.
  I've done a lot of work today. (It's still today.)
  He's written two books this year. (This year hasn't finished.)
- We use the present perfect, NOT the past simple, after *It's the first (second/third, etc.) time* and often after superlatives.
  It's the first time they've met.
  It's the most frightening experience I've had.
- *Gone to* and *been to* don't mean the same.
  He's gone to New York. = He's there now.
  He's been to New York. = He isn't there now, but he went there in the past.

1 This is this morning's TV news. Complete the headlines.

Example: This morning the Prime Minister (go) to a UN conference in Geneva.
    *This morning the Prime Minister **has gone** to a UN conference in Geneva.*

1 A cholera epidemic (break out) .... in central Africa. This week over 5,000
  people (die) ....

2 Police (arrest) .... two big international drug dealers in Edinburgh this morning.

3 The Daily Star (apologise) .... this morning to the Queen for publishing two of
  her private letters. And the Sun newspaper (report) .... that Princess Diana
  (wear) .... the same dress three times this month!

4 This year Britain (have) .... its lowest rainfall for over 100 years.

5 Manchester United (lose) .... their first four matches this season and fans
  (tell) .... the manager he must go.

2 Natalia is an Italian student at an English language school in England. She has been there for a month. She is writing to an American friend she met last summer. Complete the sentences with the right form of the verb.

I (1 not write) .... to you this year - I'm sorry. This summer I (2 be) .... very, very busy and I (3 be) .... in England for a month now. I (4 have) .... a lot of English lessons and I (5 learn) .... a lot of English. I (6 make) .... a lot of good friends at the school and I (7 meet) .... some very nice English boys. They (8 teach) .... me a lot of slang - and swear words!

  I (9 run out of) .... money twice this month - I (10 spend) .... over £500. England's expensive! I (11 buy) .... a lot of clothes and I (12 eat) .... in a lot of expensive restaurants. But I (13 not see) .... the inside of a church once this month. My mother will think I (14 become) .... an atheist!

This week I (15 not feel) .... well so I (16 see) .... the doctor a couple of times and today I (17 stay) .... in bed. This (18 give) .... me the chance to finish this letter to you. I (19 start) .... it twice this week. Now, at last, I (20 finish) .... it!

Love, Natalia

3 **Lisa is a Swedish girl, Ben is an English boy. Lisa is driving Ben's car. Read the dialogue and decide which answer, A, B, or C best fits each space.**

BEN: Why are you nervous?

LISA: Because it's the first time (1) .... on the left.

BEN: Is this your first time in England?

LISA: No it's the second time (2) .... here.

BEN: Are you enjoying it?

LISA: Yes it's the best holiday (3) ....

BEN: How do you like the weather? It's the driest summer (4) .... this century.

LISA: It's just beautiful. Today's the hottest day (5) .... in this country.

BEN: Any problems with England?

LISA: Yes, the food. It's the worst (6) ....

BEN: Hey! Slow down. You're doing 95 mph!

LISA: 95! That's the fastest (7) ....

1	A I've driven	B I've drive	C I drive
2	A I'm	B I've been	C I was
3	A I have	B I had ever	C I've ever had
4	A we've had	B we had	C we have
5	A I know	B I've known	C I knew
6	A I've ever eaten	B I've ever eat	C I've ever ate
7	A I ever drive	B I ever drove	C I've ever driven

4 **Paul Wilson wants to speak to somebody who knows about marketing in Spain. Complete the dialogue with *have gone to/has gone to* or *have been to/has been to*.**

PAUL WILSON: Hello. Can I speak to Mr Wainwright please?

RECEPTIONIST: Mr Wainwright isn't here I'm afraid. He (1) .... a conference in Barcelona. But Miss Philips is here. She (2) .... to Spain a few times. I'll try to connect you. No, I'm sorry. Miss Philips (3) .... lunch.

PAUL WILSON: Could you put me through to someone else who (4) .... Spain?

RECEPTIONIST: No, I'm sorry. The only other people who could help you (5) .... a meeting at our head office.

5 **Write down four things you have done so far this year and two you have not done.**

Example: *I've bought a new car.*
I haven't had a holiday.

Check your answers with a teacher.

Quick reference

● We use the present perfect to talk about the present results or effects of a past action or situation. The effect or the result of the action or situation isn't finished at the time of speaking. *What's the matter? - I've hurt my leg.* (His leg's hurting now.)

● We use the past simple if the action or situation took place at a particular time in the past, which is now finished. We use the past simple (not the present perfect) after *When ...?*
When did you hurt your leg? - I hurt it yesterday during a basketball match.

---

1 This is a questionnaire to find out how healthy you are. Match the questions on the left with the answers on the right.

1 What serious illnesses have you had?
2 Have you ever smoked?
3 Have you ever taken illegal drugs?
4 How many times did you go to the doctor's last year?
5 How many times have you been to the doctor's this year?
6 When did you last go to the doctor's?
7 How much alcohol have you had today?
8 How much alcohol did you drink yesterday?
9 How many times did you eat fried food last week?
10 How many hours' exercise have you taken this week?

a) Once. I had some chips on Friday.
b) I drank two glasses of wine.
c) I went three weeks ago.
d) I haven't had any today.
e) About two. I played squash yesterday.
f) I had glandular fever when I was eight.
g) Yes, but I've stopped now.
h) No, I've never taken drugs.
i) I went two or three times.
j) I've been twice.

1 .... 2 .... 3 .... 4 .... 5 .... 6 .... 7 .... 8 .... 9 .... 10 ....

2 Adam is asking Anna about a party. Put the verbs in the present perfect or the simple past.

ADAM: What (1 be) .... the party like last night?

ANNA: It (2 be) .... good. Why (3 not come) .... you .... ?

ADAM: I (4 have) .... too much work to do last night. I (5 have) .... exams all this week, so I (6 be) .... very busy. (7 see) .... you .... Lucy there?

ANNA: Yes, I (8) ....

ADAM: (9 talk) .... you .... to her?

ANNA: Yes. She (10 seem) .... really happy. She (11 apply) .... for a new job.

ADAM: That's good. And (12 be) .... Nick with her?

ANNA: No, they (13 break up) .... They (14 not be) .... together now for a month.

ADAM: Oh, I (15 not know) .... (16 find) .... Lucy .... anyone else?

ANNA: No, she (17 tell) .... me last night that she (18 not want) .... another boyfriend at the moment.

ADAM: Oh, well, I might phone her in that case.

3 Jo Thomas is a famous guitar player with the band 'Earthforce'. A journalist is asking him questions. Write her questions, using the present perfect or the simple past.

1 .... ?

JO: I started playing the guitar when I was nine.

2 .... ?

JO: I left school when I was sixteen.

3 .... ?

JO: We gave our first concert in a pub in Plymouth.

4 .... ?

JO: We got our first recording contract five years ago with Polygram Records.

5 .... ?

JO: We've made twelve albums so far.

6 .... ?

JO: I chose it. I thought 'Earthforce' was a good name for a rock band.

7 .... ?

JO: We've sold about eight million. We sold over a million records last month!

8 .... ?

JO: No, we haven't been there yet. They don't seem to like our music in the States.

4 It is 3 o'clock in the afternoon. Sally Brice is having a bad day. She is talking to her neighbour. Read the dialogue. Some of the lines are correct, and some have a mistake in them. If the line is correct, put a tick (✓). If the line has a mistake, underline the mistake and write the correction in the brackets.

SALLY: I can't use the car because I've lost the keys.	(1 ....)
NEIGHBOUR: When did you lose them?	(2 ....)
SALLY: I've lost them this morning, I think. And I can't use my	(3 ....)
word processor because I've cut my finger.	(4 ....)
NEIGHBOUR: When have you done that?	(5 ....)
SALLY: I've done it this morning on a piece of glass.	(6 ....)
Oh, and the dog's disappeared.	(7 ....)
NEIGHBOUR: The dog's disappeared!? When has that happened?	(8 ....)
SALLY: When I've let it out into the garden this morning.	(9 ....)
And worst of all, the telephone has stopped working and	(10 ....)
nobody came to repair it.	(11 ....)
NEIGHBOUR: Why has no-one come?	(12 ....)
SALLY: Because the Telecom engineers went on strike.	(13 ....)

5 Write ten sentences about your life, using the present perfect and the simple past. Say what you *have done* or *have not done* so far, and what you *did* or *did not do* at particular times in the past.

Examples: *I've walked in the Himalayas. I met the Pope in 1994.*

Check your answers with a teacher.

Quick reference

We form the present perfect continuous with *have/has* + *been* + *-ing*.

Affirmative	**Negative**	**Questions**
I've been waiting	*I haven't been waiting*	*Have I been waiting?*
You've been waiting	*You haven't been waiting*	*Have you been waiting?*
He's been waiting	*He hasn't been waiting*	*Has he been waiting?*
We've been waiting	*We haven't been waiting*	*Have we been waiting?*
They've been waiting	*They haven't been waiting*	*Have they been waiting?*

We use the present perfect continuous:

- to talk about a temporary action that started in the past, that has continued over a period of time and is still continuing now. We often use it with *for* and *since* to say how long an action has been happening.

PAST   NOW

--➤

I've   been   waiting   for   ages.

- to talk about *repeated* actions which have continued over a period of time up to *now*.

1 YEAR AGO   January   March   June   NOW

--➤

I've   been   writing   to   him   for   a   year.

- to talk about an action which started in the past, which continued over a period, and has just stopped.

PAST   NOW

--⌐

She's been doing some exercises.   *She's having a rest now.*

---

1 **Describe what has been happening in this picture. Write four sentences, using these verbs.**

fish	swim	collect	dig

1 The men ....

....

2 The woman ....

....

3 The dog ....

....

4 The girls ....

....

2 **Claudine, a French girl, lives in London. Match the sentences, giving the correct form of the verb in the second column.**

1 She's got a flat in south London.
2 Her English is very good.
3 She's got an English boyfriend.
4 They're going on holiday next month.
5 She's a bi-lingual secretary.
6 She's worried about her father.
7 She doesn't like being so far away.

a) They (go out) .... together since last May.
b) They (save) .... money for months.
c) She (work) .... for a French firm for two years.
d) She (live) .... in it for a year.
e) She (think) .... of moving back to France.
f) She (learn) .... it for eight years.
g) He (have) .... problems with his heart.

1 ....   2 ....   3 ....   4 ....   5 ....   6 ....   7 ....

3 **Four young men and two young women share a big house. It is 7 o'clock in the evening. Write sentences using the present perfect continuous + *for*. Choose from these verbs:**

watch   read   get ready   talk   lie   cook

1 Joel arrived home at 6.30 and started to read a magazine. He's still reading it.
   He .... for half an hour.
2 Michael went into the kitchen at 6.00. He's still there.
   .... for an hour.
3 Emily came home at 5.30 with a headache. She went up to her bedroom and lay down on her bed.
   She's still there. ....
4 Toby came home at 6.15 and phoned Naomi. He's still on the phone.
   He ....
5 Matthew got home at 5.00 and switched on the TV. It's still on.
   He ....
6 A boy phoned at 5.45 and invited Lucy to a party. She's still in the bathroom.
   She ....

4 **Look carefully at this dialogue in a doctor's surgery. Some of the lines are correct and some have a mistake. If a line is correct put a tick (✓) after it. If a line has a mistake in it, underline the mistake and write the correction in the brackets.**

DOCTOR: Have you been waiting long?   (1 ....)
PATIENT: No, I've only been wait for a few minutes.   (2 ....)
DOCTOR: Now, you haven't felt well, is that right?   (3 ....)
PATIENT: That's right. In fact, I've been feeling really ill.   (4 ....)
                I had terrible headaches.   (5 ....)
DOCTOR: How long have you been having these headaches?   (6 ....)
PATIENT: I had them since the beginning of the month.   (7 ....)
DOCTOR: Have you worried about anything?   (8 ....)
PATIENT: Yes, I've been worrying about an exam.   (9 ....)
                And I haven't slept.   (10 ....)
DOCTOR: Well, I suggest you try these pills. People are using   (11 ....)
                them for years and I think they'll help you.

29

Quick reference

We use the present perfect continuous:

- for an action happening over a period of time. It doesn't matter if it's finished or not.
  *This book's very good. I've **been reading** it all evening.*

- for an action happening over a short period.
  *They've **been talking** for 20 minutes.*

- when talking about *how long.*
  *'I'm sorry I'm late. How long **have** you **been waiting**?'*
  *'Don't worry. I've only **been waiting** for a few minutes.'*

We normally use the present perfect simple:

- for completed actions. *We can't get into the house, because she's **lost** the key.*

- for actions happening over a longer period. *I've always **lived** in London.*

- when we talk about *how many things* or *how many times.*
  *I've **taken** ten photos so far. She's **written** to him five times, but he **hasn't replied** once.*

- Some verbs when they describe a state, not an action, aren't used in the present perfect continuous. For example: *agree, be, believe, belong, hate, know, like, love, mind, notice, own, remember, seem, suppose, understand, want, wish.*
  *I've **been** ill for two weeks.* (NOT I've been being ill.)
  *She's **known** him for a year.* (NOT She's been knowing him.)

---

1 **Write sentences, using the present perfect simple or the present perfect continuous.**

1a It's nearly midnight and Laura/dance/all evening.

....

1b She/dance/with about five boys.

....

2a She/drink/white wine and lemonade.

....

2b She/drink/about four glasses. ....
3a Mark Roland/ask/her/to dance/all evening.

....

3b He/ask/her/several times. ....
4a But each time Laura/say/ 'No, thanks.'

....

4b She/never/like/him/very much. ....
5a It's late now and Laura/try/to phone for a taxi since 12.30.

....

5b She/try/three times. ....
6 Mark/wait/for this moment all evening.

....

'I've got a car, Laura. Do you want a lift?'

2 **It is midday on Saturday.**
What have the Hall family been doing?
What have they done?
Choose the correct question,
a or b, and give the answer.

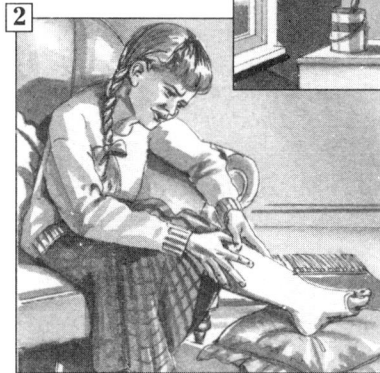

1 a) What has Harry done?   b) What has Harry been doing?
(play) .... football.

2 a) What has Sarah done?   b) What has Sarah been doing?
(break) ....

3 a) What has David Hall done?   b) What has David Hall been doing?
(paint) ....

4 a) What has Louise Hall done?   b) What has Louise Hall been doing?
(buy) ....

3 **Complete the text, using the present perfect simple or the present perfect continuous.**

Jack's a tax inspector, but he (1 be) .... out of work for six months and he (2 try) ....
.... to get another job. He (3 apply) .... for ten jobs, but he (4 have)
.... only .... one interview. While he (5 be) .... out of work he
(6 do) .... jobs around the house. So far he (7 paint) .... all the
bedrooms and he (8 build) .... a new garden shed. But all the time he (9 get) ....
.... more and more frustrated. All his life he (10 work) .... in an office
and he (11 hate) .... working in the house. He (12 not feel) .... well
recently. He (13 see) .... the doctor two or three times, and he (14 take) ....
pills for two weeks now, but they (15 not cure) .... his depression. Today he
(16 decide) .... not to get up. He (17 watch) .... television in bed. He
(18 watch) .... a documentary about unemployment and he (19 see)
.... the news three times. Now at last he (20 fall) .... asleep.
And for the last few minutes he (21 dream) .... about being back in an office again,
surrounded by computer screens full of figures. He's smiling in his sleep. He (22 not smile) ....
.... like that for months.

4 **Write ten sentences and say what *you have/have not done* recently and what *you have/have not
been doing* recently. Check your answers with a teacher.**

Quick reference

- We form the past perfect with *had* + the past participle.

Affirmative	Negative	Questions
It had started	*It hadn't started*	*Had it started?*

  Short answers: *Had it started? - Yes it had/No, it hadn't.*

- If we're already talking about the past, we use the past perfect to say that something happened before a certain time in the past. *It was 10.00. The train **had left** at 9.50.*

- When there are two actions and it's clear that the first action was completed before the other action started we use the past perfect for the first action.
  *After Simon **had eaten** his dinner, he went to bed.*

- When one action is an immediate reaction to another we use the past simple for both actions.
  *He **ran** away as soon as he **saw** me.   She **smiled** when he **spoke** to her.*

- We form the past perfect continuous with *had* + *been* + *-ing*.

Affirmative	Negative	Questions
She had been waiting	*She hadn't been waiting*	*Had she been waiting?*

- We use the past perfect continuous when we want to emphasise that something had been in progress continuously up to a certain time in the past.
  *When I met him, **he had been living** in London for ten years.*
  *Joanna **had been revising** for her exams all day, and now she was tired.*

---

1 **Rachel Gower left home when she was only 17 and went abroad. She finally returned to England and got married when she was 39. By that time she had done a lot of different things. Write complete sentences using the past perfect. Choose from these verbs.**

live	find	spend	not have	fly	have	make	break	not pay	not meet	be	lend

Example: *Rachel had lived in Brazil and Australia.*

1 She .... malaria and cholera.

2 She .... a truck driver, a sheep farmer, a helicopter pilot and a journalist.

3 She .... helicopters in the Australian outback.

4 She .... both her legs in a helicopter crash.

5 She .... gold in Northern Australia.

6 She .... a lot of money but she .... most of it.

7 She .... some of the money to friends and they .... her back.

8 But she .... any children and she .... the man she wanted to marry.

---

2 **Alexander and his wife went to a restaurant to celebrate their wedding anniversary. Complete the third sentence so that it has a similar meaning to the previous two sentences, using the word given.**

1 The waiter showed them to their table. They asked to see the menu. (had)

   When ...., they ....

2 He brought them the menu. He finished his cigarette. (had)

He .... after ....

3 Alexander took a sip of his wine. He knew it was off. (taken)

As soon as ....

4 They suddenly lost their appetite. They ate half their chicken. (eaten)

After ....

5 The waiter brought their coffee. They finished their sweet. (had)

.... before ....

6 The waiter gave them the bill. He told them that service wasn't included! (given)

After ...., he ....

3 Complete the sentences, using past perfect + past simple OR past simple + past simple.

On 9 May, 1994, a team of six skydivers took off from an airfield near Tucson, Arizona. Once the plane (1 climb) .... to 4,000 metres, five skydivers (2 jump) .... out. After they (3 jump) ...., their instructor, Greg Robertson, (4 follow) .... them five seconds later. When he (5 look) .... down at the other skydivers he (6 see) .... one of them, Debbie Williams, collide with another. He (7 see) .... immediately that the impact (8 knock) .... her unconscious. When he (9 realise) .... this he (10 make) .... an immediate decision. He still (11 not open) .... his parachute so he (12 dive) .... like Superman at a speed of 300 kph. When he (13 reach) .... her, at a height of 300 metres, he (14 put) .... her into a sitting position and (15 pull) .... her parachute cord. As soon as he (16 pull) .... it, her parachute (17 open) .... Once he (18 check) .... that her parachute was OK, he (19 open) .... his own. He (20 not take) .... his eyes off her until she (21 land) .... safely.

4 Tom Bell was involved in a car accident a month ago. Now he is in court. The magistrate is asking him questions. Complete the dialogue, using the past perfect continuous.

'Mr Bell, what/you/do that evening?' (1) ....

'I/have/a good time. I/talk/to some old friends. I/celebrate/my birthday.' (2) ....

....

'you/have/a party?' (3) ....

'Yes I/-' (4) ....

'You/drink?' (5) ....

'Yes, I/-' (6) ....

'How long/you/drink?' (7) ....

'I/drink/since about 7 o'clock.' (8) ....

'I see. Thank you Mr Bell.'

14 The future: *will/won't, shall/shan't*

> ## *Quick reference*
>
> - We use *will ('ll)* to talk about a simple prediction of a future event or situation.
> After *I* or *we* in affirmative sentences, we can use *will* or *shall*, but we normally use their short form *'ll*. In negative sentences, after *I* or *we*, we can use *won't* or *shan't*. *Won't* is more common.
>   *My brother **will be** here soon. He**'ll be** tired after his long journey.*
>   *There's a bus strike, so **I won't get/shan't get** to work on time tomorrow.*
>
> - We use *Shall we? Shall I?* to ask for suggestions and to make a suggestion or an offer.
>   *What **shall we** do? **Shall we** go to the cinema?   **Shall I** carry your suitcase?*
>
> - We can use *will ('ll)* when we decide to do something at the moment of speaking and *won't* to express a sudden decision not to do something, or a refusal.
>   *Sit down. **I'll buy** the drinks.   I **won't have** a coffee, thanks.*
>   *I **won't speak** to her again.*
>
> - We can use *will* to make a request.
>   ***Will you lend** me £5?   **Will you come** with me?*

1 Complete this conversation. using *will* (OR *'ll*) and *won't/shan't*.

'Jack's broken his leg in a car accident. He's in hospital.'

'Really? (1 he/be) .... in hospital for long?'

'No, he (2 not be) .... there for very long. Two days perhaps. He's got his leg in plaster.'

'How long (3 he/have) .... the plaster on?'

'They say it (4 be) .... about six weeks.'

'He (5 not be able to) .... play football, (6) .... he?'

'No, and he (7 not be able to) .... drive either. He (8 have to) ....

go everywhere by bus. He (9 not like) .... that.'

'I hope he (10 be) .... all right.'

'I'm sure he (11) .... They (12 look after) .... him at the hospital.'

'The trouble is I (13 not be able to) .... go and see him. I (14 not be)

.... at home for the next week.'

'Never mind. You (15 see) .... him when you get back.'

2 Helen is a social worker. She is visiting an old lady of 90 who has got some problems. In Helen's replies, complete the second question so that it has a similar meaning to the first.

Example: 1 I don't want to watch television any more.

 HELEN: Do you want me to turn it off? *Shall I turn it off?*

2 Yes, please. I'm so bored, just sitting here.

 HELEN: Why don't we look at a magazine together? .... look at a magazine together?

3 I can't see properly. My glasses are dirty.

 HELEN: Would you like me to clean them for you? .... for you?

4 I'm thirsty.

HELEN: Why don't I make you a cup of tea? .... you a cup of tea?

5 I must get out of the house more.

HELEN: Do you want us to go for a walk? .... for a walk?

6 No, I'm really not feeling well.

HELEN: Would you like me to call the doctor? .... the doctor?

3 Steve is in a hurry. He is going away for a week and he is catching a train in half an hour. But he has still got a lot of things to do. His neighbour Rachel is offering to help him. Write what they say. Use these verbs.

| answer   tell   feed   not forget   close   get |

Example: STEVE: Oh, no! The phone's ringing.   RACHEL: Don't worry. *I'll answer it*.

1 STEVE: I think my train ticket's in the desk in the living room.   RACHEL: I ....

2 STEVE: I haven't fed the cat.   RACHEL: I ....

3 STEVE: The upstairs windows are still open.   RACHEL: I ....

4 STEVE: I haven't told my mother I'm going to be away.   RACHEL: I ....

5 RACHEL: Remember to send me a postcard!   STEVE: Don't worry. I ....

4 Tom and Zoe are having a drink. Zoe is going to Rome tomorrow for three months. Complete the conversation, using *will* or *won't*.

TOM: What (1 have) .... to drink?

ZOE: I (2 have) .... anything alcoholic. I think I (3 have) .... a tomato juice.

TOM: You (4 write) .... to me while you're away, (5) .... you?

ZOE: Yes, I promise I (6 write) .... every week.

TOM: I want to know that you've arrived safely, so (7 you/phone) .... me from Rome?

ZOE: I (8 phone) .... you from the airport because I (9 have) .... time. I (10 phone) .... you from the hotel.

TOM: Do you know your address in Rome yet?

ZOE: No, but I (11 send) .... it to you as soon as I know.

TOM: Don't talk to any good-looking Italians, (12) .... you?

ZOE: I (13 talk) .... to anyone.

TOM: I want to ask you something before you go. (14 you/marry) .... me?

ZOE: Tom! I can't give you an answer now, but I (15 think) .... about it.

TOM: When (16 you/give) .... me your answer?

ZOE: We (17 talk) .... about it when I get back from Rome.

5 a) Make some predictions about the year 2010. Write five sentences, using *will* and *won't*.
b) You are at a party. How would you answer these questions?
What will you have to drink? What will you have to eat?
Check your answers with a teacher.

35

15

Going to OR Will?
It's going to rain.   He'll be 20 tomorrow

Quick reference

- We use *going to* to talk about future actions we have already decided to do.
  Why do you need your driving licence? - Because I'm going to hire a car.

- We use *going to* to predict a future event which seems certain because of present evidence.
  Look out! That tree's going to fall.

- We use *was/were going to* to talk about intentions or plans we had in the past (but we've now changed our plans).
  I was going to phone you, but I didn't have your number.

- We normally use *will/won't* for simple predictions.
  I'm sure you'll pass the exam.   It's Sunday tomorrow. There won't be much traffic.

- We use *will* for intentions where we decide at the moment of speaking.
  It's hot in here. - I'll open a window.   Do you want a drink? - Yes, I'll have a beer.

---

1 Neil is going on holiday to Spain. He is taking these things with him.

Write sentences about what he is going to do. Use these verbs.

visit	write	hire	play	sunbathe	go snorkelling	swim	read	take

Example: *He's going to swim.*

1 ....
2 ....
3 ....
4 ....
5 ....
6 ....
7 ....
8 ....

2 A hotel receptionist is talking to a guest. The things she says are all examples of:
  A intentions where we have *already decided to do something.*
  B intentions where we decide *at the moment of speaking.*
  C predictions of future events which seem certain because of present evidence.
  Read the sentences and then write A, B or C in the brackets.

  1 How long are you going to stay?   [ ]
  2 There's a big conference on in the hotel so we're going to be very busy.   [ ]

3 Are you going to pay by credit card? [ ]

4 Can I have your passport please? I'll let you have it back tomorrow. [ ]

5 I'll see if I can find you a room with a view. *visto* [ ]

6 It's going to be fine tomorrow. I've heard the weather forecast. [ ]

7 Are you going to have dinner in our restaurant? [ ]

8 I'll find a porter to take your luggage. *equipaje* [ ]

3 Jerome works in a shop. He is on the phone to a friend. These are the things he says. Match the sentences on the left and right.

1 I'm not enjoying this job.   a) so it's not going to be easy.

2 But I've got no qualifications,   b) It's going to be fine.

3 I'm free on Saturday.   c) I'll ring you back.

4 I've heard the weather forecast.   d) I'm not going to work.

5 We could meet at the river bridge at 9.00. e) I'm going to look for a new one.

6 Someone's just come in.   f) I'll bring two fishing rods.

   cañas de pescar

1 ....   2 ....   3 ....   4 ....   5 ....   6 ....

4 The following short conversations were heard at a party. Put the verb into the future with *will* or *going to*.

1 A: Red or white wine?   2 C: It's very hot in here.

   B: I (have) .... red please.   D: I (open) .... the window.

3 E: I'm tired. I (sit) .... down.   4 G: The phone's ringing.

   F: I (come) .... and sit next to you.   H: Don't worry. I (answer) .... it.

5 I: Why do you need the phone?   6 K: I (leave) .... now.

   J: Because I (phone) .... for a taxi.   L: OK. I (ring) .... you tomorrow.

   I: Don't bother. I (give) .... you a lift.
   molestia   *elevación*
   jastidio   *alzamiento*

5 Two friends are leaving work together. Some of the lines of the dialogue are correct and some have a mistake. If a line is correct put a tick (✓) after it. If a line has a mistake in it, underline the mistake and write the correction in the brackets.

'Where will you eat tonight?'   (1 ....)

'At home. I've got a new Indian cook book so I'll make a curry.'   (2 ....)

'Why not come to my place and I'm going to cook us both something.'   (3 ....)

'Won't you see Ned this evening?'   (4 ....)

'No, I've finished with Ned. I'm not going to see him again - ever.'   (5 ....)

'OK. I'm going to come round at 8 and I'll bring a bottle of wine.'   (6 ....)

'Fine. I'll see you then.'   (7 ....)

6 a) Write three simple predictions about the future. Example: *I think Italy will win the World Cup.*

b) Write three sentences about your plans or intentions for the future.

Example: *I'm going to study law at university.*

Check your answers with a teacher.

16 The future continuous and the future perfect

Quick reference

We use the future continuous (*will be/won't be + -ing*):

- to say that something will be or won't be in progress at a certain time in the future, because a) it is part of a normal routine, or b) it has been planned.
    *What **will you be doing** at 9.00 tomorrow? - **I'll be sitting** in my office, as usual.*
    *I can't come at 8.00. **I'll be watching** the match on television.*

- to talk about the present, when we say what is probably happening (or not happening) at this moment.
    *Don't phone Anna now. **She'll be having** her lunch.*
    *He's just come out of hospital. **He won't be feeling** very strong.*

We use the future perfect (*will have/won't have* + past participle):

- to talk about something that hasn't happened yet, but that will be (or won't be) completed before a certain time in the future.
    ***I'll have finished** reading this book by tomorrow evening.*
    *The car won't be ready tomorrow. **They won't have repaired** it till Thursday.*

- to talk about the present, when we say what has probably happened (or not happened) by now.
    *It's eight o'clock. **He'll have arrived** in Rome by now.*

---

1 **These are Mark's arrangements for next Saturday:**

9.00 Swim at Sports Centre   10.15 Supermarket - week's shopping
12.00 Drink with Lee at the Red Lion   13.15 Lunch with Emily   14.45 Yoga lesson in town
16.00 Optician's - eye test   17.30 Squash club. Game with Jerry.

Jenny is talking to him on the phone. Complete Mark's replies, using the future continuous.

Example: 'Hi, Mark. Can we meet at nine on Saturday morning?'
        I'm afraid not. I'll be having a swim at the Sports Centre at nine.

JENNY: Well, what about 10.30?

MARK: No, that's not possible. (1) I .... the week's shopping.

JENNY: What about lunch at about 12.15?

MARK: I can't. (2) I .... at the Red Lion.

JENNY: Well, we could meet for lunch a bit later. Say 1.30?

MARK: No. (3) I .... with Emily.

JENNY: Well, shall I come round to your place at about 3.00?

MARK: No, I won't be here. (4) I .... in town.

JENNY: Well, I'm free at about 4.00. Shall I ring you then?

MARK: No. (5) I .... at the optician's.

JENNY: How about a drink at the pub at 5.30?

MARK: That's not possible. (6) I .... with Jerry.

JENNY: OK. I've got the message!

2 Between June 5th and June 8th Nick will be taking his college exams. On June 10th he will be leaving college. On June 11th he will be moving into a new flat. On June 15th he will be starting work as a chef in a restaurant. On June 29th he will be getting his exam results. What will he have done by the end of June?

Example: *By the end of June he'll have taken his college exams.*

1 ....

2 ....

3 ....

4 ....

3 Nigel is at home in London. Sophie, his wife, is in Accra on business. When it is 8 a.m. in London, it is also 8 a.m. in Accra. Sophie is thinking about Nigel. She knows his habits very well. Complete her thoughts, using the future continuous and the future perfect. This is what Nigel does every day.

7.15 He gets up.	7.45 Breakfast.	8.15 To work.	12.30-13.15 Lunch.
18.30 Home.	19.30 Dinner.	21.00 TV news.	23.00 To bed.

Example: What is Sophie thinking at 7.15? *He'll be getting up.*
And at 8.00? *He'll have finished his breakfast.*

1 What's she thinking at 8.15? .... to work

2 At 9.00? .... work.

3 At 12.35? .... lunch.

4 At 13.20? .... lunch.

5 At 18.35? .... home.

6 At 19.35? .... dinner.

7 At 21.05? .... the news.

8 At 23.05? .... to bed.

4 Melanie Wright is meeting her cousin Camilla from Australia at the station on Saturday. This will be the first time they have met. Melanie is talking to Camilla on the phone. Write Melanie's questions, using the future continuous and the future perfect.

MELANIE: I expect you'll be tired when you arrive in London.

(1) .... on the plane?

CAMILLA: No, I won't have slept at all. I can never sleep on planes.

MELANIE: (2) ....?

CAMILLA: I'll be catching the 11.30 train from London Paddington.

MELANIE: (3) ....?

CAMILLA: Quite a lot, I'm afraid. I'll be bringing two big suitcases and a bag.

MELANIE: (4) ....?

CAMILLA: Yes, I'll have had lunch on the train.

MELANIE: (5) ....?

CAMILLA: I'll be wearing a red jacket, so you should recognise me.

5 What will you be doing this time next year? Write three sentences. What will you have done by the end of next year? Write three sentences. Check your answers with a teacher.

Quick reference

- We form the passive with the verb *be* (*is/was/has been*, etc.) + the past participle. The tense of the verb *be* changes to form the different tenses in the passive.

	Active	**Passive**
Present simple:	*He teaches*	*He is taught*
Present continuous:	*He is teaching*	*He is being taught*
Past simple:	*He taught*	*He was taught*
Past continuous:	*He was teaching*	*He was being taught*
Present perfect:	*He has taught*	*He has been taught*
Past perfect:	*He had taught*	*He had been taught*
Future *will*:	*He will teach*	*He will be taught*
Future *going to*:	*He is going to teach*	*He is going to be taught*
Modal (present):	*He may teach*	*He may be taught*
Modal (past):	*He might have taught*	*He might have been taught*

- The object of the active sentence becomes the subject of the passive sentence.
  Active: *The cat killed the mouse.*   Passive: *The mouse was killed by the cat.*

- Some verbs are followed by an infinitive, for example modal verbs (*can, must, should, will, would*, etc.). When these verbs are used in a passive construction, we use a passive infinitive (*be* + past participle).   *All tickets **must be shown**.   That **shouldn't be allowed**.*
  Note the past form of the passive infinitive - *have/has been* + past participle.
  *You **might have been hurt**.   Your room **should have been cleaned**.*
  Note that we also use the passive infinitive construction after verbs like *want to, expect to, agree to, hope to*, etc.   *She **wants to be liked**.   They **agreed to be photographed**.*

- A passive sentence is usually more formal than an active sentence. Compare:
  We'll send you a letter. (Informal) *A letter will be sent to you.* (Formal)
  Note that in a passive construction we can mention the person or thing that does the action (the agent) after the word *by*.   *The house was bought **by** a local businessman.*

- We use the passive when the person or thing doing the action isn't important, or isn't known, or is understood.   *My bike**'s been stolen**.   Ten people **were killed**.*

---

1 Put the verb in brackets into the passive.

1 The idea of a tunnel between England and France .... at the beginning of the 19th century. (put forward)

2 A tunnel .... in 1878 but it .... (start) (not complete)

3 Work on the present Channel tunnel .... in 1987. (begin)

4 Two tunnels .... side by side. (construct)

5 Seven people .... during the construction of the tunnel. (kill)

6 It .... in 1994. (open)

7 The first trains were unreliable and several .... by many hours. (delay)

8 Nowadays the tunnel .... by thousands of people every day. (use)

9 The sea crossing .... by many people. But passengers, cars and freight .... under the Channel in half the time by rail. (prefer) (transport)

2 Here are the details of a house for sale. Complete the text by putting these verbs into the past simple passive or the present perfect passive: *add, install, modernise, build, rebuild, buy.*

The house (1) .... in the 18th century. It (2) .... by the present

owners in 1980. Since then it (3) .... completely .... and central

heating (4) .... A new bedroom and a shower room (5) .... also

.... The roof (6) .... less than year ago.

3 Put a tick (✓) after the better or more natural of the two alternatives.

1 A Police are looking for a missing girl.   [ ]
   B A missing girl is being looked for by the police.   [ ]
2 A Someone last saw her on Tuesday evening.   [ ]
   B She was last seen on Tuesday evening.   [ ]
3 A A man in a red Ford Escort was talking to her in St Andrews Road.   [ ]
   B She was being talked to by a man in a red Ford Escort in St Andrews Road. [ ]
4 A She was wearing a black T-shirt and jeans.   [ ]
   B A black T-shirt and jeans were being worn by her.   [ ]
5 A None of her friends have heard from her.   [ ]
   B She has been heard from by none of her friends.   [ ]
6 A A reward is being offered for any information useful to the police.   [ ]
   B Someone is offering a reward for any information useful to the police. [ ]

4 Read the questions in this general knowledge quiz. Complete the second question so that it has a similar meaning to the first, using a passive construction.

Example: Where do they speak Dutch? *Where is Dutch spoken?*

1 In which country do they make the most bicycles?
  In which country .... *the most bicycles* ....?
2 In which country are they producing the most oil at the moment?
  In which country .... *the most oil* .... *at the moment?*
3 Who invented dynamite? *Who* .... *dynamite* ....?
4 In which city are they going to hold the next Olympics?
  In which country .... *the next Olympics* ....?
5 In which country will they play the next football World Cup?
  In which country .... *the next football World Cup* ....?
6 How many times have astronauts visited the moon?
  How many times .... *the moon* ....?

5 The workers at an engineering company are very worried. Change the following sentences from active to passive, using a passive infinitive.

Example: They don't want the management to treat them like machines.
       They don't want to be treated like machines.

1 They want the management to pay them more. ....
2 They want the management to consult them about changes.

  ....

3 They think the management should have told them about the company's problems.

  ....

4 The management ought to have offered them longer holidays.

  ....

18 The passive (2) Other constructions

Quick reference

- We can use the *-ing* form in the passive. We use *being* + a past participle.
  *I enjoy **being given** presents.   I don't like **being told** what to do.*
- With the following verbs, we can use the construction passive verb + infinitive with *to*:
  believe, consider, expect, fear, feel, find, intend, know, report, say, think, understand.
    ***He's expected to arrive** at 11.00.   **They're said to be** very rich.*
- We can also use a perfect infinitive (*to have had*) in this construction.
  *The robbers are said **to have stolen** £1,000.*
- We can use *It* + a passive verb + a *that* clause to talk about what people in general say, think or feel about a situation. We can use this construction with these verbs: *agree, announce, decide, expect, fear, feel, find, know, report, say, suggest, think, understand.*
    ***It's reported that** 20 people died in the crash.   **It was felt that** he was too old for the job.*
- Note the two meanings of *be supposed to.*
  a) Something is the general opinion of most people.
    *'Impulse' **is supposed to** be a very good film.*
  b) Something should happen because it's the rule or the plan.
    ***You're supposed to** wear a seatbelt.   **We aren't supposed to** smoke.* (This isn't permitted.)
- When the following verbs have two objects (indirect and direct), it's possible to have two passive sentences: *give, lend, offer, owe, pay, promise, sell, send, show, teach, tell.*
  (Active: Somebody gave **her a new car**.)
  Passive: ***She** was given **a new car**.   **A new car** was given **to her**.*
  (Active: Somebody showed **me the photograph**.)
  Passive: ***I** was shown **the photograph**.   **The photograph** was shown **to me**.*
  (The first construction is more common.)

---

1 When Sally was 14 she often had to stay with her grandparents, who were very strict with her. She hated it. Add what Sally says, using a passive construction.

Example: They always treated her like a child. *I hated being treated like a child.*

1 They always told her to make her bed.

   I couldn't stand ....

2 They always gave her boring jobs to do.

   I got tired of ....

3 They always sent her to the shop to buy her grandfather's tobacco.

   I got fed up with ....

4 They treated her like a servant.

   I hated ....

5 They always shouted at her when she did something wrong.

   I hated ....

6 They criticised her all the time.

   I couldn't stand ....

2 Amy Wyn lives alone. Not much is known about her. Complete the second sentence so that it has a similar meaning to the first, using the word given.

Example: People believe she's about 80. (*believed*) *She's believed to be about 80.*

1 People think she made a lot of money selling antique furniture. (*thought*)

She ....

2 Reports suggest that she's got a priceless collection of antique jewellery. (*reported*)

She ....

3 (The other day the police stopped her for speeding.) They discovered she had £25,000 in her handbag. (*found*)

She ....

4 People say she was a very good tennis player when she was young. (*said*)

She ....

5 People believe that she played at Wimbledon. (*believed*)

She ....

3 George Foster is 55 and has had a heart attack. His doctor has told him that he must change his life-style if he wants to avoid another attack. This is his advice:

> No coffee or tea.   1 litre of water a day.   Plenty of exercise.   No fried foods.   No sugar.

George is not taking the doctor's advice. Use forms of *supposed to* to remind him. Then rewrite his reply in a different way.

Example: I had a small glass of water yesterday. *But you're supposed to drink 1 litre.*
             People say the water here is polluted. *The water here is supposed to be polluted.*

1 'I fancy a nice cup of tea.' 'But ....,'

'Well, people say tea's good for you.' '...,'

2 'And I'll have two spoonfuls of sugar in it.' 'But ....,'

'Well, people say sugar gives you energy.' '..,'

3 'I had two fried eggs for breakfast.' 'But ....,'

'Well, people say eggs provide protein.' '...,'

4 'I haven't had any exercise this week.' 'But ....,'

'People say too much exercise is dangerous.' '..,'

4 Bill Graham keeps 15 dogs in his small house. His neighbours want him to get rid of the dogs. Write the following sentences in a different way, using a passive construction.

Example: The authorities have sent him three official letters of complaint.
             He's been sent three letters of complaint.

1 They say they'll find the dogs new homes. The dogs ....

2 They've promised him compensation. He ....

3 A man offered him a gun to shoot the dogs. He ....

4 Someone has sent him threatening letters. He ....

43

Quick reference

We use the construction *have something done*:

- when we don't do the job ourselves, usually because we can't.
  *I **had** my hair **cut**.*
  *We **had** the house **painted**.*
  desocioddale
- when something unpleasant happened to someone.
  *She **had** her bike **stolen**. He **had** his nose **broken**.*

- The word order is :

Subject	+	have	+	object	+	past participle
a) *We*		*had*		*the TV*		*repaired.*
b) *They*		*have had*		*their passports*		*stolen.*

- In informal English we sometimes use *get* instead of *have*. *Get* suggests a clear intention.
  *We **got** the carpet **cleaned**.*   (= We had the carpet cleaned.)

1 **Peter is practical and does a lot of things himself, but not everything. Complete these sentences with the correct forms of *have something done*.**

Example: His central heating system broke down. He couldn't fix it himself so he *had it repaired* by a
heating engineer.

He washes the car himself but normally he (1 service) .... in a garage. He always

cleans the windows himself but he (2 paint) .... by a decorator. When he bought a

new computer he (3 not install) .... the software .... at the shop. He did it

himself.

He's quite good at small building jobs but next month he (4 build) .... a new garage

.... by a building firm. And he (5 repair) .... the roof of his house ....

2 **An American tourist is talking to a Scotsman in a hotel in Glasgow. Complete the second sentence so that it has a similar meaning to the first, using the word given. Do not change the word given.**

1 I'm not enjoying my stay. On Tuesday someone stole my video camera. (I)

On Tuesday, ...

2 On Thursday someone broke my glasses in an argument in a pub. (broken)

On Thursday I .... in an argument in a pub.

3 On Friday someone took my wife's passport from our hotel room. (taken)

On Friday my wife ....

4 On Saturday the police stopped us and they searched our bags for drugs. (had)

On Saturday the police stopped us and we .... for drugs.

5 And finally, on Sunday, someone broke into our car. (broken)

And finally, on Sunday, we .... into.

So, to tell you the truth, I can't wait to get back to New York. I feel safe there!

3 Charlotte Montagu-Smith has a lot of money and a lot of spare time. She does very little for herself. Replace the words in italics with the structure *have something done.*

Example: Once a week *her hairdresser cuts and styles her hair.*
      Once a week she has her hair cut and styled.

1 Every day *a woman cleans and tidies her apartment.* ....

2 Last month *a decorator redecorated the whole apartment.* ....

3 *A carpet fitter has just laid new carpets* in every room. ....

4 Every week *a garage washes and polishes her car.* ....

5 This month *a dressmaker is making her a new collection of summer clothes.*

    ....

6 Last week *a dentist straightened her teeth.* ....

7 That was only a week after *a plastic surgeon had remodelled her nose.*

    ....

8 Next week *an artist is going to paint her portrait.* ....

9 Once a month *an astrologer tells her fortune.* ....

10 And four times a year *a dog beautician shampoos her poodle.*

    ....

4 Justin is a student living away from home. His mother is visiting him for the first time. Complete the dialogue using the construction *have something done.*

MOTHER: Your hair's too long. When did you last (1 cut) .... it ....?

    The cooker doesn't work. Why don't you (2 repair) .... it ....?

    And look at this carpet! You should (3 clean) .... it ....

    I can smell gas. You should (4 check) .... the gas fire ....

    I worry about you, Justin. Why don't you (5 install) .... a telephone ....?

JUSTIN: Because I haven't got any money.

5 Write sentences in which you describe two things you normally have done for you and two things you had done last week or last month. Check your answers with a teacher.

Examples: *I have my eyes tested once a year.*
      Last week I had my hair cut.

Quick reference

- To make a question we put the auxiliary verb (*be, have, do*) or a modal verb (*can, will, would,* etc.) before the subject.

Auxiliary/Main verb	Subject	Main verb	
Are	*you*	*staying*	*here long?*
Have	*the children*	*been*	*abroad?*
Can	*you*	*speak*	*Arabic?*

- In the present simple we use *do, does* to make questions, and *did* in the past simple.

Present simple:	*Does*	*the train*	*stop*	*at Exmouth?*
	Do	*people*	*like*	*her?*
Past simple:	*Did*	*she*	*arrive*	*yesterday?*

- We often begin questions with the question words *What? When? Where? Which? Who? Why? How?*

What	*are*	*you*	*thinking?*
How long	*does*	*the film*	*last?*

We use negative questions:

- to show surprise.

Don't	*you*	*like*	*chocolate?*

- when something seems very probable.

Aren't	*there*		*28 days in February?*

- with *Why?* to show surprise or frustration, or to make a suggestion.

Why	*won't*	*you*	*help*	*me?*
Why	*don't*	*you*	*have*	*a holiday?*

- in exclamations.

Don't	*they*	*look*	*stupid!*
Isn't	*the view*		*wonderful!*

- If we use a verb or an adjective + a preposition, the preposition remains attached to the verb/adjective in a question. *Who's she talking **to**? What are you good **at**?*

1 **Amy Price is at the new Shopping Centre in her local town. A market researcher is asking her what she thinks about the new centre. Complete the researcher's questions.**

1 .... here for the first time?

No, I'm not. I always do my shopping here now.

2 ....?

No, I don't mind. I quite like answering questions.

3 ....? Yes, I come every week.

4 ....?

Yes, I have. I've bought a lot of things this morning.

5 ....? Yes, I did. I came twice last week.

6 ....?

Yes, there is something I'd like to change. I wish they wouldn't play this music.

2 Uwe wants to get to know Pia, a girl in his English class. Write the questions he asks her.

1 He wants to know: where she comes from. *Where* .... *you* ....?

2 when she arrived in England. ....?

3 how many times she's been to England. ....?

4 how long she's been learning English. ....?

5 what she likes doing. ....?

6 what she's doing this evening. ....?

7 if they can have dinner together. ....?

3 Emma is hoping to buy a second-hand computer. She has seen an advert in the paper.

Computer (including monitor and printer) for sale. Phone 01387 874563.

Before she makes the phone call, she is writing down the questions she wants to ask the person who is selling the computer. Write her questions.

Example: IBM PC or Macintosh? *Is it an IBM PC or a Macintosh?*

1 Model? Which ....?

2 Printer type? What ....?

3 Age? How ....?

4 Cost? How ....?

5 Reason for sale? Why ....?

6 Possible to see it? Can ....?

4 Zoe is talking to her friend Chris. Complete the negative questions Chris uses to show his surprise.

ZOE: The restaurant you recommended wasn't very good.

CHRIS: Oh dear. (1 you/not like/it) ....?

ZOE: Not very much.

CHRIS: (2 the food/not be/very good) ....?

ZOE: The food was OK, but the wine was terrible.

CHRIS: (3 you/not complain) ....?

ZOE: Yes, we did. And the manager was very rude.

CHRIS: (4 he/not give/you/another bottle) ....?

ZOE: Yes, he did, but after we'd left, we realised we'd paid for two bottles!

5 Tom's friend Sue has been acting very strangely. Write the questions he wants to ask her.

Example: She's worried about something. *What are you worried about?*

1 She's angry about something. ....?

2 She seems afraid of something. ....?

3 She's obviously thinking about something. ....?

4 She was talking to someone at the station. ....?

Quick reference

- We use question tags at the end of a sentence to ask if what we said is true or not, or if the other person agrees or not.

- If we say something positive, the question tag is usually negative.

Positive	Negative
It's cold,	*isn't it?*

- If we say something negative, the question tag is positive.

Negative	Positive
It isn't easy,	*is it?*

	Positive	Negative	Negative	Positive
Present simple:	*He smokes,*	*doesn't he?*	*He doesn't smoke,*	*does he?*
Past simple:	*They won,*	*didn't they?*	*They didn't win,*	*did they?*
Present perfect:	*She's left,*	*hasn't she?*	*She hasn't left,*	*has she?*
The verb *be*:	*I'm right,*	*aren't I?*	*I'm not right,*	*am I?*
Have got:	*She's got a car,*	*hasn't she?*	*She hasn't got a car,*	*has she?*
Modal verbs:	*You can come,*	*can't you?*	*You can't come,*	*can you?*
	We should have waited,	*shouldn't we?*	*We shouldn't have waited,*	*should we?*

> ***Let's*** *go,* **shall we?** **Open** *the door,* **will you/can you?**
> ***Everybody*** *came,* **didn't they**? **Somebody** *has stolen it,* **haven't they**?
> ***There's*** *a problem,* **isn't there?** **There aren't** *any tickets,* **are there?**

- We can use a positive tag after a positive statement to express interest, sympathy, surprise or sarcasm.

> *This* **is** *your new computer,* **is it?** **You've got** *a headache,* **have you?**
> ***You had*** *too much to drink,* **did you**?

1 Two men are watching a football match. Match the two parts of each sentence.

1 They're not playing well,   a) has he?

2 And they didn't play well last week,   b) are they?

3 They lost 3-0,   c) did they?

4 Their defence isn't very good,   e) is it?

5 But the new goalkeeper's quite good,   f) didn't they?

6 The problem is, they can't score goals,   g) won't they?

7 They'll have to sack the manager,   h) can they?

8 He hasn't done very well,   i) isn't he?

1 ....   2 ....   3 ....   4 ....   5 ....   6 ....   7 ....   8 ....

2 Some tourists are going round the Oxford university colleges. Read what they say and decide which answer, A, B, or C best fits each space.

There are lots of colleges, (1) ....? But you can't see anything from the outside, (2) ....? They're beautiful inside, though, (3) ....? They've got lovely gardens, (4) ....? The students look bored, (5) ....? They must get fed up with tourists like us, (6) ....?

1	A aren't there	B isn't there	C is there
2	A can't you	B can you	C you can't
3	A are they	B they are	C aren't they
4	A haven't they got	B haven't they	C have they
5	A don't they	B aren't they	C do they
6	A must they	B they must	C mustn't they

3 Two people are watching a film on television. One of them likes to talk at the same time. Add the correct question tags.

'It's not a very good film (1) ....?'

'It's OK.'

'Those two cars are going to crash, (2) ....?'

'I don't know.'

'I said they would, (3) ....?'

'Yes, you did.'

'That man's got a gun, (4) ....?'

'Yes, I can see that.'

'He's not going to shoot her, (5) ....?'

'I don't know.'

'He looks really evil, (6) ....?'

'Shut up! You can never keep quiet, (7) ....?'

4 Two English people are lost in Barcelona. They are arguing. Complete the dialogue, using question tags.

'I've no idea where the station is.'

'We should have bought a map, (1) ....? I told you, (2) ....?'

'Well, we'll have to ask someone, (3) ....? Let's ask a policeman, (4) ....?'

'But there aren't any policemen, (5) ....? And we can't speak Spanish, (6) ....?'

'But everyone speaks English nowadays, (7) ....? So I'll go and ask that woman over there.

Look after my suitcase for me, (8) ....?'

(*Later*)

'Well, what did she say?'

'No problem. I understood everything she said, I think. We go straight on, then we turn right, er no,

left, at the lights, then we, er, ...'

'So you understood everything she said, (9) ....? You can understand Spanish,

(10) ....?'

'Don't be so sarcastic! I think we'd better get a taxi.'

'But we haven't got enough money for a taxi, (11) ....? We shouldn't have spent all our

money in that restaurant last night, (12) ....? And that was your idea, (13) ....?'

'Well, you chose the wine, (14) ....? You said it was only 400 pesetas, but it was 4,000

pesetas, (15) ....? That wasn't my fault, (16) ....?'

'Well, it doesn't matter now, (17) ...., because we've missed our train, (18) ....?'

22   *Who, what, which?*   *Do you know who/what/if,* etc?

Quick reference

- When we use *Who?/What?/Which?* as the subject of the sentence, we don't use *do, does, did* with the verb. *Who **phoned** this morning?* (NOT Who did phone this morning?)
When we use them as the object of the sentence, we use *do, does, did* with the verb.
  *Who **did you phone** this morning?* (NOT Who you phoned this morning?)

- We can use *What* and *Which* before a noun. The meaning is often the same.
  What clothes (OR ***Which clothes***) *are you going to wear?*
But *Which* is more common with people. We normally use *Which* when there's a limited choice of possibilities, and *What* when there's a large or unlimited choice.
  Which tennis player *has won the championship three times?* (*Which* + a person)
  ***Which** leg did he break?* (limited choice)   ***What** books do you read?* (large choice)

- We can use *Which* + *one/ones* and + *of*.
  There are two books here. ***Which one*** *is yours?*   ***Which of*** *those people do you know?*

- We often begin indirect questions with *Do you know...?* OR *Can/Could you tell me...?*
  *Where **are my shoes**? > Do you know where **my shoes are**?*
Do, does, did are replaced by the affirmative form of the verb.
  *What languages **does she speak**? > Can you tell me what languages **she speaks**?*
Where there is no question word, we use *if* or *whether*.
  *Does she eat fish? > Do you know **if/whether** she eats fish?*

1 Peter and Lisa were at home yesterday when there was a violent thunderstorm. At 10.00 the centre of the storm was right over the house. There was a terrific flash of lightning and the lights went out. A few seconds later there was another violent flash and the television exploded, followed by a lamp on the living room table. Lisa screamed. Peter immediately disconnected the CD player and then the video. At 10.05 the phone rang. Peter picked it up carefully. It was their neighbour asking if they were all right. When the storm had moved away, Lisa rang the electricity company to ask when the power would be restored. Complete the questions that give the following answers.

1 (happen) .... at 10.00?
The lights went out.

2 (explode) .... ?
The television and a lamp on the living room table.

3 (explode/first) .... or .... ?
The television.

4 (do) .... ?
She screamed.

5 (phone) .... ?
The neighbour.

6 (ring) .... ?
It rang at 10.05.

7 (disconnect)... ?
The CD player and the video.

8 (disconnect/first) .... or .... ?
The CD player.

9 (phone)...?
She phoned the electricity company.

2 Complete the dialogue, using *what* or *which*.

'(1) .... would you like?'

'I'd like some tomatoes, please.'

'I've got some English ones or some from Spain. (2) .... would you like?'

'(3) .... ones are cheaper?'

'The ones from Spain.'

'I'll have those. (4) .... of these avocado pears are ripe?' *maduros*

'Er, these two are OK.'

'Good. Um, (5) .... sort of cheese have you got?'

'(6) .... sort would you like? There's a big choice.'

'Have you got any goat's cheese?'

'I've got a French one or one that's produced locally. (7) .... would you prefer?'

'(8) .... do you recommend?'

'Well, I prefer the local one personally.'

'Fine.'

'(9) .... else would you like?'

'Um, (10) .... fruit juice have you got?'

'I've only got orange, I'm afraid.'

'That'll be fine. Now, (11) .... do I owe you?'

3 Read the dialogue and complete the second question so that the meaning is similar to the first.

Example: 'How do I get to Snatchwood? (1) Could you tell me *how I get to Snatchwood?*'

'Snatchwood? You need to go towards Oxford.'

'How far is it? (2) Have you any idea .... is?'

'It's about 15 miles from here.'

'Can I get a train? (3) Do you know ....?'

'No, there are no trains.'

'Is there a bus? (4) Do you know ....?'

'Yes, you can get a bus.'

'What time does it leave? (5) Could you tell me ....?'

'I think there's one every two hours, on the hour.'

'How long does it take? (6) Have you any idea ....?'

'It takes about 45 minutes.'

'How much does it cost? (7) Could you tell me ....?'

'I'm not sure.'

'Do the buses run on Sundays? (8) Do you know ....?'

'Yes, but there's a reduced service on Sundays.'

Quick reference

- In short answers, we often express agreement with *so* after the following verbs: *believe, guess, hope, imagine, presume, reckon, seem, suppose, suspect, think, be afraid.*
  They must have a lot of money. - Yes, I **suppose so**.
  And they like to spend it. - It **seems so**.

- With all of the above verbs except *guess, hope, presume, suspect, be afraid*, we often use negative forms with *so. She passed the exam, didn't she? - I* **don't think so**.

- But we must use *not* after *guess, hope, presume, suspect, be afraid.*
  Is it going to rain? - I **hope not**. (NOT I don't hope so.)

- We can use both forms with *believe, expect* and *suppose.*
  They won't win, will they? - I **don't expect so**. OR *I* **expect not**.

- When we want to say that we do the same or feel the same as someone else, we can use the short answer *So* + auxiliary verb + subject after positive statements.
  I can ski. - **So can I**. *He works hard. -* **So do I**. *I've got a headache. -* **So have I**.

- After negative statements we use *Neither* or *Nor* + auxiliary verb + subject.
  I don't like English beer. - **Neither do I/Nor do I**.
  I'm not enjoying this. - **Neither am I/Nor am I**.

- Note that when the present simple or the past simple is used in the first statement, we use *do, does* or *did* after *So/Neither/Nor.*
  We live in Manchester. - **So do we**. *I didn't want to go. -* **Neither did I**.

---

1 **Match the replies on the right with the sentences on the left.**

1 I like Indian food.
2 But I don't like very hot curries.
3 I've never eaten Thai food.
4 I'd like to try it some time.
5 But I've eaten Vietnamese.
6 I'm not very keen on Chinese food.
7 I can't use chopsticks.

a) So have I.
b) Neither can I.
c) So do I.
d) Neither am I.
e) Neither do I.
f) So would I.
g) Neither have I.

1 ....   2 ....   3 ....   4 ....   5 ....   6 ....   7 ....

---

2 **Maria is Spanish and Pascal is French. They have just met in a bar in Rome. Complete Pascal's part of the dialogue, using *So ... I* and *Neither ... I*.**

MARIA: I'm learning English.   PASCAL: (1) ....

MARIA: I've been learning it for a long time.   PASCAL: (2) ....

MARIA: I understand most of the grammar.   PASCAL: (3) ....

MARIA: But I don't find speaking English very easy.   PASCAL: (4) ....

MARIA: And I sometimes can't understand people.   PASCAL: (5) ....

MARIA: I've never been to England.   PASCAL: (6) ....

MARIA: I'd like to go one day.   PASCAL: (7) ....

MARIA: Let's have something to eat. I'm hungry.   PASCAL: (8) ....

3 Sarah is asking Zoe about her holiday plans. Zoe does not like flying. Read the dialogue and think of the word which best fits each space. Use only one word in each space.

SARAH: Are you going on holiday this summer?

ZOE: Yes, Tim and I are going to Naxos in July.

SARAH: It'll be hot there in July, won't it?

ZOE: I suppose (1) ....

SARAH: What about the language? Can Tim speak any Greek?

ZOE: I (2) .... think so.

SARAH: Well, that won't be a problem. I suppose they'll speak English in the hotels.

ZOE: I hope (3) ....

SARAH: It takes about three and a half hours to Athens, doesn't it?

ZOE: Yes, I'm (4) .... so.

SARAH: You don't like flying, do you?

ZOE: No, I'm afraid (5) ....

4 Zoe and Tim are at the airport, on their way to Naxos. Complete Tim's answers, using *I think so*, etc.

ZOE: Have we got time for a coffee?

TIM: (think) (1) .... It's only ten to four.

ZOE: Our flight hasn't been delayed, has it?

TIM: (think) (2) .... It doesn't say 'Delayed' on the board.

ZOE: So we won't have to wait long.

TIM: (expect) (3) ....

ZOE: Will they call our flight?

TIM: (expect) (4) ....

ZOE: You've got our boarding cards, haven't you?

TIM: (hope) (5) ....

ZOE: Can we change our money here?

TIM: (imagine) (6) .... There's a bank over there.

ZOE: It's quite a long flight, isn't it?

TIM: (be afraid) (7) ....

ZOE: We won't be there till 8 o'clock this evening, will we?

TIM: (be afraid) (8) ....

5 Answer these questions using *I hope so/I don't think so/I expect not*, etc. Check your answers with a teacher.
Will you live till you are 80? Will you stop work when you are 60? Will you ever use your English outside the classroom? Will you always live in your own country? Will there ever be another world war?

24 Auxiliary verbs used alone: *She likes cheese, but I don't*

Quick reference

- We often use an auxiliary verb (*be, have, might, would, can,* etc.) on its own to avoid repeating the main verb.
  *Most of my friends are going abroad this summer, but **I'm not**.*
  *Have you seen their new baby? - My sister **has**, but I **haven't**.*
- We use the full form of auxiliaries when they're affirmative.
  *I'm not going to the match, but Tom **is**.* (NOT Tom's)
- We use forms of *do* if the preceding main verb is in the present simple or past simple.
  *I **don't eat** meat, but my brother **does**.   All my friends **went** to Sally's party, but I **didn't**.*
- If the main verb has two auxiliaries, we normally repeat only the first.
  *They **won't have** finished lunch yet. - Yes, they **will**. It's quarter past two.*
  *I **would have** bought that video camera. - I **wouldn't**. It was too expensive.*
- But we use two auxiliaries if we change the verb form.
  *I **didn't buy** that car, but I **would have** if I'd had enough money.*
- We use an auxiliary on its own in reply questions to show interest or surprise.
  *I've cut my finger. - **Have you**?   He drank the whole bottle. - **Did he**?*

---

1 Sue, Zoe and Anna are sisters, but their lives are very different. Look at the chart and answer the questions, using the correct auxiliary verb.

Example: Who likes sport? *Zoe does, but Sue and Anna don't.*

	Anna	Zoe	Sue
Born in England	✓	✓	
Lived in USA			✓
Long hair		✓	
Serious illness	✓	✓	
Musical instrument			✓
Horse-riding	✓	✓	
Sport		✓	
Florida holiday		✓	
Swim	✓		✓
Boyfriend	✓		✓
Looking for a job		✓	

1 Who was born in England? .... but ....
2 Who lived for a time in the USA? .... but ....
3 Who's got long hair? .... but ....
4 Who's had a serious illness? .... but ....
5 Who plays a musical instrument? .... but ....
6 Who enjoys horse-riding? .... but ....
7 Who will be on holiday in Florida next week? .... but ....
8 Who can swim? .... but ....
9 Who's got a boyfriend at the moment? .... but ....
10 Who's looking for a job? .... but ....

2 Sam's girlfriend, Alice, has just gone to live in Scotland. Shaun and Neil live in the same flat as Sam. Decide which answer, A, B or C best fits each space.

SHAUN: I haven't seen Sam all day.

NEIL: I (1) .... either. I don't know where he is. (A *don't* B *haven't* C *have*)

SHAUN: Who left this note?

NEIL: Sam (2) .... . It's his handwriting. (A *hasn't* B *should have* C *must have*)

SHAUN: But he doesn't say where he's gone.

NEIL: He (3) .... if he'd wanted us to know. He obviously doesn't want us to know where he's gone.
(A *would have* B *would* C *hasn't*)

SHAUN: Do you think he's gone to Scotland to see Alice?

NEIL: He (4) .... . Who knows? (A *must have* B *might have* C *could*)

SHAUN: Do you think he'll telephone?

NEIL: He (5) .... . I'm not sure. (A *won't* B *couldn't* C *might*)

SHAUN: Has he taken his car?

NEIL: He (6) .... because it isn't here. (A *must have* B *would have* C *can't have*)

SHAUN: He was acting very strangely this morning.

NEIL: I know he (7) .... . We should have asked him why. (A *did* B *was* C *wasn't*)

SHAUN: I (8) ...., but I didn't have time. (A *would have* B *would* C *couldn't*)

NEIL: Can't we phone Alice?

SHAUN: We (9) ...., but we haven't got her number. (A *can't* B *could* C *won't*)

3 The Government has just announced its budget for next year. Two people are talking about it. One has heard the news, the other has not. Match the statements on the left with the reply questions on the right.

1   The Chancellor's reduced income tax by 2%.
2   He said this would help the economy.
3   But low-paid people won't benefit.
4   They think it's a big concession to the rich.
5   He should have given more money to the low-paid.
6   The price of petrol's going up.
7   But he hasn't increased the tax on wine and spirits.
8   He didn't increase spending on education.
9   I've never known a more selfish budget.
10 I reckon it's a budget for the rich.

a) Didn't he?
b) Do you?
c) Haven't you?
d) Hasn't he?
e) Won't they?
f) Has he?
g) Do they?
h) Is it?
i) Should he?
j) Did he?

1 ....   2 ....   3 ....   4 ....   5 ....   6 ....   7 ....   8 ....   9 ....   10 ....

4 Compare members of your family. Write five sentences, using auxiliary verbs on their own.

Example: *I don't like shopping, but my brother does.*

Write five sentences about things you wanted to do but that you did not do because of circumstances, or about things that you did, but that you regret now. Use the auxiliaries *would have* or *should have/shouldn't have* on their own.

Examples: *I didn't work hard at college. I should have, but I was lazy.*
I got drunk at my sister's party. I shouldn't have, but I was feeling depressed.

Check your answers with a teacher.

Quick reference

We use *can* + infinitive without *to* and *be able to* + infinitive:

- for ability/inability. *I **can** speak Spanish. I **can't** ski.*
  *He**'ll be able to** drive soon. I **won't be able to** remember your phone number.*
- for possibility/impossibility. *I **can** meet you at the station.*
  *I **can't** write to her. I don't know her address. I**'ll be able** to leave early tomorrow.*
- In the present, we usually use *can*, not *be able to*. *I **can** speak Spanish.* (NOT I'm able to)
- In the future we use *will/won't be able to*, not *can*, when we want to emphasise the future time.
  *When she's 18, she**'ll be able to drive** to school.*
- In the past we normally use *could* for a general ability and *was/were able* to for a particular action or situation. But in the negative *couldn't* is more common than *wasn't/weren't able to*.
  *He **could** write with either his left or right hand.* (a general ability)
  *I didn't have any money yesterday, but a friend **was able to lend** me some.*
  (a particular situation, so we don't use *could*)
  *I **couldn't believe** it when she said she was 20.* (NOT I wasn't able to believe it.)

1 Complete the sentences using *can/can't* or the correct form of *be able to*.

My brother (1) .... speak four languages. At the moment he's studying Japanese and by
the end of next year he (2) .... speak five languages and he (3) .... get a job
with a Japanese company. I'd like to (4) .... speak two languages! I (5) .... only
speak English and I (6) .... really speak that very well! I'm going to French evening classes
at the moment but I (7) .... go every week because I've been too busy.

2 Robert Collingwood has been a writer for 30 years. Complete the sentences with *can/can't could/couldn't* or *(not) able to*.

When I started writing books I (1) .... type so I wrote my first book with a pen and paper. A
year after the book was published, I got my first royalty cheque and I (2) .... buy a
typewriter. But I (3) .... only type with two fingers, so my second book took much longer to
write. When I got my second royalty cheque, I (4) .... buy a word processor. At first, I (5)
.... understand how to use it and I lost a whole chapter of my book! I (6) .... find it
anywhere on my computer. Fortunately, a friend, who was an expert on computers, (7) ....
find it for me and he said he (8) .... teach me how to use a word processor properly.

3 In Britain Sunday used to be a special day. Underline the better alternative.

A few years ago, on Sundays, you (1) *weren't able to/couldn't* buy anything except a newspaper. And
you (2) *weren't able to/couldn't* do anything either. The only thing you (3) *were able to/could* do was
go for a walk or go to church. But recently the law has changed and people (4) *have been able to/
could* do much more. Last Sunday I (5) *was able to/could* go shopping at the supermarket. Then, in the
afternoon, my son and I (6) *were able to/could* watch a professional football match.

26 Can, could, may, would in requests, offers and invitations

Quick reference

MAY → COULD → CAN
+   −

- We use *can, could* and *may* to ask for things or for permission. *Could* is a little more polite than *Can*. *May* is more formal than *Could*.
  Can *I come?* **Could** *I have a drink?* **Could** *I open a window?* **May** *I smoke?*

- We can use *Would you, Can you, Could you* (NOT May you) to ask someone to do something. *Would you* is more formal than *Can you* and *Could you* and is less common.
  Can *you help me?* **Could** *you pass me the salt?* **Would** *you get a taxi for me?*

- We use *Can I* or *May I* when we offer to do something. *May* is more formal and less common than *Can*. **Can I** *get you a drink?* **Can we** *help you?* **May I** *make a suggestion?*

- To give permission we usually use *can. May* is very formal.
  You **can** *stay till midnight.*   *You* **may** *leave now.* (formal)

- We use *would like* to offer something or to offer to do something, and to invite someone to do something. **Would you like** *some tea?*
  Would you like *me to get you a ticket?* **Would you like** *to stay the night?*

1

Michelle and Jean-Claude are staying at a bed and breakfast in England. They ask the owner for help, and for permission to do things. Match their needs with their requests.

1 Where can we leave the car?	a) Could we have some, please?
2 We want to visit Castle Drogo. We don't know where it is.	b) May we park in front of the house?
	c) May I smoke in the dining-room?
3 We'll be back late tonight.	d) Can you tell us where we can buy one?
4 We want to leave very early tomorrow.	e) Could you lend us a map?
5 We need to contact our bank.	f) Could we have breakfast at 7.30?
6 We need a film for our camera.	g) Can we use the phone?
7 We like bread with our meals.	h) Would you tell her we'll ring her back?
8 I like a cigarette after dinner.	i) Can you give us a key?
9 A friend might phone from Paris.	

1 ....   2 ....   3 ....   4 ....   5 ....   6 ....   7 ....   8 ....   9 ....

2

Manuela has just arrived in London to study English at a language school. She is living in a flat with a group of English girls who are very kind and helpful. Complete their offers and invitations. Use *Would you like ... ?/Would you like to ... ?/Would you like me to ... ?*

1 I'll be driving past your language school this morning. .... a lift?

2 I've just made some coffee. .... some?

3 This is our microwave. .... show you how it works?

4 You haven't got an umbrella, have you? .... borrow mine?

5 I'm afraid the bank doesn't open till 9.30. .... lend you some money?

6 There are two very nice boys living in the flat upstairs. .... meet them?

7 I know a Spanish girl at work. .... invite her round for a meal?

8 We're all going to a party tomorrow night. .... come?

Quick reference

- *Must* and *have to* sometimes mean the same - that something is necessary or obligatory. I **must go** now. OR I **have to go** now.

- In informal speech we can also use *have got to*. It usually means the same as *have to*. I've **got to go** now.

- To ask if something is necessary or obligatory, we normally use *Do I/you*, etc. *have to?* **Do you have to** be over 18? **Do I have to** come with you?

- There is sometimes a difference in meaning.
  <u>Must</u>: obligation coming from the speaker. You **must** read this book. I think it's good.
  <u>Have to</u>: obligation coming from the outside. They **have to** wear a uniform at school.
  I **didn't have to** wear a uniform when I was at school, but I **had to** have short hair.

- *Mustn't* and *don't have to* do not mean the same.
  Mustn't: You have no choice. You **mustn't** walk on the grass.
  Don't have to: You have a choice. You **don't have to** eat the soup if you don't like it.

1 Two people are on a day-trip to France. Complete the second sentence so that it has a similar meaning to the first sentence, using the word(s) given.

1 It was necessary for us to be at Dover at 10.15. (had)

   We .... at 10.15. The ferry left at 10.45.

2 It wasn't necessary for us to queue. (didn't)

   We .... queue. The ferry was half empty.

3 It wasn't necessary to take any <u>seasick pills</u>. (have)

   I .... pills. The sea wasn't <u>rough</u>.

4 Normally it's necessary to show your passport when you enter a foreign country, but when we got to Calais it was unnecessary. (have) (didn't)

   Normally .... passport when you enter a foreign country but when we

   got to Calais we ....

5 Every time I go to France I need to remind myself to drive on the right. (have)

   Every time I .... to drive on the right.

6 Some British drivers find this difficult. But it's essential not to forget it. (You)

   .... it.

7 The last ferry to Dover left at 11.00 so it was important to be at Calais by 10.30. (we)

   The last ferry to Dover left at 11.00 so .... by 10.30.

2 Look at these signs and complete the sentences using forms of *must* and *have to*.

Example: NO TALKING IN THE LIBRARY You *mustn't talk* in the library.

1 BUY NOW, PAY LATER

2 NO CYCLING ON FOOTPATH

3 OASIS CLUB MINIMUM AGE 18

4 TICKETS FREE

5 TAKE YOUR LITTER HOME

6 PARKING FREE AFTER 6 pm

7 ACE RENT-A-CAR For drivers over 25 with full British driving licence.

8 KEEP OFF THE GRASS

9 SERVICE INCLUDED

10 DRESS: JACKETS & TIES. NO JEANS OR T-SHIRTS

1 You .... pay now.

2 You .... footpath.

3 You .... 18 to get into the club.

4 You .... pay .... tickets.

5 You .... home.

6 You .... pay for parking after 6 pm.

7 You .... over 25 and you

.... a full British licence.

8 You .... walk .... grass.

9 You .... pay for service.

10 You .... wear a jacket and tie and

you .... wear jeans or a T-shirt.

3 One person is in a hurry, the other is more relaxed. Which sentences on the right match the ones on the left?

1 We must hurry.
2 We don't have to panic.
3 We mustn't miss the train.
4 We must leave enough time to buy tickets.
5 We must call for a taxi.
6 We don't have to go by taxi.
7 We mustn't forget to set the burglar alarm.
8 We don't have to worry about the house.

a) John will give us a lift.
b) It's too far to walk.
c) The neighbours will keep an eye on it.
d) The house will be empty for three weeks.
e) We've got plenty of time.
f) We haven't got much time.
g) There might be a queue at the ticket office.
h) There isn't another one till much later.

1 ....   2 ....   3 ....   4 ....   5 ....   6 ....   7 ....   8 ....

4 Put the following pieces of advice in the correct columns.

ADVICE TO VISITORS TO THE USA

A) have a valid passport   B) stay in motels   C) visit New York   D) work unless you've got a work permit
E) have an American Express credit card   F) stay longer than your visa permits   G) drive on the right
H) have enough money for the duration of your stay   I) drive at more than 55 mph on most roads
J) have air conditioning in your car   K) have alcohol, in a bottle or can, in your car

You must/have to	You mustn't	You don't have to
....	....	....

Quick reference

We use:

- *must* + infinitive without *to* or *must be* + *-ing* when we feel certain something is true.
  He **must live** here. That's his car outside.   The television's on. He **must be watching** TV.
  Note the short answers.
  Is he in? - He **must be**.
  Does he know we're here? - He **must do**. I told him we were coming at 8.00.

- *can't* + infinitive without *to* or *can't be* + *-ing* when we think something is impossible.
  She's just lost her job. She **can't have** much money. She **can't be feeling** very happy.

- *must have* + a past participle or *must have been* + *-ing* when we feel certain something was true in the past.
  The video's disappeared. Burglars **must have taken** it. They **must have been watching** the house when I went out. - Did they get in through a window? - They **must have done**.

- *can't have* + past participle or *can't have been* + *-ing* when we think something was impossible.
  He hit a motorcyclist. He **can't have seen** him. He **can't have been watching** the road.
  Was he driving carefully? - He **can't have been**.

---

1 Claire has got a maths exam soon. Her parents are talking about her. Complete the second sentence so that it has a similar meaning to the first, using the word(s) given.

Example: I'm sure it's a difficult time for her. (must) *It must be a difficult time for her.*

'I'm sure she's feeling worried.' (must) (1) .... worried.

'Do you think she's feeling nervous?'

'I'm sure she is.' (must) (2) .... be.

'I'm sure she isn't sleeping well.' (can't) (3) She ....

'I don't suppose she likes all this hard work.'

'I'm sure she doesn't.' (can't) (4) .... do.

'I'm sure she thinks she's going to fail the exam.' (must)

(5) She .... to fail the exam.

'Yes, I'm sure that's the problem.' (must) (6) Yes, that ....

'But she's good at maths. I'm sure she knows that.' (must) (7) She .... that.

'I'm sure she isn't feeling very confident, that's all.' (can't)

(8) She .... very confident, that's all.

After the maths exam Claire comes home, looking miserable. Her parents are talking about her again.

'I'm sure the exam was difficult.' (must have) (9) The exam .... difficult.

'It looks as if she didn't do very well.' (can't have) (10) She .... very well.

2 Andy Caswell has been shopping in town. He is talking to his wife, Jenny. Complete the sentences, using *must have* or *can't have* + past participle, or *must have been/can't have been* + *-ing*.

ANDY: I bought myself a new mobile phone. It's one of the best you can buy. Look!

JENNY: (1 be) It .... expensive.

ANDY: No, I got it at a special price.

JENNY: Well, it (2 be) .... cheap if it's the best you can buy. (3 cost) It

.... at least £200!

ANDY: Well, nearly. By the way, I think I've lost my credit card. (4 drop) I .... it

somewhere. But I had it when I bought the phone.

JENNY: Well, (5 leave) you .... at the shop.

ANDY: (6 leave) I .... it there, because I used it to buy some petrol on the way

home. Oh, I forgot to tell you, I had a small accident in the car. I hit a tree.

JENNY: (7 damage) You .... the car. (8 go) You .... too fast.

ANDY: No, I wasn't going fast.

JENNY: Well, (9 concentrate) you ....

ANDY: No, I was concentrating. I was trying to ring you on my new phone.

3 The police are looking for Meg Sharp. Look at the pictures, and make your conclusions. Answer the questions, using the short answers: *She must have been/She must have done. She can't have been/She can't have done.*

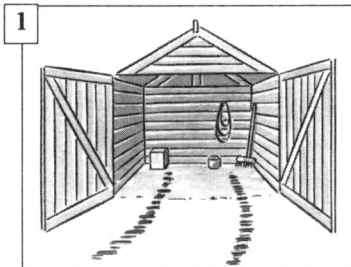

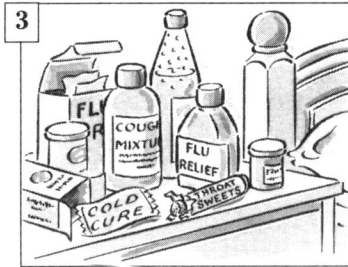

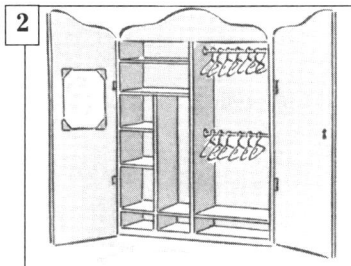

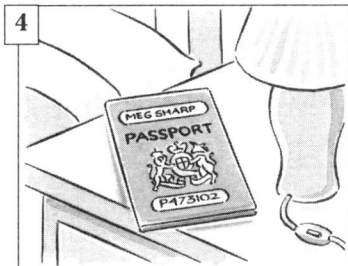

1   Did she take her car?

....

2   Was she planning to be away for a long time?

....

3   Was she feeling well?

....

4   Has she gone abroad?

....

4 Think of an important time in the past. Imagine how people felt and make deductions. Write three sentences using *must have* + past participle.   Example: *They must have been very excited.*
Write three sentences using *can't have* + past participle.   Example: *They can't have had much to eat.*

Check your answers with a teacher.

29 — *May (have), might (have), could (have)*

Quick reference

- We use *may, might* or *could* when we say that something is possible (in the present or the future). *It **may/might/could** rain this afternoon.*
- We use the negative forms *may not/might not* to talk about possibility, but not *couldn't*. *I **may not/might not** see you tomorrow.* (NOT I couldn't see you tomorrow.)
- *Couldn't* means something is impossible. *He **couldn't** be American. He's got a British passport.*
- We often use a continuous form: *may be, might be, could be* + *-ing* to talk about a present possibility. *She **may be lying**. They **could be waiting** for us to ring.*
- We can use either *may have, might have* or *could have* + a past participle to say that something was possible in the past. *Where is she? - She **might have gone** to town already. She **could have left** early.*
- *Could have* can also mean that something was possible but didn't happen. *The police **could have** caught him.* (= They didn't catch him.)
- Note the negative forms *may not have/might not have*. *I **may not have remembered** to lock the door.* (= It's possible I didn't remember.)
- *Couldn't have* means that something was totally impossible. *He **couldn't have passed** the exam. He never did any work.* (= It wasn't possible.)
- We often use the continuous form *may have been, might have been, could have been* + *-ing* to talk about a past possibility. *He didn't answer the phone. He **might have been having** a bath.*

1 Complete this weather forecast, using *may/might/could* or *may not/might not/couldn't*.

All parts of the country will have rain tomorrow but the rain (1) .... reach the south till the evening. It will be quite warm. Temperatures (2) .... reach 25°. Winds will increase from the west and (3) .... reach speeds of 45 mph on the coast but they (4) .... be as strong inland. And the forecast for the weekend? It (5) .... be better really. Dry, warm and sunny for both Saturday and Sunday.

2 This man is in hospital. Complete what his friends are saying about him, using each of these verb forms.

| couldn't | may have | may not | could | may | might have |

'He (1) .... be in hospital for weeks.'

'He (2) .... recover completely.'

'But it (3) .... be worse. He (4) .... been killed.'

'This is a very good hospital. He (5) .... get better medical treatment anywhere else.'

'The other car was on the wrong side of the road. The driver (6) .... been drunk.'

3 Helen Goodman was driving to an important meeting when her car broke down. Now she is phoning her office. Some of the lines are correct and some have a mistake. If a line is correct put a tick (✓) after it. If a line has a mistake in it, underline the mistake and write the correction in the brackets.

1 My car's broken down. I couldn't get to the meeting on time.   (.................)

2 I mightn't have contacted you earlier because I couldn't find a phone.   (.................)

3 I may be as much as an hour late.   (.................)

4 I might have left home earlier.   (.................)

5 But I may not have known that my car was going to break down.   (.................)

6 This delay wouldn't have happened at a worse time.   (.................)

7 I may have to wait for hours for someone to come and repair the car.   (.................)

8 I might leave my car here and take a taxi.   (.................)

4 An office building is on fire. Two firefighters are discussing the situation. Complete the dialogue using each of these verb forms.

couldn't   might have   may not   couldn't have   may   could

'We (1) .... have got everybody out of the building. There (2) .... be more

people trapped inside. But they (3) .... still be alive in there. The heat's too intense.'

'We (4) .... got here sooner. We came as soon as we (5) ....'

'I wonder what started the fire.'

'It (6) .... been a gas leak. I smelt gas when we first arrived.'

5 On 15 May 1979 David Booth of Cincinnati dreamed that he saw a three-engined American Airlines plane crashing. He had the same dream for seven nights. On 22 May he told aviation officials in Washington about it. They interviewed him and wrote down the details of his dream but did nothing more. On 25 May American Airlines flight 191, a DC 10 with three engines, crashed shortly after take-off at O'Hare Airport, Chicago, killing 273 people.
Which of the alternatives are correct? (One, two or three alternatives may be correct.)

1 Booth a) *may have* b) *could have* c) *might have* had powers to see into the future. ......

2 He a) *couldn't have* b) *might not have* c) *may not have* lied about his dreams after the crash,

   because the interview was recorded. ......

3 The dream a) *may not have* b) *couldn't have* c) *might not have* been clearer and he had the same

   dream seven times. ......

4 He a) *couldn't have done anything* b) *may not have done anything* c) *could have done nothing* about

   his dreams but in fact he contacted Washington. ......

5 American Airlines a) *couldn't have* b) *mightn't have* c) *may not have* grounded all its planes. ......

6 The plane a) *might not have* b) *couldn't have* c) *may not have* crashed if Booth hadn't had his

   dream. ......

Quick reference

We use:

- *should/shouldn't* or *ought to/oughtn't to* + infinitive to say something is or isn't the right thing to do.
  *You **should go** to the dentist's.   You **oughtn't to smoke**.*

- *should/shouldn't*, etc. + *be* + *-ing* to say that something should (shouldn't) be in progress now.
  *You **shouldn't be watching** television. You **ought to be working**.*

- *had ('d) better (not)* + an infinitive without *to* to say that something is (isn't) the right thing to
  do. We use it with *I* and *we* to talk about an immediate intention.
    *It's late. **I'd better** go.   This liquid may be poisonous. **We'd better not** touch it.*
  We use it with *you* or *he, she, it, they* when we're giving advice or a warning about the present or
  the immediate future.
    *She looks ill. **She'd better** stay in bed.   You've had too much to drink. **You'd better not** drive.*

- *should have/ought to have/shouldn't have/oughtn't to have* + a past participle to say that
  something in the past was a mistake.
    *I didn't pass the exam. I **oughtn't to have been** so lazy. I **should have worked** harder.*

- *should(n't) have been* or *ought(n't) to have been* + *-ing* when we talk about something that
  should(n't) have been in progress at a particular moment in the past.
    *When he was knocked down, he was using his mobile phone. He **should have been watching**
    the traffic. He **oughtn't to have been** using his phone.*

- *should/shouldn't* and *ought to/oughtn't to* to talk about how probable something is, or what we
  expect to happen in the future.
    *I don't have to work late today, so I **should** be home by 6.00.*
    *I gave her a map, so she **shouldn't** get lost.*

1 Stephanie Reed works for a computer software company. She is a workaholic. She works at least
12 hours a day. She only gets home from the office at 9 p.m. She smokes a lot. She eats a lot of junk
food. She does not spend much time with her family. At the moment she is driving home from
work. She is very tired and she is doing 160 k.p.h. on the motorway. She has got one hand on the
steering wheel. With the other she is eating a pizza. Is Stephanie doing the right thing? What do
you think? Write eight sentences, using *should/ought to* + infinitive and *should/ought to* + *be* +
-ing (or their negative forms).

1 .... work so hard.

2 .... home earlier.

3 .... smoke so much.

4 .... so much junk food.

5 .... more time with her family.

6 And now .... so fast.

7 .... both hands on the steering wheel.

8 .... a pizza when she's driving.

2 Last night Lucy Cage went to a country pub near her home to listen to a new Australian group. She did not tell her parents where she was going. She did not look at the bus timetable and when she arrived at the bus-stop she found there were no buses. She decided not to get a taxi. She walked alone along the dark road that led to the pub. She tried to get into the concert without paying, but the doorman saw her and made her pay. During the evening she behaved very stupidly. She went up to the group and tried to kiss the lead singer. The doorman told her to leave and got her a taxi. When the taxi arrived at her house, she refused to pay the driver. Her father was angry with her and called her an idiot. Her mother tried to calm things down. Lucy said she would not come into the house until her father had apologised. He would not apologise. Her mother told her to come in and they would talk about it the next day. But Lucy would not listen. Write eight sentences about what you think Lucy and her father did wrong. Use *should(n't) have* or *ought(n't) to have* + past participle.

1 ....

2 ....

3 ....

4 ....

5 ....

6 ....

7 ....

8 ....

3 Match what one person says on the left with the replies of the other on the right.

1 The travel agent said the hotels on Anguilla get full very quickly.

2 When shall we go?

3 I'm not sure when I can get two weeks off work.

4 I'll ask my boss tomorrow.

5 It's going to cost us twice as much as last year's holiday.

6 And we were going to change the car this year.

7 We could spend less money on the house and on clothes.

a) Is it? Perhaps we'd better go somewhere cheaper.

b) Yes, we could. I'd better not buy that new suit.

c) Well, we'd better not. We can't afford that as well.

d) We'd better book straight away then.

e) Yes, you'd better.

f) Well, you'd better find out.

g) I don't know, but we'd better decide quickly.

1 ....   2 ....   3 ....   4 ....   5 ....   6 ....   7 ....

4 Tom is telling a friend that he can probably meet him later. Complete the second sentence so that it has a similar meaning to the first, using forms of *should*.

1 I'll probably have finished work by 4.15.

I .... by 4.15.

2 So I'll probably be able to catch a bus at about 4.30.

So I .... at about 4.30.

3 There probably won't be much traffic at that time.

There .... at that time.

4 So I'll probably be able to meet you in town at 5.00.

So I .... at 5.00.

Have got/have:
I've got £200. She's having a bath

Quick reference

- *Have got* and *have* mean the same. But in informal English we normally use *have got* rather than *have* when we talk about:
Possessions: *I've got a motorbike.* Relatives: *She's got two brothers.*
Personal characteristics: *He's got blue eyes.* Illnesses: *I've got a cold.*

- In American English we rarely use *have got* in questions or negatives.
*We **haven't got** a video.* (British English) *We **don't have** a video.* (American English)

- Note the short answers *Yes, I have/No, they haven't*, etc.
Has she got a flat? - **Yes, she has**.

- In the past simple we use *had/didn't have*. We can use *had got/hadn't got*, but they're less common.
*When I was 20, I **had** long hair, but I **didn't have** a moustache.*

- Note that we don't include *got* in these forms:
Future: *When the baby is born, they**'ll have** four children.*
Present perfect: *I've had this cold for a week.* Infinitive: *He might **have** malaria.*

- We use *have* for actions or activities. *She's **having** a swim. They **had** an argument.*
*We've **had** a long walk. How often **do you have** a bath?*

- Note that we don't use contractions with *have* when it's describing an action.
*They **have** two holidays a year.* (NOT They've two holidays.)

1 **Complete the sentences with forms of *have got* where possible or, where not possible, with forms of *have*.**

This year Tom Carter (1) .... a job with a company called Club 18-30 which specialises in holidays for young people between the ages of 18 and 30.

'I (2) .... an interview in London last May. I (3) .... any qualifications but they offered me the job. I (4) .... a week's <u>training</u> in London and then they sent me out here to Torremolinos. Now I (5) .... a room in a small flat above a restaurant. It (6) .... a bed and a chair but it (7) .... any other furniture. It's a good thing I (8) .... many clothes. I (9) .... my 18-30 uniform (a T-shirt with the company logo on it) and some jeans but that's about all.

My friends at home think I (10) .... a four-month holiday but it's not like that at all. It's hard work. I (11) .... only .... two days off since I started work here. I get up at about 9. I (12) .... much sleep, five or six hours at the most. Then I (13) .... a shower and a shave. For breakfast I just (14) .... a cup of coffee and a bread roll. I (15) .... lunch - I (16) .... time! In the afternoon I sometimes (17) .... a short siesta.

My job is to make sure our customers (18) .... a good time. I (19) .... a lot of friends here. Most of them are people like me who (20) .... jobs with holiday companies. I (21) .... a girlfriend back home in Manchester so I (22) .... any serious <u>relationships</u> since I've been here.

Last week I (23) .... food <u>poisoning</u> and I remembered too late that I (24) .... any <u>insurance.</u> The medicine cost me half a week's wages! I (25) .... six more weeks' work here and then I go back to England. I hope I (26) .... some money in my pocket!'

2 **Read this dialogue. Decide which answer, A, B, or C best fits each space.**

DOCTOR: What's the problem?

PATIENT: I (1) .... a lot of headaches recently.

DOCTOR: (2) .... a headache at the moment?

PATIENT: Yes I (3) ....

DOCTOR: When was the last time you (4) .... one?

PATIENT: On Monday.

DOCTOR: (5) .... any particular problems at the moment?

PATIENT: Well, (6) .... plenty of problems but I (7) .... any particular ones.

DOCTOR: (8) .... any children?

PATIENT: Yes, (9) .... three.

DOCTOR: (10) .... a husband?

PATIENT: Yes, (11) ....

DOCTOR: (12) .... a job?

PATIENT: (13) No, he ....

DOCTOR: How much sleep (14) .... ?

PATIENT: About seven hours a night normally, but lately I (15) ℞. less than that.

DOCTOR: (16) .... a holiday recently?

PATIENT: No, we (17) .... enough money for holidays!

DOCTOR: So you (18) .... a holiday this year.

PATIENT: No, I'm afraid we can't afford one.

DOCTOR: I see. Well, (19) .... lots of patients like you. I think these pills might help.

1 A I've got	B I have	C I've been having
2 A Have you got	B You have	C Have you had
3 A had	B have	C got
4 A have	B had got	C had
5 A Have you got	B Got you	C You have
6 A I got	B I've got	C I'm having
7 A haven't got	B not have	C not got
8 A Do you got	B Have you got	C You have
9 A I've got	B I got	C I'm having
10 A You have	B Have you got	C Did you have
11 A I got	B I do	C I havc
12 A Has he got	B Have he got	C Have he
13 A hasn't got	B hasn't	C doesn't
14 A do you have	B have you got	C have you
15 A I've got	B I've had	C I had
16 A Did you have	B Have you got	C Have you had
17 A haven't got	B don't have	C aren't having
18 A haven't had	B haven't got	C aren't having
19 A I had	B I got	C I've got

3 **Describe yourself or a person you know well, using four sentences with *have got* and four with *have*. Check your answers with a teacher.**

Example: *I've got blue eyes and long, blond hair. I've got three brothers, but I haven't got any sisters. I haven't got a driver's licence, so I'm having driving lessons at the moment. When I pass my driving test, I'm going to have a party.*

32 Phrasal verbs:
I got up and turned off the light

Quick reference

- Phrasal verbs are usually two-word verbs (verb + adverbial particle): *go out, put on, give up*, etc.
- We can use different particles with the same verb. The meaning changes.
  *I **got up** at 7.00 this morning.* (= got out of bed)
  *The police arrested the thief, but he **got away**.* (= escaped)
- Most phrasal verbs can take an object. The object can usually go before or after the particle.
  *I turned on **the radio**.* OR *I turned **the radio** on.*
- But if the object is a pronoun, the pronoun always goes before the particle.
  *Here's your coat. Put **it** on.* (NOT Put on it.)
- 'Long' objects go after the particle.
  *Why don't you throw away **the clothes you don't wear any more**.*
  (NOT Why don't you throw the clothes you don't wear any more away.)
- Some phrasal verbs are three-word verbs (verb + particle + preposition): *get on with, run out of*, etc. Here, the object must go after the preposition.
  *I don't get on with **my parents**. I don't get on with **them**.*

---

1 **A girl is describing the first episode of a TV series she has just watched. Replace the words in italics with the correct forms of these phrasal verbs.**

| pick up (x2) think over get out hand over come back get up wake up set off get away from |
| run out of go on go down get on with lie down go out with take off come up to talk over |

Brad, an American teenager, *had a bad relationship with* (1) .... his parents. He

wanted to *escape* (2) .... from them. He *considered it* (3) ....

for several days before he finally decided to *leave* (4) .... He said to himself he

would never *return* (5) .... He *was having a relationship with* (6) ....

.... Donna, a girl who was also unhappy at home. One night he *got out of bed*

(7) .... at 3 a.m. He took his father's car. He *collected his girlfriend* (8) ....

.... and they *started their journey* (9) .... for the Mexican

border. They *suddenly had no more* (10) .... petrol in the middle of Texas. What

were they going to do? They *discussed it* (11) .... for a long time, and finally they

started to walk. They *continued* (12) .... for hours in the hot sun. Brad *removed*

(13) .... his shirt so Donna could put it over her head. They tried to get a lift, but

no-one stopped to *take them* (14) .... The nearest town was 25 miles away and the

sun *was sinking* (15) .... They *stretched out on the ground* (16) ....

.... by the side of the road and fell asleep. Two hours later a man *approached* (17) ....

.... them. His voice *wakened them* (18) .... It was a truck

driver. Would he take them to Mexico, or would he *let the police have them* (19) ....

to the police?

2 **Doris Griggs has got a very difficult husband. When she wants something, he wants the opposite. Use the word given in capitals at the end of each line to form a phrasal verb that fits in the space in the same line.**

Example: When I turn up the television because I can't hear it, he *turns it down*.   TURN

Sometimes when I switch the television on, he (1) ....   SWITCH

When I want to go out, he wants to (2) .... When I get a   STAY

drink out of the cupboard, he (3) .... When I put up a nice   PUT

picture in the living room, he (4) .... When I want to go   TAKE

to bed early, he wants to (5) .... When I say I like the shirt   STAY

he's wearing, he (6) .... When I say I want him to stop talking,   TAKE

he just (7) .... When I ask him to come home early, he automatically   CARRY

(8) .... late. He thinks I like him, but to be honest I really can't   GET

(9) .... him for much longer.   PUT

3 **Helen is 20 but she is still living at home. Her mother is talking to her. Replace the words in italics with a pronoun (*it, him, them,* etc.) and rewrite the sentence.**

1   You watch too much television. Turn *the television* off.

....

2   Why are you smoking? You should give up *smoking*.

....

3   Why are you wearing that old sweater. Take off *that old sweater*!

....

4   You've left your clothes all over the floor. Put *your clothes* away.

....

5   Your room's full of old magazines. Why don't you throw away *the old magazines*?

....

6   In fact your room's in an awful mess. Clear up *the mess*!

....

7   You're so lazy. I can't put up with *your laziness* any more.

....

8   You owe me £10. You haven't paid *the £10* back yet.

....

9   What about this job application form? You haven't filled in *this job application form*.

....

10   What about the manager of the new supermarket ? He might have a job for you. Why don't you ring up *the manager*?

....

11   You don't know his telephone number? Well, look up *his number* in the telephone book!

....

12   One day you might get a job. I'm really looking forward to *the day when you get a job*.

....

33 Verbs of perception: see, watch, notice, hear, feel, taste, smell

Quick reference

- We normally use *can* and *can't* with the verbs of perception (*see, hear, feel, taste, smell*) in the present. *I **can see** our hotel. I **can't hear** you. I **can smell** gas.*
We don't normally use the present continuous or the present simple with these verbs.
   (NOT I see our hotel. I don't hear you. I'm smelling gas.)

- In the past we use *could* and *couldn't* with these verbs when we talk about a **continuing** perception. *I **could hear** the noise of the traffic, but I **couldn't see** the sea.*
We use these verbs in the past simple if the perception was **momentary**.
   *Suddenly, I **heard** a noise. When the children **saw** the sea, they got very excited.*

- We use the *-ing* form after these verbs when an action or an event is or was in progress.
   *I can hear somebody **singing**. She watched them **playing**. I saw him **smoking**.*

- But we use the infinitive without *to* when we talk about a completed action or event that we saw, heard or felt from beginning to end.
   *I heard him **sing** that song in 1975. She watched him **get into** his car and **drive away**.*

---

1 Harry McCann was in prison for ten years. He is out now, but he cannot forget what it was like. Write complete sentences, matching the verbs with the other part of the sentence.

He can still	see	the awful prison food.
	hear	the unwashed bodies of other prisoners.
	feel	the sound of the prison guards shouting.
	taste	the four walls of his prison cell.
	smell	the hard mattress on his bed.

1 ....

2 ....

3 ....

4 ....

5 ....

2 Katherine and James are on holiday. James is still in bed. Katherine is on the balcony of their room, talking to him. Read the text and decide which answer, A, B, C or D best fits each space.

I (1) .... some people down by the swimming pool. There's a good-looking boy down by the pool. He's saying something to me but I (2) .... what he's saying - he's too far away. I (3) .... a man singing but I (4) .... him - he's in the room below us I think. It's quite hot out here - I (5) .... the warmth of the sun on my face.

1 A see	B can see	C am seeing	D do see
2 A don't hear	B am not hearing	C can't hear	D don't can hear
3 A can hear	B am hearing	C hear	D do hear
4 A don't see	B can't see	C can't seeing	D am not seeing
5 A am feeling	B feel	C can feel	D can feeling

3 A motorcycle rider was involved in a road accident. Complete the sentences using *could/couldn't* + *see, feel, taste, hear, smell.*

He (1) .... the sound of the siren and through the window of the ambulance he

(2) .... its blue light flashing. He (3) .... that one of the ambulance men was

trying to say something to him - he (4) .... his lips moving - but he (5) ....

him through the bandage that covered his ears. He (6) .... disinfectant, and on his lips he

(7) .... blood. But what alarmed him most was that he (8) .... his right leg.

4 Use the past simple to complete the text, or *could/couldn't* + infinitive without *to*, **where you think it is preferable.**

I was flying from London to Barcelona. On the plane everything was normal. I (1 hear) ....

the engines running smoothly. We were flying over the Pyrenees, and I (2 see) .... the

snow-covered mountain tops. The flight attendants were serving lunch. I (3 smell) ....

coffee. Suddenly we flew into some severe turbulence, and I (4 feel) .... the plane fall

several metres. I (5 feel) .... a sudden panic. I (6 hear) .... a woman behind me

drop her food tray. The plane was shaking, and everyone was very quiet. I (7 not hear) ....

.... anyone talking now.

Then, five minutes later, we were all very relieved when we (8 hear) .... the captain say

we had left the turbulence behind.

5 Complete these sentences, using the verbs in the box in the *-ing* form or the infinitive without *to.*

approach   burn   slam   come   get   explode   shout   jump   begin   take   put

I woke up when I heard a door (1) .... I could hear some people (2) ....

Seconds later I heard something (3) .... downstairs. Then I smelt something

(4) .... The house was on fire! I listened to the sound of flames (5) .... nearer

and nearer and I felt heat (6) .... up through the floor. I looked out of my window and saw

a woman suddenly (7) .... from her first floor balcony. But I couldn't jump - I was on the

third floor! I heard the sound of a siren (8) .... Two minutes later the fire engine

arrived. I watched the firefighters (9) .... the ladder off the fire engine and then

(10) .... it up against the building. As I climbed out of the window and onto the ladder I

could see flames (11) .... to burn through the door of my bedroom!

6 a) **Write sentences about what you can or cannot see, hear, etc. at this moment.**
   I can/can't see ...   I can hear someone/I can't hear anyone ...
   I can/can't smell ...   I can/can't feel ...

b) **Write four sentences in which you describe something which you saw happen or happening recently. Use these verbs + the *-ing* form or the infinitive without *to*: *see, watch, hear, notice, smell.***

   Check your answers with a teacher.

Look, sound, feel, taste, smell, seem + adjective OR like OR as if/as though

Quick reference

- We use *look, sound, feel, taste, smell, seem* to talk about our impression of things. We use an adjective after them, not an adverb.
  *I **feel terrible**.* (NOT terribly) *This soup **tastes good**.* (NOT well)
- For visual appearance we use *look*. *You **look** happy.* *The children **looked** frightened.*
- We use *sound* to talk about the things we hear.
  *She **sounded** tired on the phone.* *That music **sounds** awful.*
- We use *like* + a noun after these verbs to say what someone or something is similar to.
  *She **looks like** her mother.* *What's that noise? - It **sounds like** thunder.*
- We use *of*, not *like*, after *taste* and *smell* when there's a particular taste or smell on something.
  *This cup **tastes of** washing-up liquid.* *These gloves **smell of** petrol.*
- We can use *as if/as though* + a subject and a verb after these verbs to describe our impressions.
  As if and *as though* mean the same. *You **look as though** you've seen a ghost.*
  *I **feel as if** I'm going to be sick.* *He **sounded as if** he had a cold.*
- We often use the impersonal *it* with *look, sound, feel, + as if/as though*, with the meaning 'It seems as if/as though'. *Look at those clouds. **It** looks as if it's going to rain.*
  *I spoke to James. **It** sounds as if he isn't coming to the party.*

1 Gemma is ill. Her boyfriend Rick has come to see her. Complete the sentences using the verb in brackets and each of these adjectives/adjectival phrases once: *quite good, worse, very well, terrible, hot, pale, very nice.*

RICK: How do you feel?

GEMMA: I (1 not feel) .... What do I look like?

RICK: Well, your face (2 look) .... And you've almost lost your voice. You

(3 sound) .... I thought you were getting better yesterday, but you

(4 seem) .... today. Have you got a temperature?

GEMMA: Yes, my forehead (5 feel) ....

RICK: Try this medicine.

GEMMA: Ugh! It (6 not smell) ....

RICK: What does it taste like?

GEMMA: Mmm! It (7 taste) ....

2 Kate has just given Amy a present. She wants Amy to guess what it is before she opens it. Look at the pictures and complete Kate's questions and Amy's answers.

KATE: Look at it. (1) What .... like?

AMY: (2) It .... a book.

KATE: Feel it. (3) What ....?

AMY: (4) It .... a box.

KATE: Shake it. (5 sound) What ....?

AMY: (6) It .... chocolates.

3 Complete the dialogue with *like* or *of*.

'Ugh! You smell awful.'

'What do I smell (1) ....?'

'You smell (2) .... varnish. What have you been doing?'

'I've been varnishing the kitchen cupboards.'

'Yes, they look good. Well, I'm going to have a cup of tea. Would you like one?'

'Oh, thanks. Ugh! This cup tastes (3) .... varnish. Give me another one.'

'There's some sugar in that jar.'

'Are you sure this is sugar? It tastes (4) .... salt.'

'Oh, sorry. Here's the sugar.'

'Now, why don't you go and change your clothes? You smell (5) .... a chemical factory.'

4 Helen has just arrived home after work. She is talking to her husband Paul. Complete the second sentence so that it has a similar meaning to the first, using the word given.

HELEN: Phew! I'm tired!

PAUL: You give me the impression you've had a bad day. (sound)

Example: *You sound as if (as though) you've had a bad day.*

HELEN: Yes, it's as if someone's hit me over the head. (feel)

1 Yes, I .... over the head.

PAUL: What about a glass of wine?

HELEN: I think I could drink a whole bottle. (feel)

2 I .... a whole bottle.

PAUL: Oh no. I don't think we've got any wine. (look)

3 Oh, no. It .... we've got any wine. I think we'll have to go to the pub. (looks)

4 It .... go to the pub.

HELEN: Oh. I don't think I could go out again this evening. (feel)

5 Oh. I .... I could go out again this evening.

5 Match each item on the left with the correct one on the right.

1 There's Lisa. She doesn't look

2 She says she feels

3 But I feel

4 She looks

5 It's Nathan, I think. It looks

6 He doesn't sound

7 I saw him in town with Zoe. And it looks

8 And Zoe is Lisa's best friend. It seems

a) as though he hasn't told Lisa.

b) like a very nice boy.

c) as if she's treating Lisa very badly.

d) fine.

e) as if he's found another girlfriend.

f) like someone who's got boyfriend problems.

g) very happy today.

h) sure she isn't telling the truth.

1 ....   2 ....   3 ....   4 ....   5 ....   6 ....   7 ....   8 ....

Quick reference

We use *There is/There are*:

- to introduce a piece of information. ***There's** a new teacher at college.*

- to describe what we can see. *Look. **There's** a fly in my soup.*

- Singular: ***There's (is)** a man at the door. **Is there** a bank here? **There isn't** a park here.*
  Plural: ***There are** two cars outside. **Are there** any buses? **There aren't** any taxis.*

- We use *There is* before a list of things if the first item is singular.
  ***There's** a book, a newspaper and some magazines on the table.*

- We use *There is* or *There are* when we mention something for the first time. If we then want to
  give more information about it, we use *It's* and *They're*.
  ***There's** a car outside. **It's** red. **There are** two letters. **They're** both for you.*

1 Use forms of *there is/there are* to complete this telephone conversation between an estate agent
and a person interested in buying a large three-storey house in London.

'How many bedrooms (1) .... on the top floor?'

'(2) .... three.'

'And how many bathrooms (3) ....?'

'(4) .... only one bathroom on the top floor but (5) .... another on the first floor.'

'(6) .... much noise from traffic?'

'Well, (7) .... quite a lot of traffic, but (8) .... much noise.'

'(9) .... room to park a car?'

'No, (10) .... But (11) .... usually plenty of parking spaces in the street.'

'(12) .... an underground station nearby?'

'Yes, (13) .... two in fact.'

'(14) .... any people living in the house at the moment?'

'No, (15) .... So, if you're interested, I can show you round the house at any time.'

2 Read the text below about a Greek island and look carefully at each line. Some of the lines are
correct, and some have a mistake. If a line is correct put a tick (✓) after it. If a line has a mistake in
it, underline the mistake and write the correction in the brackets.

Example: Two kilometres from the only big town on the island, there <u>are</u> an airport. (*is*)

(1) It isn't a very big airport - it's only got one very short runway. (................)

(2) There are only one real road on the island and it's only 18 kilometres long. (................)

(3) There's buses which go backwards and forwards along this road every half an hour. (................)

(4) In the summer they're usually very full because there's dozens of hotels on the (................)

(5) island. There are on the south coast where there are several good beaches. (................)

(6) Every summer there are thousands of tourists from Northern Europe. But in the (................)

(7) winter it's very different. There's only a few hundred people left on the (................)

(8) island and they are mostly old people. (................)

Quick reference

- We use *used to* + infinitive to talk about a habit or a regular activity in the past that doesn't happen now (or that might or might not happen now).
  *I **used to smoke**, but I don't now.   My father **used to be** a professional footballer.*

- Note the question form *did I/you/*etc. *use to* + infinitive.
  ***Did you use to** eat frogs' legs when you lived in France?*
  ***Did your parents use to criticise** you a lot when you were young?*

- Note the negative forms *didn't use to* or *used not to* and *never used to* + infinitive.
  *Laura drinks beer now. - Does she? She **didn't use to/used not to** like it. She **never used to drink** it.*

---

1 **Oliver Stratton is telling a journalist how his life has changed. Complete the sentences about his past with *used to*.**   Example: I live in London now. *(Manchester)* *I used to live in Manchester.*

1   I'm a professional actor now. *(history teacher)* ....

2   I travel a lot now. *(not travel/much)* ....

3   I often go abroad now. *(never go abroad)* ....

4   I've got a lot of friends. *(not have/many)* ....

5   *(never like/getting up in the morning)* Now I look forward to each day.

   ....

6   *(not like/hard work)* Now I enjoy it. ....

7   *(My old pupils/not be/interested in me)* Now they ask for my autograph!

   ....

2 **Neil and Sue are both 30. They are talking about the time when they were teenagers. Use forms of *used to* to complete their conversation.**

SUE: My parents were very strict. They never (1) .... trust me.

NEIL: Didn't they? What (2) .... do?

SUE: Whenever I went out, they (3) .... ask me where I was going.

NEIL: (4) .... let you go out with boys?

SUE: No, they didn't. All my friends (5) .... go out with boys. I (6) .... envy them.

NEIL: (7) .... get angry?

SUE: Yes, I did. I (8) .... have arguments with them. And I often (9) ....
   speak to them for days.

NEIL: My parents were the same. They found relationships with the opposite sex very embarrassing.
   They (10) .... talk about them. They (11) .... make me feel
   guilty if I wanted to go out with a girl. I (12) .... get very angry with them sometimes.

3 **Have your tastes and habits changed? Write five sentences about things you used to do and that you do not do now, and five sentences about things you did not use to do and that you do now. Check your answers with a teacher.**
Examples: *I used to smoke a lot. I didn't use to read much, but I read a lot now.*

Quick reference

● We use *get used to something* or *get used to doing something* when we talk about the process of becoming accustomed to something. Something that was strange or unfamiliar, at first, becomes familiar and normal.

   *I can't **get used to** speaking English.* (It's still strange to me.)
   *I'm **getting used to** speaking English.* (It's becoming less strange.)
   *I've **got used to** speaking English.* (It isn't a problem now.)

● We use *be used to something* or *be used to doing something* when we say that we are(n't) or we were(n't) accustomed to something.

   *I'm **used to** the job.   They **were used to** an easy life.   He **wasn't used to** sleeping in a tent.*

● Note the difference between the verbs *used to* and *be used to*.

   *I **used to** eat seafood.* (= It was my habit in the past. I don't do it now.)
   *I'm **used to** eating seafood.* (= It's familiar, not strange to me.)

1 **An American journalist from Washington has been living in London for six months. Some things he still finds strange, others he is accustomed to. Complete the second sentence so that it has a similar meaning to the first sentence, using the words given.**

1 He sees police officers without guns every day. (seeing)

   He .... police officers without guns.

2 He finds it normal that he gets free medical treatment. (used)

   He .... free medical treatment.

3 He normally travels by public transport now. (is)

   He .... travelling by public transport.

4 He still finds it strange to have a small refrigerator. (having)

   He still .... a small refrigerator.

5 He still isn't accustomed to living in a city centre. (used)

   He still .... living in a city centre.

2 **A month ago Maggie Sullivan won half a million pounds on the lottery. A journalist is interviewing her. Complete the text using forms of *be used to* or *get used to* + noun or *-ing*.**

JOURNALIST: (1) .... you .... (be) rich yet?

MAGGIE: No, not yet. I'm trying (2) .... all this money, but it isn't easy.

JOURNALIST: What's the biggest problem?

MAGGIE: I (3) .... (get up) early when I had a job. That wasn't difficult. Now I don't have to go to work but I can't (4) .... (stay) in bed till 9.00.

JOURNALIST: (5) .... you .... (live) in this big house?

MAGGIE: Oh yes, that isn't a problem. I soon (6) .... that. I don't think I could ever (7) .... (live) in a small flat again. But I (8) .... (be) so far from all my friends. And there's another thing I'll never (9) .... I still look for bargains and special offers in the supermarket. I don't think I'll ever (10) .... (spend) as much as I like in the shops.

38 Verb + indirect object/direct object: *I gave the man some money*

Quick reference

- An indirect object normally refers to a person and comes before a direct object.

	Indirect object	**Direct object**
I sent	*my brother*	*a postcard.*
He lent	*her*	*his car.*

- We put the object that gives more important information second.
  *What did you give your wife? - I gave her **some flowers**.*
  *Who did he give the flowers to? - He gave them **to his wife**.*

- We use *to* or *for* when we want to emphasise the indirect object.
  *He left his London apartment **to his son** and his villa in Monte Carlo **to his daughter**.*
  *I've saved this seat **for you**.   He made a meal **for all the family**.*

- An indirect object with *to* or *for* goes after the direct object.
  *She left all her money **to her children**.* (NOT She left to her children all her money.)

- If the direct object is a pronoun, we normally use *to* or *for* with the indirect object.
  *Show it **to him**.*   (NOT Show it him.)   *I've posted it **for you**.* (NOT I've posted you it.)

1 Put the following sentences in the right order.

1 Every year Doris Slocombe/her sister Mary/a birthday card/sends.

....

2 Last week she/the card/to her husband George/gave. (She asked him to post it.)

....

3 Two days later Mary/a letter/sent/to Doris.

....

4 She told/some shocking news/her. ....

5 The postman had only given/half the card/her.

....

6 He told/the reason/Mary. ....

('Snails in the post box have eaten the other half of the card.')

2 A film director is telling his actors and technicians what he wants them to do.
a) Complete the sentences with *to* or *for*. b) Then rewrite the sentences without *to* or *for*.

Example: Fetch my glasses *for* me. *Fetch me my glasses.*

1 Make some coffee .... everyone. ....

2 Send this fax .... the producer. ....

3 Buy a packet of cigarettes .... me. ....

4 Book a table .... me at Doyle's Bar. ....

5 Order a taxi .... me for 6.30. ....

6 Give this note .... my assistant. ....

7 Take this reel of film .... the editor. ....

Quick reference

- We use *need* + a noun when we talk about the things it's necessary to have.
  *You **need** an umbrella. It's raining. She'll **need** a visa to go to the States.
  The mechanic told me I **needed** two new tyres on my car.*

- *Need* has two negative forms: *don't/doesn't need* and *needn't*. *Needn't* can never be followed by a noun.
  *You **don't need a ticket** to get in.* (NOT You needn't a ticket.)

- We use *need* + infinitive with *to* to talk about a necessity in the present or the future.
  *She's very ill. She **needs to see** a doctor. I can't stay any longer. I **need to go** now.*

- In the negative, we can use either *don't/doesn't need* + infinitive with *to* OR *needn't* + infinitive without *to*. The meaning is the same.
  *It's only 11.00. You **needn't leave** yet.* OR *You **don't need to leave** yet.*

In the past, note the difference between *didn't need to* and *needn't have*.

- We use *needn't have* + a past participle when someone did something that wasn't necessary. It was a waste of time or effort. But at the time they didn't know this.
  *She **needn't have taken** her umbrella, because it didn't rain.* (But she took it.)

- We use *didn't need to* + infinitive when it wasn't necessary to do something. But it isn't always clear if it was done or not.
  *She **didn't need to take** an umbrella, because the weather forecast was good.*
  (Perhaps she took an umbrella. Perhaps she didn't.)

1 **It is November, and this Italian woman is going to England to do an English language course. She is packing her suitcase. Look at the pictures and write what things are necessary or not necessary. Use the verb *need*.**

1 ....
2 ....
3 ....
4 ....
5 ....
6 ....
7 ....
8 ....

2 Peter Clegg is going to Paris for a business meeting next Monday. His wife is asking him about it. Put in the correct form of the verb *need*.

'(1) .... book a hotel room in Paris?'

'I don't think so. The last time I went I (2) .... to, because the company had already booked one. I just (3) .... check that they've booked one this time, that's all.'

'What train (4) .... catch?'

'I (5) .... catch an early one. I (6) .... be at the airport till 18.30.'

'I'm going into town this afternoon. (7) .... any French currency?'

'Yes, but you (8) .... go to the bank. I'll get some at the airport.'

'What clothes (9) .... take?'

'I (10) .... take many. I just (11) .... my suit and a change of underwear.'

'You might (12) .... a raincoat.'

'Oh, I don't think so. I (13) .... one the last time I went.'

3 Complete the sentences by matching the items in the two columns.

1 It's great. I needn't	a) to go into work.
2 So I don't need	b) to feel the sun on my face.
3 I told my boss I needed	c) the money.
4 He said he didn't need	d) me next week.
5 So I didn't need	e) to get up early in the morning.
6 I won't be paid, but I don't really need	f) go to work tomorrow.
7 I've needed	g) a holiday for months.
8 I'm going to North Africa. I need	h) a week's holiday.

1 ....   2 ....   3 ....   4 ....   5 ....   6 ....   7 ....   8 ....

4 Dan Price went to a concert last night to see an American blues band. The evening cost him nothing. Read the text and decide which answer, A, B, C or D best fits each space.

1 He .... in a queue because he already had a ticket. He just walked in.

2 He bought a programme for £5, but he .... because he found one on his seat.

3 Then he told the woman sitting next to him that she .... £5 for a programme - he would sell her one for £2.50.

4 At the interval he had a drink. He .... his own money. He used the £2.50.

5 After the concert he phoned for a taxi, but he .... because while he was waiting a friend stopped and gave him a lift home.

6 The taxi driver arrived, but he .... because Dan wasn't there.

1	A needn't stand	B didn't need to stand	C needn't have stood	D needn't to stand
2	A didn't need to do	B needn't do	C needn't done	D needn't have done
3	A needn't have paid	B didn't need to pay	C needn't to pay	D didn't need pay
4	A needn't have used	B didn't need to use	C needed not to use	D needed not use
5	A needn't have	B needed not	C didn't need to	D needn't to
6	A needn't have come	B didn't need come	C didn't need to come	D needn't come

Quick reference

- We use the 1st conditional (*if* + a verb in the present simple) to talk about a possible future action or situation. The *if* clause is often followed by a main clause with *will/won't*.
  *If the weather **gets** better, we **'ll go** for a walk.* (NOT If the weather will get better.)
  OR *We **'ll go** for a walk if the weather **gets** better.*

- In addition to the future *will*, we can also use *can, should, ought to, may, might, must* or an imperative in the main clause.
  *If you want to go to London, you **can** catch a bus.*
  *We **shouldn't** be late, if the train's on time.*   ***Phone me** if you want anything.*

- To talk about something that's always true, we use *if* + present simple + present simple.
  *If you **heat** plastic, it **melts**.*   *If I **travel** by car, I always **get** carsick.*

- We use the 2nd conditional *if* + a verb in the past simple + *would/wouldn't, could, might* to talk about an action or situation in the present or the future which is improbable, hypothetical or imaginary.
  *If public transport **was** better, there **would be** fewer cars on the road.*
  *You **might feel** better if you **took** some of these tablets.*
  *If you **found** £100 in the street, what **would** you **do** with it?*

---

1 **Jack Rice is in a hotel room in Saint Lucia. It is very hot. He cannot sleep. Write sentences about his problem, using *If* and choosing the correct main clause from the list on the right.**

Example: (Leave his door open) *If he leaves his door open, it'll be too noisy.*

1	(Leave the window open)	he'll have mosquito bites all over his body.
2	(Close the window)	he might drown.
3	(Take off his pyjamas)	there'll be no fresh air in the room.
4	(Not take off his pyjamas)	the mosquitoes will get into the room.
5	(Try to sleep in a cold bath)	he'll be too hot.

1 ....

2 ....

3 ....

4 ....

5 ....

---

2 **Anna is going to London for an interview for her first job. She is very worried. She is thinking of possible problems. Make sentences with *What will I do if ...?***

Example: I might not get there on time. *What will I do if I don't get there on time?*

1 My train might be late. What will I do if ....?

2 I might not be able to get a taxi. What will I do if ....?

3 The interviewer might not like me. What will I do if ....?

4 She might ask difficult questions. What will I do ....?

5 They might not offer me the job. What will I do ....?

3 At the interview (see Exercise 2) Anna was asked to talk about herself. She said some general things (general truths) about herself. Complete her sentences, using *If* ...

Example: (worry a lot/be late for something) *I worry a lot if I'm late for something.*

1 (I/get embarrassed   people/say nice things about me)

....

2 (I/not feel good   I/not be wearing smart clothes)

....

3 (anyone/criticise me   I/feel guilty)

....

4 (my boyfriend/not listen to me   it/make me angry)

....

4 Emily is learning Spanish, and she is thinking of going to Spain. A friend is giving her some advice. Make sentences with *If* ...

Example: Try to go for at least a month. (go for a month/learn a lot of Spanish)
      If you went for a month, you'd learn a lot of Spanish.

1 (It/be better/go on your own)

....

2 (go with a group of English friends/not speak much Spanish)

....

3 (go on your own/not be able to speak English)

....

4 Stay with a Spanish family. (learn the language quickly/stay with a family)

....

5 Find a Spanish boy. (have a Spanish boyfriend/soon speak Spanish well!)

....

5 Read the text. If a line is correct, put a tick (✓). If a line has a mistake in it, underline the mistake and write the correction in the brackets.

Example: (1) If I <u>went</u> to London next Saturday, I'll have to hitchhike. If there were (*go*)

(2) more buses, that was all right. But there's only one bus a day and that leaves   (.......................)

(3) at 5.30 in the morning. If it leaves a bit later, I'd catch it. If they stop that   (.......................)

(4) early morning bus service, there'll be no way of getting to London by   (.......................)

(5) public transport. If I would have a car, I could get there in three hours. If   (.......................)

(6) public transport will get any worse, a lot of people won't be able to travel.   (.......................)

6 a) Using *if* + present simple + present simple, write five general truths about yourself and your opinions. Example: *If people smoke in a restaurant, I get angry.*

b) Imagine you are going to England. Talk about the alternative means of travel. Write five sentences, using *if* + present simple + *will/won't*.

Examples: *If I go from Santander, I'll have to drive for three hours. If I go by plane, it'll cost a lot more.*

c) Write five questions you would ask someone you were thinking of marrying. Use *if* + past simple + *would/wouldn't*. Example: *Would you be angry if I criticised you?*

Check your answers with a teacher.

41 *If* in past situations (3rd conditional)

Quick reference

- We use the past perfect in the *if* clause to talk about something that didn't happen or a situation that didn't exist in the past. We use the past conditional in the main clause.

  If* + past perfect** + ***would have/could have/might have
  If Jack had worked hard,   *he would (could/might) have passed the exam.*
  (= He didn't work hard. He didn't pass the exam.)
  If Sue had taken a taxi,   *she wouldn't have been late for work.*
  (= She didn't take a taxi. She was late for work.)
  Note that we don't use the past conditional in the *if* clause. (NOT *If Sue would have taken*)

- We sometimes use the past perfect continuous (*would have been + -ing*) in the *if* clause.
  You weren't concentrating. If you'd (had) been concentrating, you would have seen that the traffic lights were red.

- We sometimes link the past with the present by using *would* or *would be + -ing*.
  If* + past perfect** + ***would or would be + -ing
  If I hadn't lost my lottery ticket,   *I'd (would) be rich now. I'd be living in luxury.*
  (= He lost his ticket. He isn't rich now. He isn't living in luxury now.)

1 Becky and Polly went to Scotland for the weekend. They have just got back and they are talking about it. Read the dialogue and decide which answer, A, B, C or D best fits each space.

BECKY: We (1) .... the weekend if it (2) .... the whole time.

POLLY: Yes, if it (3) .... raining, we (4) .... out more.

BECKY: And it was cold! If we (5) .... it was so cold in Scotland, we (6) .... some warm clothes.

POLLY: And if your car (7) .... we (8) .... much more of Scotland.

BECKY: And what about Saturday night? If you (9) .... the front door key of the guest house we were staying at, we (10) .... sleep in the car!

1 A would have enjoyed	B enjoyed	C had enjoyed	D would enjoy
2 A wouldn't have rained	B hadn't rained	C didn't rain	D wouldn't rain
3 A stopped	B would have stopped	C had stopped	D has stopped
4 A could have gone	B can have gone	C had gone	D went
5 A would have known	B know	C knew	D had known
6 A might have take	B might to take	C might have taken	D might take
7 A didn't break down	B hadn't broken down	C doesn't break down	D wouldn't have broken down
8 A had seen	B mightn't have seen	C could see	D could have seen
9 A wouldn't have lost	B haven't lost	C hadn't lost	D didn't lose
10 A wouldn't have had to	B wouldn't have to	C didn't have to	D hadn't to

2 An old man is thinking about his past life. Write sentences with *If* + past perfect + *would have* or *wouldn't have*.

Example: I didn't have any brothers or sisters. I had a lonely childhood.
If I'd had brothers or sisters, I wouldn't have had such a lonely childhood.

1 My parents were poor. I didn't have many clothes.

If my parents ...., I .... more clothes.

2 I missed a lot of school lessons. I didn't learn a lot.

If I ...., I could .... more.

3 I wasn't very clever. I didn't do very well at school.

If .... more clever, ... better at school.

4 I didn't pass any exams. I never got a well-paid job.

If ...., I might ....

5 I was shy. I didn't have many friends.

If ...., I .... friends.

6 I worked on a farm. I didn't fight in the war.

If ...., I ....

7 I didn't leave this village. I never got a better job.

If ...., I could ....

8 I never got married. I never had any children.

If ...., I might ....

3 Four people are talking about big events in their lives. Complete their stories, using *if* + past perfect continuous + *would(n't) have* and *would(n't)* OR *would(n't) be* + *-ing*.

1 ANDY: In a recent storm, lightning struck a tree, fifty metres from where I was standing. If I (stand) .... under the tree, I (be) .... killed. I (be) ....
here now.

2 CARLA: I first met my husband Larry on a cross-Channel ferry. I was feeling ill and he asked me if he could help me. If I (feel) .... ill, he (speak) ....
to me. And we (live) .... together now.

3 LOUISE: When I had my accident, I wasn't watching the road, so I hit the car in front. If I (watch) .... the road, I (hit) .... that car.

4 ADAM: I applied for a job in Australia. At the interview I was feeling tired and they didn't offer me the job. If I (feel) .... tired, they (offer) .... me the job.
I (be) .... in Australia now. I (surf) .... on Bondi Beach.

4 Complete these sentences about yourself. Check your answers with a teacher.

1 If I'd been born a boy/girl ...

2 If I'd chosen my own name ...

3 If I'd been born ten years earlier ...

4 If I'd lived in the last century ...

Quick reference

- *Unless* + an affirmative verb = *if* + a negative verb.
  *I won't go to London, **unless** you **come** with me.* (= if you don't come with me)
- We use *as long as, provided (that), providing (that)* to talk about a condition. They're stronger than *if*, and they all mean *only if*.
  *You can borrow my CD player, **as long as** you give it back to me tomorrow.*
  (= You can borrow my CD player, only if you give it back to me tomorrow.)
  We could use *provided (that)* or *providing (that)* here. The meaning would be the same.
  Note that we often leave out *that* after *provided/providing*.
  *You can borrow my CD player, **provided** you give it back to me tomorrow.*
- We use *in case* to talk about the precautions we take because something might happen.
  *I'll take an umbrella **in case** it rains.*
  (= It might rain, so I'll take an umbrella as a precaution.)
  *Take some sea-sick tablets **in case** you don't feel well on the boat.*
  (= You might not feel well on the boat, so take some tablets as a precaution.)
- Note that *unless, as long as, provided (that), providing (that), in case* are followed by the same tenses as *if* in the 1st and 2nd conditional. (See Unit 40.)

---

1 **Anna has got some very strict rules for her boyfriends. In the sentences rewrite the clause in italics, using *unless*.**

1 If a boy smokes, she won't go out with him *if he doesn't stop smoking.*

....

2 She won't go to the cinema with him *if he doesn't let her pay for herself.*

....

3 When he's away she isn't happy *if he doesn't phone her every day.*

....

4 If they have problems, she gets angry *if he isn't prepared to talk about them.*

....

5 If she asks him questions, she isn't satisfied *if he doesn't answer her honestly.*

....

2 **Look at these notices. Complete the sentences that explain them, using *as long as/provided/ providing*.**

1 ENTRANCE FOR TICKETHOLDERS ONLY
  You can go in ....

2 SWIMMING POOL: UNDER 7s MUST BE ACCOMPANIED BY AN ADULT
  Under 7s can swim ....

3 PARKING FOR RESIDENTS ONLY
  You can park in the street ....

4 NON-SMOKING COMPARTMENT
  You can travel in this compartment ....

3 Jenny Railton teaches French in an English school. She is taking a group of young students to Paris. She is telling them what they can and cannot do. Write the word(s) that best fit(s) each space.

Examples: The coach leaves school at 7.30. If you're late, I'll be angry (1) *unless* you've got a very
          good excuse. You can wear any clothes you like (2) *as long as* you look reasonably smart.

You can bring your personal stereos (3) .... you don't play them too loudly on the coach.

In Paris on your free evenings you can go out (4) .... you tell me where you're going. You

can't go out in the evening (5) .... you're with at least two other students. You can go into

cafés (6) .... you don't drink alcohol. There'll be an excursion every day. I'll expect you all

to come (7) .... you're ill. The trip won't be a success (8) .... you try to speak as

much French as possible. Which of you are vegetarians? Vegetarian food will be available for you at

the hotel (9) .... you let me know before we leave. The hotel won't be responsible for your

valuables (10) .... you leave them in the hotel safe. There shouldn't be any problems

(11) .... you keep to the rules and behave sensibly.

4 Katie Wain is going to Copenhagen tomorrow on a business trip. The Danish company is sending Andrea to meet her at the airport. Katie is preparing for her trip. Make the two sentences into one, using *in case*.

Example: I'll put my passport in my bag now. I might forget it tomorrow morning.
          I'll put my passport in my bag now in case I forget it tomorrow morning.

1 I'll pack my case now. I might not have time tomorrow morning.

   ....

2 I'll take my hairdryer. There might not be one at the hotel.

   ....

3 I'll take my winter coat. It might be cold in the evening.

   ....

4 I'll phone to confirm my hotel booking. They might not have got my letter.

   ....

5 I'll take Andrea's phone number. She might not be at the airport to meet me.

   ....

6 I'll book a taxi now. There might not be any available at 8.00 tomorrow.

   ....

5 On what conditions would you accept a job in Alaska? Use *provided/providing/as long as* or *unless*.

Examples: *I'd take the job as long as they offered me a very good salary.*
          I wouldn't take the job unless they gave me long holidays.

If you were going to sail round the world alone, what precautions would you take and why? Write five sentences using *in case*.

Examples: *I'd take my cat in case I got lonely. I'd say goodbye to all my friends in case I didn't come
          back.*

Check your answers with a teacher.

85

43

Quick reference

- We use *wish* or *If only* + *would* to say that we want something to change, or that we want someone to do something. It often means we're feeling impatient or annoyed.
    *I **wish** it **would** stop raining.   **If only** he'**d** **(would)** be quiet.*
  Note that we can't say 'I wish **I** would ...' or 'I wish **we** would ...'

- We use *could* after *I* and *we* to talk about a regret about a present or future inability.
    *I wish **I could** come with you.   I wish **we could** have a holiday.*

- We use *wish* or *If only* + the past simple or the past continuous when we talk about a regret we have about a present situation.
    *I wish I **had** more money.   I wish she **was** my girlfriend.   If only it **wasn't raining**.*

- We use *wish* or *if only* + the past perfect when we talk about a regret we have about something that happened or didn't happen in the past.
    *I wish you'**d (had) come** earlier.* (but you didn't come earlier.)
    *I wish I **hadn't said** that.   If only the train **had been** on time.*

- We don't use *would have* after *wish/if only*.
  (NOT I wish I would have seen it.   NOT If only you would have worked harder.)

---

1 Luke is revising for an important exam. He is feeling stressed. Complete the second sentence so that it has a similar meaning to the first sentence, using the words given.

Example: The phone's ringing - why doesn't someone answer it? (wish)
          The phone's ringing - I wish somebody would answer it.

1 I want my sister to turn the television down. (wish)

....

2 I want my brother to stop playing his music so loudly. (If only)

....

3 I don't want my mother to keep coming up to my room. (wish)

....

4 I don't want her to worry so much. (If only)

....

5 I want to know what the exam questions are. (wish)

....

6 I don't want to have to do the exam. (If only)

....

2 Albert Street is 85. He is thinking back over his life. Complete what he says using *I wish* + the past perfect. Use these verbs.

| marry   have (x2)   learn   go   travel   read   stay |

Example: *I wish I'd (had) stayed at school longer.*

1 .... to university.
2 .... a foreign language.
3 .... to more foreign countries.
4 .... more books.
5 .... a more interesting job.
6 .... the first girl I fell in love with.
7 .... a son as well as three daughters.

3 Complete what the people in the picture are saying, using *wish/if only* + *would/wouldn't* or *wish/if only* + the past simple or the past perfect of these verbs.

| not forget   stop   not buy   live   have   come |

Example: 1 *I wish my bus would come.*

2 I wish .... raining. 3 If only .... more money.
4 If only .... in the country. 5 I wish .... my raincoat.
6 I wish .... so many things.

4 **a) Write three sentences about the regrets you have about the situation you are in at present.**
Examples: *I wish I was on a beach in the sun. I wish I wasn't studying English grammar.*
       I wish I could go on holiday.

b) Write three sentences about things you wish you had or had not done in the past.
Example: *I wish I'd started to learn English at an earlier age.*

Check your answers with a teacher.

44 Purpose: *to/in order to* + infinitive *So that/so* + clause *So as not to* + infinitive

Quick reference

- We use *to* + infinitive and *in order to* + infinitive to talk about the purpose of an action, where the subject of each part of the sentence is the same.
  *I went to London **to buy** some new clothes.* (= **I** went/**I** bought)
  *She stopped **in order to look** at the map.* (= **She** stopped/**she** looked.)
  In order to + infinitive is more formal than *to* + infinitive.

- We use *to* + infinitive (NOT *in order to*) to talk about the purpose or use of a thing or person.
  *I'll buy a magazine **to read** on the train. I must find someone **to help** me.*

- Note that the preposition stays with the verb. And when the verb has an object, the preposition comes after the object.
  (He wants to **talk to** someone) *He's looking for someone **to talk to**.*
  (I want to put **my books** in a bag.) *Can I have a bag **to put** my books **in**?*

- We use *so that* or *so* (usually followed by *can, can't, could, couldn't, will, won't, would, wouldn't*) if there is a different subject in each part of the sentence, or if the purpose of an action is negative.
  *I'll phone my father **so that** (OR **so**) he can come and pick us up.* (I/he)
  *She hung her key round her neck, **so that** (OR **so**) she wouldn't lose it.*

- If the purpose is negative and the subject is the same in each part of the sentence, we can also use *so as not to* + infinitive. *She hung her key round her neck, **so as not to** lose it.*

---

1 **Burglars broke into James Hart's house three times last year. This year the cost of insuring the contents of his house was very high. James also needed a way of protecting his property, so he bought a dog. The insurance company said they would reduce the cost of his insurance if he bought an alarm system. So he bought one. The alarm system cost so much money that he had to sell some of the valuable things he owned. Now he can only get into the house by remembering a special alarm code. And he has to shut the dog in the kitchen, because it is the only way he can stop it activating the alarm!**
Answer these questions, giving the purpose of the actions.

Example: Why did James have to pay a lot this year? *To insure the contents of his house.*

1 Why did James buy a dog? ....

2 Why did he buy an alarm system? ....

3 Why did he have to sell some of his valuable things? ....

4 Why does he need to remember a special alarm code? ....

5 Why does he shut the dog in the kitchen? ....

---

2 **Melanie Wright has just moved to an isolated part of the country. She is lonely and unhappy.**
Complete the second sentence so that it has a similar meaning to the first.

Example: 1 She wants to talk to someone. *She wants someone to talk to.*

2 She wants to go out with a friend. She wants a friend ....

3 Only her cat keeps her company. She's only got her cat ....

4 She can't spend her money anywhere. There's nowhere ....

5 She wants to share her life with someone. She wants someone ....

3 Stewart Price does everything he can to save energy. Read the text and replace the words in brackets with a clause, using *to* + infinitive, *in order to*, *so that/so* or *so as not to* + infinitive.

(1 *He wants to reduce his energy costs*) .... , he has installed a solar heating system in his house. (2 *He doesn't want to lose any heat*) ...., he has insulated the roof and the walls of his house. (3 *He intends to keep fit*) ...., he uses his bicycle a lot, and, when he travels long distances, he always uses public transport, (4 *this means he can leave his car at home*) .... He also advises his friends to stop using their cars, (5 *by doing so they will reduce air pollution*) ....

(6 *He intends to travel less*) .... , he has asked his office manager if he can work at home. He has bought a computer (7 *he wants to communicate*) .... with his office by e-mail.

He thinks that world trade is a bad thing. He feels a lot of energy is wasted by importing and exporting goods. He checks the origin of all the things he buys (8 *he wants to make sure*) .... they were produced locally in Britain.

(9 *He doesn't intend to waste anything*) .... , he doesn't throw things away. He keeps all his vegetable waste (10 *in this way it can be used on the garden*) .... When he goes shopping he always keeps the plastic bags (11 *in this way they can be used again*) .... He keeps all his waste paper in a big box (12 *in this way he can take it*) .... to the recycling factory at the end of every month.

He's got his own web-site on the Internet and he uses it (13 *he wants to tell the world*) .... about his ideas on energy-saving methods.

4 Violet Horn is an eccentric old lady of 80. Complete the sentences, using *to, in order to, so that/so* or *so as not to*. Sometimes there is more than one possible answer.

1 She puts salt on her strawberries .... they don't taste too sweet.

2 She puts sugar on her tomatoes .... make them taste sweeter.

3 She reads by candlelight .... save electricity.

4 She talks politely to her plants .... hurt their feelings.

5 She never wears her best clothes .... spoil them.

6 She always empties the bags from her vacuum cleaner .... she can use them again.

5 Say why you do certain things. Write five sentences, using a) *to* + infinitive; b) *in order to* + infinitive; c) *so that* + clause; d) *so* + clause; e) *so as not to* + infinitive.

Examples: *To save money I sometimes walk to work instead of taking the bus.*
In winter I often wear socks in bed so that my feet don't get cold.

Check your answers with a teacher.

45

Verb + infinitive with *to*: *I want to come*
She promised not to be late

Quick reference

- Many verbs can be followed by the infinitive with *to*. The most common are:
  afford, agree, appear, arrange, ask, attempt, choose, decide, demand, deserve, expect, fail, forget, happen, help, hesitate, hope, hurry, intend, learn, manage, mean (= intend), offer, plan, prepare, pretend, promise, refuse, remember, seem, tend, threaten, train, want, wish.
  She **learned to** swim.   They **arranged to** meet.   We **intend to** sell it.   He **promised to** write.

- Note the negative form of the infinitive.
  *He decided **not to go**.   He promised **not to laugh**.   She pretended **not to listen** to him.*

- The verb *dare*.
  Present: *I daren't look* OR *I don't dare (to) look.*   Past: *I didn't dare (to) look.*
  Questions: *Do you dare (to) look?   Did you dare (to) look?*

- The verb *help*.
  *I helped **to make** dinner.* OR *I helped **make** dinner.*

- With some verbs we often use a question word + the infinitive with *to*.

Verb	+	question word	+	infinitive
I don't know		*what*		*to do.*
He explained		*how*		*to use the machine.*
I can't decide		*where*		*to go.*

1 **Richard Yates, from Bristol in the west of England, plays football for a top London team. But he is not happy. A London journalist is interviewing him. Complete the interview, using these verbs:**
leave (x 2), not have, worry, see, be, come, admit, let, give up (x 2), talk, not understand, earn, tell, pay, change, play.

JOURNALIST: Why did you decide (1) .... to London?

RICHARD: I didn't decide. The manager of Arsenal happened (2) .... me in a match on
             TV. Two days later they offered (3) .... over £4 million for me.

JOURNALIST: So why have you decided (4) .... London?

RICHARD: It's my wife. At first she seemed (5) .... happy in London. She got a job
             because we'd decided (6) .... children for a few years. But she wasn't happy.
             She refused (7) .... that she was unhappy. She didn't dare (8) ....
             me, because she didn't want (9) .... me. But finally she agreed
             (10) .... to me about it. She told me that the problem was her Bristol accent.
             Everybody at work laughed at her when she spoke. They pretended (11) ....
             .... her. She worked for an insurance company for a month. But they refused
             (12) .... her answer the phone! So she decided (13) .... jobs. But
             the same thing happened in the next job. And now she's even threatening (14) ....
             me and go back to Bristol on her own.

JOURNALIST: So are you intending (15) .... football?

RICHARD: No, I daren't (16) .... it .... It's the only thing I can do. I'm hoping
             (17) .... for a Bristol team and I'm prepared (18) .... much less
             money as long as my wife is happy.

2 Carina has just got a job as an au pair girl with an English family called the Harveys. There are a lot of things she is not sure about. Write the two sentences as one, using an infinitive with *to*.

Example: What shall I call Mrs Harvey?/She doesn't know.
She doesn't know what to call Mrs Harvey.

1 Where shall I put my dirty clothes?/She doesn't know.

   ....

2 How do I set this alarm clock?/She doesn't understand.

   ....

3 What time should I get up in the morning?/She wants to know.

   ....

4 How do I use the dishwasher?/She hasn't discovered yet.

   ....

5 How much are they going pay me?/They haven't discussed it yet.

   ....

6 How do I cook food in a microwave?/She's never learned.

   ....

7 Where can I go to learn more English?/She's wondering.

   ....

8 What shall I do on my day off?/She hasn't decided.

   ....

3 Some tourists have just arrived at London Airport. Read the text below and think of the word which best fits each space. Use only one word in each space.

1 A porter's helping two Americans .... get a taxi.

2 A Frenchman's wondering .... to leave his luggage while he goes to the toilet.

3 A businessman's having problems. He doesn't know .... to use an English telephone.

4 A group of Australians aren't sure .... to catch a bus to the centre of London - they can't find the bus stop.

5 They've asked three people and they didn't know. Now they don't know .... to ask.

6 A German businesswoman's in the souvenir shop. She can't decide .... to buy.

7 Two French girls at the Tourist Information desk are discussing .... hotel to stay at in London.

8 A woman from Nigeria wants to know .... to contact the Nigerian embassy.

4 Complete these sentences about yourself with an infinitive.
Check your answers with a teacher.

1 Next weekend I want ...

2 I can't afford ...

3 In five years' time I hope ...

4 I've decided ...

5 I don't dare ...

6 I sometimes help ...

7 I don't know who ...

8 I understand how ...

9 I often forget when ...

10 I've discovered where ...

46

Quick reference

We often use the construction verb + object (noun or pronoun) + infinitive with *to* when we say or do something to influence somebody else. We use it:

- with verbs like: *advise, allow, ask, encourage, expect, force, get, help, invite, persuade, recommend, remind, teach, tell, warn,* etc.

Verb	+	object	+	infinitive with *to*
I persuaded		*my father*		*to lend me the car.*
Remind		*me*		*to post this letter.*
I advise		*you*		*to go by train.*

- with the verbs *want, would like, would love, would hate, would prefer.*

Verb	+	object	+	infinitive with *to*
What do you want		*me*		*to do?* (NOT What do you want that I do?)
I don't want		*her*		*to know.* (NOT I don't want that she knows.)
Would you like		*the doctor*		*to come?*
I'd like		*people*		*to listen to me.*
I'd prefer		*you*		*to stay.*

- Note the negative infinitive.
  *They asked him **not to smoke**.   I'd prefer you **not to say** anything.*

---

1 **Manworth school is different from conventional schools. A teacher is telling a parent about it. Complete the second sentence so that it has a similar meaning to the first, using the word given.**

Example: The students can call us by our first names. (allow)
> *We allow students to call us by our first names.*

1 It isn't necessary for students to attend all the lessons. (expect)

We .... attend all the lessons.

2 Students can choose what they want to do. (encourage)

We .... choose what they want to do.

3 Students should have self-respect and respect for others. (teach)

We .... self-respect and respect for others.

4 Students don't have to do homework. (force)

We .... do homework.

5 All students must help with the cooking and the cleaning. (ask)

We .... with the cooking and the cleaning.

2 **Some people's jobs are often difficult. Look at these situations and write two sentences each time. Say a) What does he/she want? and b) What does he/she say?**

Example: A doctor's examining a patient who is very tense.
> *He wants the patient to relax. 'I want you to relax.'*

1 A mother's talking to her child, Amy, who has only eaten a little of her lunch.

   a) She .... Amy .... lunch.   b) 'I .... lunch.'

2 A teacher's annoyed because the students in her class aren't listening.

   a) She .... the students ....   b) 'I ....'

3 A dentist's talking to a very young patient who's keeping her mouth closed.

   a) He .... the patient ....   b) 'I ....'

4 A driving instructor's annoyed because his student has just turned left instead of right.

   a) He .... his student ....   b) 'I ....'

3 Jenny Kite is at college. She is training to be a teacher, but she also plays the drums. She wants to be a professional musician. She talked to her drum teacher, and now she is telling her boyfriend, Rick, what he said to her. Read the dialogue. Some of the lines are correct, and some have a word that should not be there. If a line is correct, put a tick (✓). If a line has a word that should not be there, write the word in the brackets.

1 RICK: What did he tell to you to do?   (.................)

2 JENNY: He told me for to think about it for a while. He warned me not   (.................)

3   to make any quick decisions.   (.................)

4 RICK: What did he tell you to do about college?   (.................)

5 JENNY: He advised that me not to give up my studies. He told me to get as   (.................)

6   many qualifications as possible. He told me I to talk to my teachers   (.................)

7   about it. He expected of my teachers to say the same thing. He   (.................)

8   recommended me to keep music as a hobby.   (.................)

4 An old man has stopped someone outside his house. Complete the dialogue, using *want* or *would like, would prefer, would hate* + object + infinitive.

'Excuse me. I (1 like/you/help) .... me, please. I've lost my parrot.'

'Your parrot? What (2 you/want/me) .... do?'

'I (3 like/you/stand) .... here, while I go round to the back of the house to

look for him there. And I (4 want/you/make) .... this noise: "Skreeeeeeee!"'

'I (5 hate/you/think) .... that I'm being unkind, but I (6 prefer/you/ask)

.... someone else.'

'(7 you/prefer/go) .... round to the back of the house?'

'No, I wouldn't. I haven't got time. My husband (8 want/me/post) .... this letter

before midday.'

'(9 you/like/me/show) .... you how to make the noise?'

'No, thank you. I'm in a hurry.'

'You see, I'm worried. He escaped from his cage about five minutes ago. I (10 want/someone/help)

.... me find him.'

'Well, I'm sorry, but I can't. And anyway, I don't like parrots.'

'Oh dear. I (11 prefer/you/not say) .... that. If he hears you, he can

be very aggressive. (12 you/want/me/show) .... you a photo of him?

In case you see him. ... Hey! Where are you going? Come back!'

47

Quick reference

Note these three constructions.

	Adjective	+	**infinitive with *to***
It isn't	easy		*to find a job.*
I'm	pleased		*to meet you.*
It's	important		*not to forget your ticket.*

Some other adjectives used in the construction: *advisable, amazed, cheap, dangerous, difficult, disappointed, exciting, expensive, good, hard, impossible, interesting, lucky, nice, possible, ready, safe, sensible, silly, surprised, terrible, wonderful.*

	Adjective	+	***for***	+	**noun/pronoun**	+	**infinitive with *to***
It's	impossible		*for*		*me*		*to say.*
It was	difficult		*for*		*him*		*not to laugh.*

Some other adjectives used in this construction: *common, easy, essential, important, necessary, normal, rare, unnecessary, unusual, usual.*

	Adjective	+	***of***	+	**noun/pronoun**	+	**infinitive with *to***
It was	silly		*of*		*your brother*		*to do that.*
It's	nice		*of*		*you*		*to come and see me.*

Some other adjectives used in this construction: *careless, clever, generous, good, kind, mean, polite, stupid, unkind, wrong.*

---

1 **Some Greek friends of Claire Long are coming to visit the area where she lives. She is telling them what they must do. Complete the second sentence so that it has a similar meaning to the first sentence, using the word given. Do not change the word given.**

Example: You'll easily find places to stay. (easy)
> *It's easy to find places to stay.*

1 Staying in a bed and breakfast is less expensive than staying in a hotel. (cheaper)

It's .... in a bed and breakfast.

2 Hiring a car isn't cheap in July and August. (expensive)

It's ....

3 Parking is difficult in the town centres. (easy)

It ....

4 Buy a map of the area. (sensible)

It would be ....

5 You must walk along the cliffs. (wonderful)

It's ....

6 You must visit Land's End. (silly)

You'd ....

7 Don't leave valuables in your car. (advisable)

It's ....

8 Unfortunately, I won't be here in July. (disappointed)

You'll be .... know that ....

2 Marie is complaining to a friend about her sister's three-year-old son. Complete the friend's replies, using adjective + *for* + object + infinitive.

Example: MARIE: 'He just can't sit still.' - (not easy) `It isn't easy for children to sit still for long.´

MARIE: He seems to shout all the time.

'(1 common) .... young children .... sometimes.'

MARIE: He doesn't eat what she gives him.

'(2 rare) .... children .... everything you give them.'

MARIE: That child has too much freedom!

'(3 important) .... young children .... a lot of freedom.'

MARIE: I just don't understand why she doesn't control him better.

'(4 difficult) .... you .... until you have children of your own.'

3 Read the text and make sentences, using adjective + *of* + object + infinitive.

Alan Badger recently gave £20 to a woman in the street who said she hadn't eaten for three days and had nowhere to live. But this wasn't true. She wasn't homeless and she had a job. She spent his money on things she didn't need. The following week he saw her again. She asked him for some more money. Alan handed her another £20. The next day Alan saw her in the pub buying drinks for her friends. When he told her she hadn't told him the truth, she just laughed at him.

Example: *It was good of Alan to help the woman.*

1 (generous) It was .... £20.

2 (dishonest) It was .... she was homeless.

3 (stupid) It was .... she didn't need.

4 (silly) It was .... why she wanted the money.

5 (wrong) It was .... laugh at him.

4 Louise Betts is in hospital with a broken leg. Her friend, Ryan, has come to see her. Complete the dialogue, using the three constructions you have practised in Exercises 1, 2 and 3.

LOUISE: Hi, Ryan. It's (1 good/you/come) .... And it was (2 nice/you/phone)

.... yesterday.

RYAN: How's the leg?

LOUISE: Painful. It isn't (3 easy/me/walk) ....

RYAN: How long will you be here?

LOUISE: It's (4 difficult/say) .... Three days, perhaps.

RYAN: How did it happen?

LOUISE: I tripped over the dog. It's (5 hard/not laugh) .... really.

RYAN: Well, is there anything I can do? I'm always (6 happy/help) ....

LOUISE: Yes, there is something you can do. Would it be (7 possible/you/scratch) ....

.... my right foot? It's itching and I can't reach it.

5 Write five sentences giving your opinion of the way you or other people have behaved. Check your answers with a teacher.

Examples: *It was silly of me not to learn to play a musical instrument when I was young.*
It was wrong of the government to increase taxes last year.

48 — Make and *let*: *You make me laugh. He let her go*

Quick reference

- In the following construction, *make* can mean 'force' or 'cause'.

Make	+	**object**	+	**infinitive without** *to*
His mother makes		*him*		*work hard.* (= force)
The seafood made		*me*		*feel ill.* (= cause)

- *Make* can also be followed by object + adjective.

Make	+	**object**	+	**adjective**
You make		*me*		*angry.*

- *Let* (meaning *allow*) is used in this construction.

Let	+	**object**	+	**infinitive without** *to*
My father let		*me*		*borrow the car.*
They don't let		*passengers*		*smoke.*

- We can use *make* in the passive. It is followed by the infinitive with *to*.
  The children **were made to go** to bed.   Passengers **are made to show** their passports.

---

1 Brian and Ann Price do not approve of the way their neighbours are bringing up their children. Complete the second sentence so that it has a similar meaning to the first, using the word given.

Example: ANN: They don't force the younger ones to go to bed at a reasonable time. (make)
They don't make the younger ones go to bed at a reasonable time.

BRIAN: They allow them to go to bed when they like. (let)
1 They .... when they like.

ANN: They allow them to watch anything they like on television. (let)
2 They .... anything they like on television.

BRIAN: They aren't forced to go to school. (made)
3 They .... to school.

ANN: They allow them to stay at home if they want to. (let)
4 They .... if they want to.

BRIAN: They allow their eldest daughter to go out with a man ten years older than her. (let)
5 They .... with a man ten years older than her.

---

2 Stephanie is telling her mother about her boyfriend. Complete what she says, using *make* or *(not) let* with the verbs in brackets.

He's very funny. He always (1 laugh) .... And when I'm feeling miserable he (2 happy) .... But he also (3 angry) .... sometimes. He's very old-fashioned. He never (4 decide) .... what we're going to do and he (5 pay) .... for myself when we go out. And he always tries to (6 wear) .... smart clothes when we go out. He (7 wear) .... old jeans. He also (8 impatient) .... sometimes - he does everything so slowly! I want to shake him sometimes to (9 hurry) ....

96

49 Verb + -ing: I enjoy eating

Quick reference

- If these verbs are followed by another verb, we use the -ing form of the second verb:
  admit, avoid, consider, delay, deny, detest, dislike, enjoy, escape, fancy, finish, go on, imagine, involve, keep, miss, postpone, practise, recall, regret, risk, suggest.
  *I **avoided meeting** her.   They **finished arguing**.   The manager **risked losing** his job.*

- We use *go* and *come + -ing* when we talk about sports or free-time activities outside the home.
  *He **went shopping**.   Do you want to **come sailing**?   Shall we **go swimming**?*

1 These are some of the results of a recent survey in the USA in which Americans were asked about their likes and dislikes. Read the text below and think of one word which best fits each space.

63% said they enjoyed (1) .... to sleep at night.

38% of American husbands fancied the idea of dating other women but only 13% admitted

(2) .... it regularly.

32% said they hated (3) .... the dirty dishes and pans after a meal.

29% of drivers said they delayed (4) .... up their cars with petrol for as long as possible.

27% of Americans couldn't imagine not (5) .... no matter how rich they were, because they enjoyed their jobs.

23% said they were considering (6) .... jobs because they were bored at work.

21% said they disliked (7) .... up in the morning and admitted (8) .... it to the last moment.

19% said they didn't mind just (9) .... in front of the TV, whatever was on.

17% of Americans went on (10) .... computer games even when they were adults.

15% said they regretted not (11) .... to play a musical instrument.

5% said they detested (12) .... their teeth.

2 What are the people in this picture doing?

1 They're going sailing.   2 ....
3 ....   4 ....

3 Complete these sentences about yourself using the verb + -ing form. Check your answers with a teacher.

1 I enjoy ...   2 I hate ...   3 I avoid ...   4 I fancy ...   5 I regret ...   6 I dislike ...

Quick reference

Preposition + -*ing*

Before going to bed, I fed the cat. She left **without saying** goodbye.
I got into the house **by breaking** a window. **After leaving** college, I got a job.

Adjective	+	preposition	+	-*ing*
She's interested		in		learning foreign languages.
Are you afraid		of		not getting a job?

Some other common adjectives + preposition: *angry about, bad at, clever at, excited about, fed up with, fond of, good at, keen on, proud of, worried about.*

Verb	+	preposition	+	-*ing*
I feel		like		going to the cinema.
I don't approve		of		people smoking in restaurants.

Some other common verbs + preposition: *apologise for, approve of, decide against, dream of, insist on, talk about, think of/about.*

Verb	+	object	+	preposition	+	-*ing*
She thanked		me		for		helping her.
They accused		me		of		not trying hard enough.

Some other verbs + object + preposition: *blame someone for, congratulate someone on, forgive someone for, prevent (or stop) someone from, suspect someone of.*

1 Katie Stevens is telling her new boyfriend about her life so far. Make the two sentences into one, using *before, after, by* and *without* + -*ing*.

1 I studied physics at university./I left school.

....

2 I started work./I spent a year travelling in Asia.

....

3 In India I paid for my food and accommodation./I gave English lessons.

....

4 I got back to England last month./I didn't know what I was going to do.

....

2 This is some publicity for a new book for men called 'How to get on with girls'. Write the questions, using the construction adjective + preposition + -*ing*.

Example: You don't want to look stupid when you meet that new girl. (Afraid?)
Are you afraid of looking stupid when you meet that new girl?

1 You haven't got a girlfriend. (Fed up?)

Are you fed up ....?

2 Do you want to improve your chances? (Keen?)

Are you keen ....?

3 You don't want to say the wrong thing. (Worried?)

Are you worried ....?

4 You lost that last girl because you said something wrong. (Angry?)

Are you angry ....?

5 Do you want to know all the answers? (Interested?)

Are you interested ....?

3 **Simon Welch is talking about his likes and dislikes and his habits. Read the text below and decide which answer, A, B, C or D best fits each space.**

I don't approve (1) .... in the street. I don't like people who never apologise (2) .... a mistake.

I never feel (3) .... early on Monday morning. I always look forward (4) .... in the morning.

I always insist (5) .... white wine ice-cold. I never believe people who accuse me (6) .... intolerant. I

suspect all politicians (7) .... hypocrites. Oh, and I'd like to prevent people (8) .... too slowly on

motorways.

1 A of women smoking	B of smoking women	C for women to smoke	D of women to smoke
2 A to have made	B for to make	C for make	D for making
3 A like to get up	B like get up	C like getting up	D like to get up
4 A to the coming postman	B to the postman come	C to the postman coming	D to the postman
5 A to drink	B on to drink	C to drink	D on drinking
6 A of being	B for being	C of be	D to be
7 A to be	B for being	C of being	D being
8 A of driving	B from driving	C from drive	D to drive

4 **This is an advertisement for Sun Villas in the Seychelles. Read the text. Some of the lines are correct. Some have a mistake in them. If a line is correct, put a tick (✓). If a line has a mistake, underline the mistake and write the correction in the brackets.**

1 Are you bored about living an ordinary life? Are you afraid of spending   (......................)

2 the rest of your life in the same place? Are you tired of do the   (......................)

3 same thing every day? Does your job stop you from being the person you   (......................)

4 want to be? Do you ever blame yourself with being unadventurous? Do   (......................)

5 you only talk about changing your life? Do you ever dream of get   (......................)

6 away from it all? Have you ever thought of owning your own house in   (......................)

7 paradise? Why not buy a Sun Villa in the Seychelles?   (......................)

8 Then you'll thank us for save your life!   (......................)

5 **What frightens you? What makes you angry? What do you do well? What do you do badly? What interests you? What do you really enjoy? Answer these questions, using the construction** *adjective + preposition + -ing.* **Write two answers for each question.**

Examples: *I'm afraid of losing my job. I get angry about not being able to play the guitar well. I'm good at speaking English. I'm bad at spelling. I'm interested in making money. I'm keen on playing volleyball.*

Check your answers with a teacher.

Quick reference

● When *mind* is followed by a verb, we always use the *-ing* form.
Do you mind and *Would you mind* are polite ways of asking someone to do something.

mind +	(noun or pronoun) +	*-ing*
Do you mind		*waiting?*
I don't mind	*Katie*	*coming.*
They don't mind	*me*	*wearing jeans at work.*

● We use *can't stand* to show strong dislike. It means 'hate' or 'detest'. When it is followed by a verb, we always use the *-ing* form.

Can't stand +	(noun or pronoun) +	*-ing*
I can't stand		*fighting.*
They can't stand	*people*	*smoking.*

● *It's no use* (OR *It's no good*)/*There's no point*/*It's (not) worth* are followed by the *-ing* form of the verb. *I can't help* **laughing**. *It's no use* **crying**. *It's not worth* **trying**. *There's no point (in)* **asking**.

1 A hotel receptionist is talking to a guest. Write what they say using *Would you mind + -ing*?

1 She wants him to show her his passport. ....

2 She wants him to leave his passport with her. ....

3 She wants him to fill in the registration card. ....

4 He wants her to put his travellers cheques in the hotel safe.

....

5 He wants her to order him a taxi. ....

2 Annika is an au pair girl. Complete the dialogue between her and Jane Forsyth, the woman she works for, using *(not) mind* + the *-ing* form of these verbs.

clean   do   stay   cook   look after   read

JANE: (1) .... Emily this evening? We're going to the theatre. I'm sure
Emily (2) .... you .... her a bedtime story for a change.

ANNIKA: No, that's fine. I (3) .... in this evening. I've been out twice this week.

JANE: And (4) .... the kitchen floor?

ANNIKA: No, I'm sorry Jane. I (5) .... light housework and last week I (6) ....
.... all the meals when you were ill. But I'm an au pair, not a cleaner!

3 Look at what these airline passengers are saying and think of one word which best fits each space.

'I can't stand (1) .... I know it's very safe really, but I can't help (2) .... scared.'

'Stay in that seat. It's no use (3) .... by the window. There's nothing to see except cloud.'

'There's no point (4) .... to the toilet now. There's a long queue.'

'That meal wasn't worth (5) .... It didn't taste of anything.'

52

Like, love, hate + infinitive with *to* or *-ing*:
I hate flying. I'd love to come

Quick reference

- The verbs *like, love, hate* are usually followed by the *-ing* form, but can be followed by the infinitive with *to*. *I like **singing**.* (OR *I like **to sing**.*)
- The verb *enjoy* must be followed by *-ing*, not the infinitive with *to*.
  *I enjoy **reading**.* (NOT I enjoy to read.)
- When we think something is a good idea, we use *like* + the infinitive with *to*.
  *I like **to go** to the dentist's twice a year.* (Here, we don't say *I like going*.)
- We must use the infinitive with *to* after *would like/love/hate*. *I'd love **to come**.*
- For present regrets and opinions about the past, we use *would like/love/hate* + *to have* + past participle. *I'm a taxi driver. I'd love **to have been** a pilot.*

---

1 Some people were asked about the things they liked and hated. Complete the sentences using these verbs: *get, go back, talk, see, put, not know, find, answer, wake up.*

1 I hate .... a pair of shoes I really like in a shop window and then .... they haven't got them in my size.

2 I don't like .... the phone and .... who the person at the other end is, because he doesn't give his name.

3 I love .... on Saturday morning and then .... to sleep again.

4 I hate .... money in a vending machine and then .... nothing out of it.

5 I don't like .... to an answer-phone.

2 Sophie Carr writes best-selling novels. Complete these sentences using an infinitive with *to* when something is a good idea, and *-ing* when something is/is not enjoyable.

1 She enjoys (write) .... She likes (write) .... five pages every morning.

2 She likes (revise) .... those five pages in the afternoon.

3 She likes (talk) .... to her editor because he's a good friend. She likes (phone) .... him once a month to talk about her latest book.

4 She likes (keep) .... a copy of everything she writes on a floppy disk.

5 She doesn't like people (ask) .... her questions about her next book.

3 Eileen Parry is talking about the £2 million she has just won in the National Lottery. Complete the sentences using *would ('d) like/hate* + infinitive or *would ('d) like/hate* + *to have* + past participle.

I (1 like/go on) .... working. I (2 hate/give up) .... my job. But I (3 like/move) .... to a house with a garden. I (4 not like/live) .... in a different area because I (5 hate/lose) .... touch with all my friends. And I (6 love/go) .... on a world cruise - just once. But I (7 not like/spend) .... all the money. I (8 like/leave) .... a lot of it to my children. I'm glad I won only two million pounds. I (9 not like/have/win) .... £20 million. I (10 hate/have/be) .... on television. I'm just sorry my husband George isn't still alive. He (11 love/have/go) .... on that cruise with me.

Quick reference

We can use an *-ing* clause to talk about:

- two actions happening at the same time (often after the verbs *be, stand, sit, lie*).
  *She's in the bar **waiting for you**.   They sat **talking**.   He lay on the bed **reading**.*
- an action happening while another is going on. *He fell asleep **watching television**.*
- an action immediately preceding another. ***Closing the door quietly**, he left the house.*
- an action that was completed before another started.
  ***Having paid the bill**, we left the restaurant.*
- We can also use an *-ing* clause to explain why something happened.
  ***Not knowing which way to go**, he asked a policeman.*
  ***Having lost my ticket**, I had to buy another one.*

1 **This is a newspaper report of a big gas explosion in central London. Complete the sentences, using the correct form of the verbs in brackets.**

I arrived on the scene soon after the blast. One woman was sitting on the pavement (1 cry)
.... An old man was lying in the road (2 bleed) .... heavily from a head wound.
Another woman was walking up and down (3 hold) .... her head and (4 scream)
.... Several cars were on fire, (5 send) .... a column of black smoke into the sky.
Three teams of paramedics were there (6 treat) .... people for shock. Workers from the gas
company were already in the building (7 try) .... to discover the cause of the blast.

2 **Last year was a bad one for Andrea. Write complete sentences, using an *-ing* clause.**

Example: In February she/break/her leg/ski *In February she broke her leg skiing.*

1 In May she/have/a car accident/come/home from work

   ....

2 In June her father/have/a heart attack/play/tennis

   ....

3 In August she/break/arm/fall/down the stairs

   ....

4 In October she nearly/electrocute herself/try/mend her guitar amplifier

   ....

3 **A bank robbery that went wrong. Match items in the two columns to make complete sentences.**

1 Taking a gun out of his pocket,	a) the cashier pressed the alarm bell.
2 Pushing his way to the front of the queue,	b) he rushed out into the street.
3 Seeing him coming,	c) the man panicked.
4 Hearing the alarm,	d) the robber ran into the bank.
5 Pushing people out of the way,	e) he spoke to the cashier.

1 ....   2 ....   3 ....   4 ....   5 ....

4 **How to make a mushroom omelette. Make the two sentences into one, using an *-ing* clause.**

1 Beat the eggs. Then add a little salt and pepper to them.

   Having ....

2 Chop the mushrooms. Add them to the eggs.

   ....

3 Melt the butter in the frying pan. Pour in the mixture.

   ....

4 Cook the omelette for three minutes. Serve it with a little fresh parsley.

   ....

5 **Read the text about Tim Bell. Complete the second sentence so that it has a similar meaning to the first sentence, using an *-ing* clause.**

Example: Because he didn't want to stay at school Tim left when he was 16.
   Not wanting to stay at school, Tim left when he was 16.

1 Now, because he can't find a job, he spends most of his time at home.

   Now, ... at home.

2 One day last month, because he had nothing to do, he bought some juggling balls.

   One day last month, ...

3 After two weeks, because he'd practised three hours a day, he could juggle five balls.

   After two weeks, ...

4 Because he feels that this might be his career, he practises regularly every day.

   .... every day.

5 His friends, because they've seen him juggle, think that he could earn some money as an

   entertainer.

   His friends, ...

6 This week, because he's done three performances, he's earned over £150.

   This week, ... over £150.

7 Because he's a very cautious person, Tim has put half the money in the bank.

   .... in the bank.

8 Because he's found something he can do well, Tim's now a lot happier than he was.

   .... than he was.

6 **Write five sentences, using *-ing* clauses. Say what you have done so far in your life, and say how one thing has led to another. Check your answers with a teacher.**

Examples: *Being an only child, I felt a bit lonely at home. When I was 12, not having many friends, I moved to a new school. Having liked rock music all my life, I started to learn to play the drums last year.*

Quick reference

- General preference: we can use *prefer* + infinitive with *to* OR *prefer* + *-ing*.
  *He doesn't like watching television. He prefers **to read**. OR He prefers **reading**.*

- A particular situation: we can use *would prefer (not)* + infinitive with *to* OR *would rather (not)* + infinitive without *to*.
  I'd prefer not to go *by bus tomorrow.* OR ***I'd rather not go** by bus tomorrow.*
  I'd prefer to go *by train.* OR ***I'd rather go** by train.*

- Two alternatives
  *He prefers to read **rather than** watch TV.* OR *He prefers reading **to** watching TV.*
  *I'd prefer to stay at a hotel tonight **rather than** sleep in the car.* OR *I'd **rather** stay at a hotel tonight **than** sleep in the car.*

- *Would prefer* someone *to do* something/*would rather* someone *did* (simple past) something.
  *I'd prefer **you to buy** a car.* OR *I'd rather **you bought** a car.*
  *I'd prefer **you not to buy** a motorbike.* OR *I'd rather **you didn't buy** a motorbike.*

- Regrets about the past: *Would prefer (not) to have done/would rather (not) have done.*
  *I'd prefer **not to have gone** to China.* OR *I'd rather **not have gone** to China.* (but I did)
  *I'd prefer **to have gone** to India.* OR *I'd rather **have gone** to India.* (but I didn't)

1 Look at the Griggs family's general preferences. Make sentences, using *prefer* + infinitive or *-ing*, and including the two alternatives. Use the following verbs.

| read   study   watch (x2)   ride   play (x2)   drive |

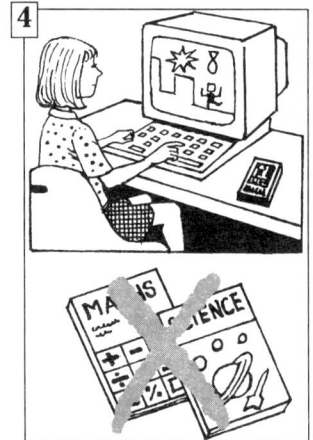

1 Jerry Griggs ....

2 Katherine Griggs ....

3 Tim ....

4 Jessica ....

2 Harold Maw is an invalid who lives on the seventh floor of an old block of flats near the centre of Liverpool. He is telling a social worker about his problems and preferences. Complete the sentences, using *would prefer* or *would rather* with these verbs.

| have to   live   talk   be (x2)   have |

I like living in Liverpool, but (1 not) I .... in this flat. It's difficult being on the seventh floor. (2) I .... in a ground-floor flat rather than this one. When the lift's not working, I have to walk up the stairs. (3 not) I .... do that three times a day. I'm not married and I don't like living alone. (4) I .... married. I've got three cats and a budgerigar, but (5) I .... some children. Nobody comes to see me, so I watch television for hours. (6) I .... to people than watch television.

3 Milly Jones teaches in a primary school. She is talking to her class of five-year-olds. Complete the second sentence so that it has a similar meaning to the first, using the word given.

Example: William, I'd prefer you not to write all over the walls. (rather)
  William, I'd rather you didn't write all over the walls.

1 Gabby, I'd rather you didn't pull Beth's hair. (prefer)
  I'd .... pull Beth's hair.
2 Jessica, I'd prefer you not to eat your lunch on the floor. (rather)
  Jessica, I'd .... eat your lunch on the floor.
3 Jack, I'd prefer your feet to be on the floor, not on Matthew's head. (rather)
  Jack, ... on the floor, not on Matthew's head.
4 Alice, I'd rather you talked quietly than shouted like that. (prefer)
  Alice, ... like that.
5 Nicola, I'd prefer you to eat your sandwiches rather than throw them at Amy. (rather)
  Nicola, ... them at Amy.
6 Carla, I'd rather you sat on your chair than stood on the table. (prefer)
  Carla, ... on the table.
7 Neil, I'd prefer your coat to be in the cloakroom rather than on my desk. (rather)
  Neil, ... on my desk.
8 Charles, I'd prefer you not to pour your orange juice over Zoe. (rather)
  Charles, ... your orange juice over Zoe.

4 Louise and Chris went to London to do some shopping yesterday. Chris is talking about the trip. Read the text and decide which sentence, A, B, C or D best follows the first sentence.

1 I didn't really want to go. .....
  A I'd prefer to have gone to London.   B I'd rather have spent the day at home.
  C I'd rather spend the day at home.   D I'd prefer to stay at home.
2 I had to get up at 6.30. .....
  A I'd rather get up at 8.00.   B I'd rather have stayed in bed.
  C I prefer getting up early.   D I'd prefer to stay in bed.
3 We went by car. .....
  A I'd prefer to have gone by car.   B I'd rather go by train.
  C I'd rather have gone by car.   D I'd prefer to have gone by train.
4 Louise insisted on driving. .....
  A I'd rather have driven.   B I'd prefer Louise to have driven.
  C I'd rather not have driven.   D I'd prefer not to have driven.
5 We had lunch at a McDonald's. .....
  A I prefer not to go to fast-food restaurants.   B I'd rather have gone to a McDonald's.
  C I'd prefer to have gone to a McDonald's.   D I'd rather eat in fast-food restaurants.
6 In the end we didn't buy anything. .....
  A I'd prefer not to have bought anything.   B I'd rather not have bought anything.
  C I'd rather have stayed at home.   D I'd prefer to stay at home.

Quick reference

- These verbs can be followed by the infinitive with *to* or *-ing*. The meaning is the same: *begin, bother, continue, intend, start.*
  *He continued **to work**.* OR *He continued **working**. It started **to rain**.* OR *It started **raining**.*
  But note that we don't use the *-ing* form after a verb in a continuous tense.
  *We're **intending to leave** soon.* (NOT *We're intending leaving soon.*)

- These verbs can also be followed by the infinitive with *to* or *-ing* but the meaning is not the same: *forget, go on, need, regret, remember, stop, try.*

- *Go on* + the infinitive with *to*: a situation or an action comes later.
  *He studied law and **went on to become** a judge.*
  Go on + *-ing*: someone continues doing the same thing. *He **went on talking**.*

- *Need* + the infinitive with *to*: to say what it's necessary to do. *We **need to leave** now.*
  Need + *-ing*: if something is in need of attention. *This window's broken. It **needs repairing**.*

- *Stop* + the infinitive with *to*: when someone stops one thing to do another.
  *We walked for ten kilometres and then we **stopped to have** a rest.*
  Stop + *ing*: when an action finishes. *It **stopped raining**.*

- *Forget* + the infinitive with *to*: to say we didn't do something we should have done.
  *I **forgot to lock** the door.*
  Forget + *ing*: to talk about memories of things we did in the past.
  *I'll never **forget driving** a car for the first time.*

- *Remember* + the infinitive with *to*: when we remember that we have to do something.
  *She **remembered to post** the letter.*
  Remember + *-ing*: to talk about something we did in the past.
  *I **remember falling** in love for the first time.*

- *Try* + the infinitive with *to*: when we make an effort to do something.
  *I **tried to remember** her name.*
  Try + *-ing*: when we talk about a possible solution to a problem.
  *I had a headache. I **tried taking** some aspirin, but it didn't help.*

- *Regret* + the infinitive with *to*: to announce bad news.
  *I **regret to announce** the death of the president.*
  Regret + *-ing*: when we wish we had or hadn't done something.
  *I **regret saying** that. He **regrets not going** to university.*

1 **A group of people on holiday are sitting round the hotel swimming pool. Read what they are saying and think of the word(s) which best fit(s) each space.**

'We're intending (1) .... for two more days at this hotel and then to move on.'

'Now the weather's better I'm beginning (2) .... myself.'

'You're starting (3) .... a suntan already. You're really quite brown.'

'I'm lucky. I never bother (4) .... suncream on but I never get sunburnt.'

'If the people above us continue (5) .... parties every night, I'm going to complain.'

2 **Complete the following story from a local newspaper using either the infinitive or the *-ing* form of the verb in brackets.**

Twenty-two-year-old telephone engineer, Kevin Hooper, went to the house of pensioner Mrs Edith Reed. Her husband had died recently and she needed (1 have) .... another phone in her bedroom. Mrs Reed told him she missed her dead husband because he was so practical. Whenever something in the house needed (2 repair) .... he fixed it immediately. She went on (3 talk) .... about him for some time. In fact she didn't stop (4 talk) .... about him for half an hour. Kevin, meanwhile, went on (5 work) .... She then said she needed (6 go) .... shopping and left Kevin on his own.

Soon after that Kevin stopped (7 make) .... himself a cup of coffee. He put the kettle on the cooker and switched on the gas. But then the phone rang and he forgot (8 light) .... it. Twenty minutes later he suddenly remembered (9 leave) .... the gas on. He ran back into the kitchen. The room was full of gas and Mrs Reed's pet budgerigar was lying on the floor of its cage. He tried desperately (10 revive) .... it. He even tried (11 shake) .... it. But that didn't do any good. So, finally, he glued the dead budgerigar's feet to its perch.

When Mrs Reed returned she thought her budgerigar was asleep. Kevin finished the job and left as soon as he could.

He really regretted (12 deceive) .... Mrs Reed and said he'd never forget (13 see) .... the budgerigar on the floor of its cage with its feet up in the air.

3 **Suzanne Ford is talking to an old school friend who she has not seen for ten years. Rewrite the sentences, using an infinitive with *to* or an *-ing* form.**

1 I left school when I was only 16. I regret it. I regret ....

2 I didn't go to university. I didn't even try. I didn't ....

3 I didn't work hard when I was at school. I regret it.
   I regret ....

4 I didn't go to the last class reunion. I forgot. I forgot ....

5 I got a job in a supermarket. I worked there till I had a baby.
   I went on ....

6 Do you remember Nick Edwards, the captain of the school football team? He became a professional player. He went on ....

7 I met him a year ago in a London night club. I'll never forget it.
   I'll never forget ....

8 I smoked when I was at school. I've stopped now. I've stopped ....

4 **Finish these sentences about yourself. Use an infinitive with *to* or an *-ing* form. Check your answers with a teacher.**

When I was very young I remember ...
This morning I remembered ...
I regret not ...
When I'm older I intend ...
I try ... every day.
After I've finished doing this exercise I'll go on ...

I'll never forget ...
I sometimes forget ...
I can't stop ...
At the weekend I need ...
When I can't sleep I try ...

Quick reference

- If the reporting verb is in the past (*He said ... He told me ...*) the verb in reported speech usually 'goes back' one tense into the past.
  Present simple: *'I **come** from Greece.'* > Past simple: *She said (that) she **came** from Greece.*
  Present continuous: *'I'm **working**.'* > Past continuous: *He said (that) he **was working**.*
  Past simple > Past perfect   Past continuous > Past perfect continuous
  Present perfect > Past perfect   Future *will* > *would*
  We usually leave out *that* after the reporting verb.

- The past simple in direct speech can stay the same in reported speech.
  *'We **fell** into the lake.'* He said they **fell** into the lake. (OR *they had fallen*)

- Modal verbs
  Can > *could*   *may* > *might*
  Must stays the same or changes to *had to*.
  *'You **must** work harder.'* > He told me I **must** (OR *I had to*) work harder.
  Would, could, should, might, ought to and *mustn't* don't change in reported speech.

- If the reporting verb is in the past, but the situation still exists, we can use the same tense.
  'I'll see you in town tomorrow.' > He said he'll (OR *he'd*) see me in town tomorrow.

- Note these changes in reported speech:

tomorrow	> *the following day*		*yesterday*	> *the day before/the previous day*
today	> *that day*		*last week*	> *the week before/the previous week*
now	> *then*		*next week*	> *the following week*
this morning	> *that morning*		*tonight*	> *that night*
three days ago	> *three days before*			

1 **Jenny Broad is interested in the supernatural. She went to see a medium in the hope of contacting some dead relatives. This was their conversation.**

MEDIUM: I can see a man. He's your uncle Walter who died in 1994.

JENNY: I've never had an uncle Walter.

MEDIUM: You often went to see him in Manchester.

JENNY: I've never been to Manchester. I don't know anyone in Manchester.

MEDIUM: You must try to remember. He gave you the necklace you're wearing.

JENNY: Nobody gave me the necklace. I bought it myself.

MEDIUM: The man looks sad because you didn't go to his funeral. He's trying to give you a message.
          But he can't speak.

JENNY: I'm sorry, but you've made a mistake.

MEDIUM: He'll come and see you again in a dream.

Now Jenny's reporting the conversation to a friend. Put the dialogue into reported speech.

1 She said she .... a man. She said he .... in 1994.

2 I told her I .... Walter.

3 She said I .... Manchester.

4 I told her I .... Manchester. I said I .... Manchester.

5 She said I .... to remember. She told me he ....
   .... wearing.

6 I told her that nobody .... the necklace. I said .... myself.

7 She said the man .... sad because I .... funeral. She

said he .... a message. But he .... speak.

8 I told her I .... sorry, but she .... a mistake.

9 She said the man .... in a dream.

2 **Phil Mather is writing a love song. The girl does not love the boy any more. The boy is reminding her of what she said to him. The song is called 'You said ...' Phil wrote the words by putting these sentences into reported speech. Write the words of his song.**

Example: I'll love you for ever. *You said you'd love me for ever.*

1 'I can't live without you.' You said ....

2 'I'll never leave you.' You said ....

3 'You're the only one for me.' You said ....

4 'I feel fine when I'm with you.' You said ....

5 'I won't ever be untrue.' You said ....

6 'I've never felt this way before.' You said ....

3 **When Lauren lost her job, her friend Camilla lent her £200. Three weeks later Lauren left a message on Camilla's answer-phone.**

'I can't give you the money now, but I'll pay you back tomorrow or next week.

I did some temporary work for a travel agency last week and I think they're going to pay me today. I'll certainly be able to give you £50, and I hope that will be all right. I'm really sorry I haven't paid you back yet. You can phone me tonight if you want to talk about it. I won't go out till you've phoned.'

It is now three weeks since Lauren left the message. Camilla is talking to her on the phone. Complete what she says, using reported speech.

When you left the message you said you (1) .... the money .... but ....

.... or .... You said you (2) .... some

temporary work for a travel agency .... and you .... to pay

.... You said you (3) .... £50, and you

.... all right.

You told me you (4) .... sorry you .... yet.

You said I (5) .... if I .... to talk about it. You

said you (6) .... But you weren't in when I

phoned and I haven't heard from you since.

4 **Think of something that someone has recently said to you that really interested you, surprised you or irritated you. Write your version of it, using reported speech.**

Examples: *My English teacher said that she'd (had) once had lunch with the US president. I told her I didn't believe her. She said it was true and she said she'd (would) show me a photograph to prove it.*

Check your text with a teacher.

Quick reference

- In direct questions the word order is verb + subject. In reported questions the word order changes to subject + verb and there is no question mark.

Direct question:	**verb** +	**subject**	**Reported question:**	**subject** +	**verb**
How old	*are*	*you?*	*He asked me how old*	*I*	*was.*
Where	*do*	*you come from?*	*She asked where*	*I*	*came from.*
What	*did*	*the man say?*	*He asked me what*	*the man*	*said/had said.*

- If there is no question word (*what, where, how,* etc.), we use *if* or *whether* in the reported question. *Are you English? He asked **if/whether** I was English.*

- We use this construction in reported commands, warnings, requests and advice.

	Subject +	**verb** +	**object** +	**infinitive with *to***
('Shut up!')	*He*	*told*	*me*	*to shut up.*
('Don't go.')	*He*	*advised*	*us*	*not to go.*

- We can use *agree, invite, offer, promise, refuse, remind, threaten* as reporting verbs.

	Subject +	**Verb** +	**(object)** +	**infinitive with *to***
('Please come with us.')	*They*	*invited*	*me*	*to come with them.*
('I promise I'll pay.')	*I*	*promised*		*to pay.*

- We can use *add, admit, agree, claim, comment, complain, deny, explain, insist, mention, promise, remind, suggest* as reporting verbs.

	Subject +	**verb** +	***that* clause**
('I love him.')	*She*	*admitted*	*that she loved him.*
('Why don't you go to bed?')	*She*	*suggested*	*that I went to bed.*

1 Change this telephone conversation from direct to reported speech.

ROBERT: Can I speak to Tess please?

JILL: I'm sorry, she isn't in. Who's speaking?

ROBERT: My name's Robert. Um, do you know what time she'll be back?

JILL: She won't be back till ten.

ROBERT: Can you give her a message? Can you ask her to ring me?

JILL: What's your number?

ROBERT: It's 9298465.

JILL: What time do you go to bed?

ROBERT: I won't be in bed before midnight.

Robert asked if ....

....

....

....

....

....

....

....

2 These are some of the things a driving instructor said to Sophie during her first driving lesson. Sophie is telling a friend about the lesson. Complete the second sentence in reported speech so that it has a similar meaning to the first sentence. Use the words given.

1 'Could I see your driving licence please?' (asked)

He .... my driving licence.

2 'Now, start the engine.' (told)

He .... the engine.

3 'Don't forget that there's a 30 mph speed limit in town.' (reminded)

He .... a 30mph speed limit in town.

4 'Why don't you drive a little more slowly?' (suggested)

He .... a little more slowly.

5 'Don't drive so fast!' (told)

He .... fast.

6 'I'm going to get out and walk if you don't drive more slowly.' (threatened)

He .... drive more slowly.

3 Mateo is a Spanish student. He is talking to the receptionist at an English youth hostel. Complete the report of their conversation.

MATEO: Have you got any beds free for tonight please?

RECEPTIONIST: Yes, I have. You can have a bed in a room with four other people.

MATEO: That's OK.

RECEPTIONIST: How many nights do you want to stay?

MATEO: I only want to stay for one night.

RECEPTIONIST: OK. Now, breakfast is at 8.00 and you must make your own bed. And remember, alcohol isn't allowed in the hostel.

MATEO: OK. I won't be late for breakfast.

RECEPTIONIST: I can look after your passport and valuables if you want. It's a bit risky leaving them in your room. But don't forget to collect them before you leave.

He asked .... night. She said ....

She offered .... four other people. He said

.... She then asked .... to stay. He

replied .... one night. She told him ....

and added .... She warned him ....

.... in the hostel. He promised ....

for breakfast. She offered .... wanted.

She explained ....

room. She reminded him .... left.

4 Report a conversation which you have had recently with a teacher, a friend or a member of your family. Use at least six of these reporting verbs.

ask tell say warn advise agree invite offer promise refuse remind threaten add
admit agree comment claim complain deny explain insist mention suggest

Check your text with a teacher.

Quick reference

We use *the*:

- when we talk about a particular person or thing. *I met **the** man she's going to marry.*
- with superlatives. *Mount Everest is **the highest** mountain in the world.*
- with parts of the day. *in **the** morning   in **the** afternoon   in **the** evening* (BUT *at night*)
- with words describing geographical position and place. *in **the** north   on **the** left*
- with the names of rivers, oceans, groups of mountains and islands. ***the** Thames   **the** Alps*
BUT NOT with most lakes and individual mountains and islands. *Lake Superior   Cuba*
- with the names of buildings, cinemas, hotels, etc. ***the** Eiffel Tower   **the** Imperial Hotel*
BUT NOT with most churches, castles, squares, streets. *Ely Cathedral   Walton Street*
- with 'plural' countries. ***the** United States   **the** West Indies   **the** Netherlands*
BUT NOT with continents and most countries. *Asia   Europe   North America   Spain   Britain*
- with an adjective used for the people of a country. ***the** British   **the** French   **the** Japanese*
BUT when we use a plural noun, *the* is usually optional. *(**the**) Americans   (**the**) Europeans*
- with an adjective describing groups of people. ***the** rich   **the** homeless*

We don't use *the*:

- in the phrases *in bed/to bed   at work/to work   at home   by bus, by train*, etc.
- before days, months and festivals. *It was **Sunday**.   in **June**   at **Christmas***
- before meals. *We have **breakfast**, **lunch** and **dinner** at the hotel.*
- before school subjects/languages. *I'm studying **French** and **Geography** this year.*
- before time expressions like *last week   next month   last Tuesday   next Thursday*
- before *church, hospital, school, college, university, prison, court* when we're talking about the main purpose of these places. *He's very ill. He's **in hospital**.*
BUT we use *the* when we go to these places for an alternative purpose, or when we're talking about a particular church, a particular hospital, etc.
*He went to **the hospital** to see his mother.   She works at **the school** in Miller Street.*

1 **Match the items in the two columns, and complete the sentences, using *the* where necessary.**

1 ..... River Nile is

2 ..... Volga is

3 ..... Mount Kilimanjaro is

4 ..... Downing Street is

5 ..... White House is

6 ..... rich and ..... famous

7 ..... Trafalgar Square is

8 ..... English, ... French and ..... Spanish

a) colonised ..... West Indies.

b) where ..... President of ..... the USA lives.

c) ..... most famous square in ..... London.

d) ..... longest river in ..... Europe.

e) ..... residence of ..... Britain's Prime Minister.

f) ..... highest mountain in ..... Africa.

g) stay at ..... Ritz Hotel in ..... London.

h) ..... longest river in ..... world.

1 ....   2 ....   3 ....   4 ....   5 ....   6 ....   7 ....   8 ....

2 Mikael is learning English. He finds the use of *the* very difficult. Read what he says. Some of the lines are correct, and some have a *the* which should not be there. If a line is correct, put a tick (✓). If a line has a *the* which should not be there, underline it and write *the* in the brackets.

1 I've been learning English since the last year. I came to England   (..........)

2 the last April, just before Easter. I go to a language school in the   (..........)

3 centre of London near the Leicester Square. We do three hours   (..........)

4 in the morning, then we have lunch. After the lunch we do two hours   (..........)

5 and finish at 4 o'clock. We don't work on Friday afternoons or on   (..........)

6 Saturdays. The last month I met an English girl, Rebecca, who   (..........)

7 wants to learn the Russian. It's Christmas next week. Next   (..........)

8 Saturday we're going to the north of England to spend Christmas with   (..........)

9 her parents. We're going by the bus because it's the cheapest way to   (..........)

10 travel. The next summer Rebecca is coming to Russia to stay with me.   (..........)

3 Complete the text, using *a* or *the*.

Sophie and Larry are looking for (1) ...... new house in (2) ...... town where they live. They like (3) ...... house they're living in, but (4) ...... rooms are too small, and it's difficult to find (5) ...... parking-place. (6) ...... street's noisy too. Sophie wants (7) ...... bigger house away from the city centre. They both want (8) ...... house in (9) ...... quiet part of (10) ...... town. Yesterday they looked at (11) ...... nice house with (12) ...... garage and (13) ...... garden. Larry liked (14) ...... garage, but Sophie thought (15) ...... garden was too small. And there was only (16) ...... shower in (17) ...... bathroom. Was it really (18) ...... house they wanted?

4 Complete the text, using *the* where necessary.

Jerry Walsh's father is in (1) ...... prison. Jerry lives with his sister and his mother. They try to look after him, but his mother's at (2) ...... work all day and his sister's at (3) ...... college. At the moment his mother's ill in (4) ...... hospital. He's never been to (5) ...... hospital to see her. He's supposed to be at (6) ...... school every day, but he stays in (7) ...... bed a lot of the time. He goes to (8) ...... school at (9) ...... end of his street, but he doesn't go to (10) ...... school very often. He never goes to (11) ...... church on (12) ...... Sundays, but on (13) ...... Tuesdays he sometimes goes to (14) ...... church near his house because there's a youth club there. Jerry's only 12, but he's often in trouble with the police and he's already been in (15) ...... court three times.

1 **Do these sentences refer to the particular or the general? Write *Particular* or *General* after each sentence.**

1 Murder is becoming more and more common nowadays.   ....

2 Have you heard the news about the murder of the London school teacher?   ....

3 The pupils at the teacher's school saw it happen.   ....

4 People say crime is getting out of control.   ....

5 Statistics prove it is increasing.   ....

6 The increase last year was particularly bad.   ....

7 Violence is certainly increasing.   ....

8 The violence people see on television may be partly responsible.   ....

9 Politicians are very worried about this.   ....

10 Violence in big cities is very worrying.   ....

2 **Read the radio news headlines below. Look carefully at each line. Some of the lines are correct, and some have a word which should not be there. If a line is correct put a tick (✓) after it. If a line has a word in it which should not be there, underline the mistake and write the word in the brackets.**

Example: The government has announced that <u>the</u> alcohol is good for you. (*alcohol*)

1 Government scientists have confirmed that one or two glasses of the wine or   (.....................)

2 beer are good for the heart.   (.....................)

3 The price of petrol is going up but the diesel stays the same.   (.....................)

4 The unemployment has gone down by 125.000 in the last six months.   (.....................)

5 The Prime Minister says he is worried by the increase in the sex and (.....................)

6 violence on the British television.   (.....................)

7 The weather tomorrow will be hot and sunny.   (.....................)

3 A speaker at an international conference on the environment wants to make the following points in his speech. He finds the use of the definite article *the* difficult. Rewrite the sentences correctly.

1 Ozone layer that protects the Earth from the radiation has been damaged by CFC gases coming from the aerosols and the refrigerators.

   ....
   ....

2 The scientists believe that emissions of the carbon dioxide are causing the global warming, and that the temperatures will continue to rise worldwide.

   ....
   ....

3 The water is being polluted. The fertilisers and the pesticides are killing fish and insect life in the world's rivers. The oceans of the world are full of the industrial waste.

   ....
   ....

4 The acid rain caused by the air pollution is damaging forest trees and the plant growth.

   ....

5 The world's rain forests are disappearing because of the demand for the hardwoods, and millions of hectares are burnt every year to provide the farming land.

   ....
   ....

6 Energy resources, like the oil and the coal, are being rapidly exhausted, and the burning of these fuels adds to the atmospheric pollution.

   ....
   ....

7 Air pollution in big cities is mainly caused by the cars.

   ....

4 Complete these sentences in any way you like. Check your answers with a teacher.

1 Coffee ...

2 The coffee ...

3 Money ...

4 The money ...

5 Girls ...

6 The girls ...

7 Young people ...

8 The young people ...

Quick reference

- We use *a* before words that begin with a consonant sound. *a man   a big dog   a uniform*
We use *an* before words that begin with a vowel sound. ***an** egg   **an** unusual man   **an** hour*
We usually use *a/an*:

- with singular countable nouns when we talk about a person or thing for the first time. We don't identify the person or thing. *She's got **a** car.*
- before jobs, occupations and religions. *He's **a** waiter.   I'm **a** student.   She's **a** Buddhist.*
- before some numbers and quantities.
***a** dozen eggs   **a** hundred men   **a** few friends   **a** lot of time   **a** number of people*
- with the meaning of 'per'. *twice **a** day   three days **a** week   £5 **a** kilo*
- in exclamations with 'What'. *What **a** lovely day!   What **an** interesting story!*

We don't use *a/an* before uncountable nouns.
***Work** is difficult to find.   I like **bread** and **cheese**.*

- We often use *some* as the plural of *a/an*. It means 'a certain number, but not all'.
***Some** people have bacon and eggs for breakfast.   **Some** cars have air conditioning.*

We don't use *some*:

- when we talk about things or people in general.
*I don't like **cats**. (= all cats)   **Bananas** are cheap at the moment.*
- when we're interested in the things or people themselves, not the number of them.
*He hasn't got **big feet**.   I like **people** who smile.   I like wearing **new clothes**.*

---

1 These are questions from an English language quiz. Answer them, using *a* or *an*.

1   What's another way of saying '90 minutes'? ....

2   If a return ticket is 'a two-way ticket', what's a single ticket? ....

3   What do you call someone who lives in Europe? ....

4   What do you call someone who lives in the United States? ....

5   What do you call the centre of learning where students can go after they've left school?

   ....

6   What's the opposite of 'It's a difficult job'? ....

7   What do you call a place where a traveller can get food and a room to stay in? ....

8   What's the opposite of 'a comfortable bed'? ....

9   What do you call a group of musicians who play together, under a conductor?

   ....

10   What's the opposite of 'a dishonest person'? ....

11   What's another way of saying 'a second-hand car'? (Use an adjective beginning with *u*.)

   ....

12   A teacher who, for example, describes life in the 18th century, is ....

2 Complete the text, using *a*, *an* or *some* where necessary.

My friend is (1) .... Irish, but she's got (2) .... unusual name - Manuela. She's got (3) .... rich parents who live in Ireland. Her father's (4) .... Spanish but he married (5) .... Irish girl. She's got two brothers and they've both got (6) .... jobs in England. Manuela's (7) .... photo-journalist. (8) .... people in Ireland don't see themselves as (9) .... Europeans, but she sees herself as (10) .... European citizen. She works as (11) .... freelance photographer all over the continent, selling (12) .... photographs to (13) .... newspapers and magazines. (14) .... photo-journalists concentrate on (15) .... violent and tragic stories, but Manuela prefers (16) .... stories of human strength and happiness. The other day she took (17) .... wonderful pictures of a woman in Italy who had just returned home to her child after spending six months in (18) .... prison. She called her story 'What (19) .... wonderful present!' because the mother came home on her child's birthday. (20) .... days Manuela doesn't have any work. She relaxes by reading (21) .... books, watching (22) .... videos and taking her dogs for (23) .... long walks in the Irish countryside. She loves (24) .... animals, and her house is full of (25) .... cats and dogs.

3 Vladimir is a new student in an English class. He is telling the class about himself. He finds the use of *a/an* and *some* difficult. Rewrite what he says correctly.

'I'm a Russian. I'm architect. But I haven't got job at the moment. Getting job is problem for me, because some jobs for some architects aren't easy to find in Russia at the moment. I haven't got some rich parents, so I must find a work soon. Russian architects go abroad to find some jobs. I've got American friend in California who has offered me job with his company that builds some swimming pools. I want to speak a good English before I go to the USA. My friend is a very successful. He makes lot of money. He's got enormous house near the beach at Malibu. I hope I'll be a rich like him in few years.'

....
....
....
....
....
....
....
....

4 Write eight sentences about yourself, using *a/an* and *some*.

Examples: *I'm a student. I live in a big city. I have English lessons three days a week. I've got some English friends in London.*

Check your answers with a teacher.

61 Nouns (singular and plural)

Quick reference

- Most nouns have a plural ending in -s or -es.
  a girl   two girls,   a box   two boxes,   a church   two churches
- Common irregular plural forms: *man > men, woman > women, person > people, child > children, foot > feet, tooth > teeth, mouse > mice*
- The plural of compound nouns: *a car radio   two car radios*
- Some numbers don't change in the plural.
  two dozen   three hundred   five thousand   twelve million
- Some nouns look singular but are used with a plural verb.
  People are *interested.*   *The* **police are** *coming.*
- Collective or group nouns can be followed by a singular verb (if we think of the group as a single unit) or by a plural verb (if we think of the group as a number of individuals).
  His **family is** *very big.*   *His* **family are** *all very tall.*
  The **government has** *changed the law.*   *The* **government have** *discussed the situation.*
- When we think of a quantity of money, etc. as a single unit, we use a singular verb.
  £500 is *a lot of money.* (NOT £500 are a lot of money.)
  10 kilometres isn't *far.* (NOT 10 kilometres aren't far.)
- Some nouns are only plural. The most common are: *clothes, contents, earnings, headquarters, outskirts, surroundings, thanks, valuables; glasses, pants, knickers, pyjamas, jeans, scissors, shorts, tights, trousers.*
  His **clothes are** *new.*   *My* **glasses are** *broken.*   *These* **jeans are** *too small.*
- Some nouns end in -s but are followed by a singular verb. The most common are: *news, politics, mathematics, physics, economics.*
  The **news isn't** *good.*   **Mathematics is** *his best subject.*

1 Put the words in italics into the plural, using the words in brackets.

The millionaire industrialist Alexander Crenshaw died last night.

1 During his life he had *an American wife*. (two) ....

2 He had *a child* with each of them. (three) ....

3 He had *an electronics factory* in Scotland. (two) ....

4 He owned *a computer company* in Taiwan. (two) ....

5 He had *a large house* in England. (two) ....

6 He had *a party* for his staff every year. (two) ....

7 He employed *a man* and *a woman* to look after his *gorilla*. (three) (two) (six)

  ....

8 He also had *a person* to look after his *pet monkey*. (two) (twelve)

  ....

2 **Complete the sentences with the plural form of the word in brackets. Sometimes a plural form is not necessary.**

Fifteen (1 man) .... and their (2 wife) ...., four single (3 woman) ....
and five (4 child) ...., two of them (5 baby) ...., were on holiday in the south of
Spain. They booked seats on a sight-seeing tour of the old (6 city) .... and (7 church)
.... of Andalucia. They each paid three (8 thousand) .... pesetas for the trip.
The trip was a disaster! Two (9 coach) .... arrived at the hotel. Neither was big enough. A
third coach arrived and took them up into the (10 mountain) .... and (11 valley)
.... of the Sierra Nevada. An hour later this coach ran out of fuel. While they were waiting
for help they had a picnic. 'We had a few (12 tomato) .... and a few (13 loaf) ....
of bread, so we made some (14 tomato sandwich) .... We also had a few
(15 bottle) .... of water,' one passenger reported. No help arrived so all the passengers
helped to push the coach for over eight (16 hundred) .... metres to the nearest petrol
station. Another passenger commented, 'The (17 fly) .... and (18 mosquito) ....
were terrible and several of us had very sore (19 foot) ....' Then the driver became ill. A
passenger who was a coach driver in England drove them back to Malaga. Unfortunately he had
never driven on the right before and by the time they got back they'd had four minor (20 crash)
........................, two old (21 lady) .... had swallowed their false (22 tooth) ....
and several (23 person) .... had been repeatedly sick. All, however, agreed they had had
the trip of their (24 life) .... and exchanged (25 address) .... so they could go
on another coach trip together the following year.

3 **Read the text below and look carefully at each line. Some of the lines are correct, and some have a mistake in them. If a line is correct put a tick (✓) after it. If a line has a mistake in it, underline the mistake and write the correction in the brackets.**

Example: I met a very interesting man on the train. 200 kilometres <u>aren't</u> a long way.   *(isn't)*

1 And two hours isn't a long time but in that time I learnt a lot about him.   (.............)
2 Physics were his main subject at university. Then he'd written a book about   (.............)
3 mathematics which were his real interest. His earnings from the book were very   (.............)
4 small - £5,000 a year aren't a lot of money. But for years he'd lived on this income.   (.............)
5 He certainly looked poor. His glasses were broken. His clothes were all very old   (.............)
6 and his trousers was torn.   (.............)
7 He said he didn't care what his surroundings was like.   (.............)
8 The news on radio and TV weren't of any interest to him.   (.............)
9 People were of no interest to him either.   (.............)
10 Even his family was total strangers to him.   (.............)
11 The only thing that interested him was ideas.   (.............)

4 **Write a paragraph about yourself and your family using the plural of as many of these words as possible. Check your answers with a teacher.**

man   woman   child   grandchild   person   wife   baby

Quick reference

Countable nouns	Uncountable nouns
• can be counted.	can't be counted.
Two restaurants/several hotels	Materials/substances: *air/water/milk/butter*
	Feelings/qualities: *love/anger/intelligence*
	Abstract ideas: *freedom/beauty/safety*
• can be singular or plural.	don't have plural forms, and take a singular verb.
A hotel/three hotels	*Our luggage is in the car.*
• can be used with *a/an*	if used in a general sense, can't be used with *a/an*.
*I want **a drink** and **an ice cream**.*	*I like **beer** and **ice cream**.*

• Note that the following nouns are uncountable in English:

accommodation, advice, baggage, behaviour, damage, equipment, evidence, furniture, garbage, homework, information, knowledge, luck, luggage, money, news, nonsense, progress, research, rubbish, spaghetti, traffic, transport, weather.

• Some words can be used as uncountable nouns when they are used in a general sense, and as countable nouns when they are used to talk about a particular example of something, or a number of examples of something: *cheese, coffee, exercise, fire, glass, success,* etc.
   ***Exercise** is good for you. I do two or three yoga **exercises** every morning.*
   *I like **cheese**. Cantal and camembert are two **cheeses** I particularly like.*
   *Plastic is less fragile than **glass**. I'd like **a glass** of water.*

1 A puzzle. Find the 'odd man out' in each group. It is either a countable or an uncountable noun in the wrong place.

children	table	hope
water	freedom	knowledge
enthusiasm	train	luck
food	child	problem
1	2	3 ....
police officer	health	woman
factory	sickness	actress
furniture	doctor	profession
people	happiness	satisfaction
4	5	6 ....
minute	child	milk
hour	love	egg
sleep	parent	sugar
clock	mother	bread
7	8	9 ....

2 a) Read the text and decide which answer, A, B or C best fits each space.

b) Which nouns in this text are uncountable? Write a list.

When I was young my grandfather gave me (1) .... advice. He said 'People (2) .... too much. The important thing is to listen. Don't depend on money. Money (3) .... bring happiness. Work hard. Progress (4) .... always the result of hard work. A house needn't be full of tables and chairs. Fine furniture (5) .... important, but the house should be full of warmth and love. Visit different countries, because knowledge about other parts of the world (6) .... important, and travel (7) .... you independence and tolerance.'

a) 1 A an   B some   C the   2 A talks B talk   C doesn't talk
   3 A doesn't   B don't   C does   4 A are   B aren't C is
   5 A isn't   B isn't being C aren't   6 A isn't   B are   C is
   7 A teaches   B teach   C show

b) Uncountable

....
....
....
....
....
....

3 This is a conversation at the Tourist Information Centre at Paddington Station in London. Complete the sentences by choosing the correct alternative.

'I'd like (1 some/an) .... information, please. Is it easy to find (2 an/—) .... accommodation in this part of London?'

'Are you looking for (3 a/—) .... hotel?'

'Yes, but it mustn't be too expensive or too far away because our luggage (4 is/are) .... heavy and we can't afford (5 a/—) .... taxi.'

'Well, here are the names of some hotels less than a mile from here. Public transport (6 is/are) .... quite cheap. You can catch (7 a/—) .... bus.'

'Fine. Thanks. Is there anywhere we can buy (8 a/—) .... wine round here? You see it's my girlfriend's birthday today and I want to buy (9 a/—) .... good red wine to celebrate.'

'Yes, there's a shop that sells (10 a/—) .... wine just outside the station.'

4 Write six sentences, beginning with the following nouns.
1 The traffic in big cities ... 2 Money ... 3 Spaghetti ... 4 Scientific research ...
5 Food ... 6 Scuba-diving equipment ...

Check your answers with a teacher.

Much, many, a lot of, plenty
(Very) little, (very) few   A little, a few

Quick reference

- We use *a lot of, many, plenty of, a few, very few* + countable nouns to say *how many*.

  Affirmative   **Negative**
  *There are **a lot of** shops in the city.*   *There aren't **many** cars on the road.*
  ***Many** people never go abroad.*   **Questions**
  *I bought **a few** bottles of wine.*   *Has he got **many** friends?*

- We use *a lot of, plenty of, very little, a little, much* + uncountable nouns to say *how much*.

  Affirmative   **Negative**
  *He drank **a lot of** water.*   *There isn't **much** food in the house.*
  *I've got **plenty of** time.*   **Questions**
  *She's got **very little** patience.*   *How **much** sugar do you want?*
                                          *Is there **much** milk left?*

- *Plenty (of)* means 'more than enough'.

- *Very little/little* and *very few/few* have a negative meaning.
  A little and *a few* have a more positive meaning.
    *He's worried. He's got **very little** money.   It's OK. I've got **a little** money left.*
    *He's lonely. He knows **very few** people.   She isn't lonely. She's got **a few** friends.*

- Note the use of *too much/too many* and *so much/so many*. Unlike *much, so much* and *too much* can be used in affirmative sentences.
    *There's **too much** traffic.   You talk **too much**.   There are **too many** people in the lift.*
    ***So much** money is wasted.   I've seen **so many** bad films this year.*

---

1 **Canterbury in the south of England and Billingham in the north of England both have a population of about 35,000. But apart from that they are very different.**

	Canterbury	Billingham
% unemployment	9%	29%
% families with 2 cars	17%	2%
% empty shops	7%	31%
Number of tourists	1.2 million	5,000

Use the words in the box to complete the questions and answers.

> a lot   a lot of   a few   much   many   very few   not much

1 How .... unemployment is there in Billingham? - There's ....

2 Is there .... in Canterbury? - No, ...

3 How .... families with two cars are there in Canterbury? - There are quite ....

4 Are there .... in Billingham? - No, there are ....

5 Are there .... empty shops in Billingham? - Yes, ...

6 Are there .... in Canterbury? - No, there are only ....

7 How .... tourists visit Canterbury each year? ....

8 How .... visit Billingham? ....

2 Read the text below about a hairdresser, Gary St John. Look carefully at each line. Some of the lines are correct, and some have a mistake in them. If a line is correct put a tick (✓) after it. If a line has a mistake in it, underline the mistake and write the correction in the brackets.

Example: How <u>many</u> training did you have?   (*much*)

GARY: (1) Not much. I remember I made a lot of mistakes when I first started. (.....................)

INTERVIEWER: (2) How many years have you been a qualified hairdresser?   (.....................)

GARY: (3) Only a little. Three in fact.   (.....................)

INTERVIEWER: (4) How much customers do you have a day?   (.....................)

GARY: (5) Quite many. Between 10 and 15 usually.   (.....................)

INTERVIEWER: (6) How much do you speak to them?   (.....................)

GARY: (7) Much. In fact, some people say I talk too much!   (.....................)

INTERVIEWER: (8) And how much of them are friends?   (.....................)

GARY: (9) Oh very little. I see a lot of them every week.   (.....................)

              (10) But I only know a few of them outside the salon.   (.....................)

INTERVIEWER: (11) How much hours a week do you work?   (.....................)

GARY: (12) Quite a few. I suppose about 45 on average.   (.....................)

INTERVIEWER: (13) Do you make many money from tips?   (.....................)

GARY: (14) Yes, a few. But I have to pay tax on it.   (.....................)

INTERVIEWER: (15) And how much do you earn altogether?   (.....................)

GARY: (16) Too few !   (.....................)

3 Alan Burnside is a successful businessman. Read the facts about his lifestyle and then match the questions on the left with the answers on the right.

Cigarettes: *5 a day.*
Exercise: *He walks upstairs to bed.*
Alcohol: *4 glasses of whisky a night.*
Sleep: *5 hours.*
Time with his family: *Most evenings and weekends.*
Money: *£150,000 a year.*

1 Does he smoke many cigarettes?   a) Yes, a lot.
2 How much exercise does he get?   b) No, only a few.
3 Does he drink much alcohol?   c) No, not much.
4 Does he get much sleep?   d) Yes, quite a lot.
5 How much time does he spend with his family?   e) Quite a lot.
6 Does he make much money?   f) Very little.

1 ....   2 ....   3 ....   4 ....   5 ....   6 ....

4 A ship has sunk. Two sailors have swum to an island. Make sentences, using *there is/there are* + *plenty of* + these nouns: *ships, fruit, fresh water, fish, wood.*

1 We won't starve. .... on the trees.

2 We can make a fire. ....

3 It rains a lot on the island so .... to drink.

4 .... in the sea so we can catch them and eat them.

5 We'll soon be rescued. .... in the area.

64 Some, any, no, none

1 **A couple have arrived at their rented holiday villa. They are checking to see if the villa has got everything they need. Complete the dialogue, using *some* and *any, no* and *none*.**

'Is there (1) .... cutlery?'

'Well, there are (2) .... knives and forks in this drawer, but I can't see (3) .... spoons.'

'I don't think there are (4) .... glasses. Can you see (5) ....?'

'No, there are (6) .... in the kitchen cupboards. Perhaps there are (7) .... in the other room.'

'There are (8) .... bulbs in the bedside lamps.'

'I'll ask the agent to get us (9) .... '

'There aren't (10) .... pillows on the bed.'

'Look in the wardrobe. There may be (11) .... there.'

'No, there are (12) .... there. There are (13) .... cushions on the sofa. We'll have to use those.'

'Oh, no. We're going to have a bad night tonight. There are (14) .... mosquito nets over the windows.'

'The agent said there was a nice garden and a swimming pool. I can see the garden, but there's (15) .... swimming pool.'

'Yes, there is. It's over there, near the trees. But there's (16) .... water in it!'

'I'll phone the agent. But let's have (17) .... tea first.'

'Yes, OK. Oh, no! I can't light the gas. There aren't (18) .... matches.'

2 Read this local radio news report. Complete the sentence in italics so that it has a similar meaning to the sentence before it, using the word given.

Example: Good morning! Welcome to GWR radio. I've got no good news for you this morning. (any)
I haven't got any good news for you this morning.

The transport workers are still on strike. I had to walk to the studio. (1) There were no buses or trains. (any) .... *buses or trains.*

(2) There are no flights out of Bristol Airport today. (any) .... *out of Bristol Airport today.* (3) And there won't be any trains to London. (no) *And ....*

.... *trains to London.* Roads around Bristol are jammed with cars.

(4) There are no places left in the city car parks. (any) .... *places left in the city car parks.* There's a fifteen-mile queue on the M4 motorway into Bristol. (5) And there isn't any movement on the M5 at Junction 19. (no) *And .... movement on the M5 at Junction 19.*

Leaders of the Transport Workers Union are meeting the government today. (6) Union officials don't see any chance of a breakthrough in negotiations. (no) *Union officials ....*
chance of a breakthrough in negotiations. (7) So there'll be no improvement in the situation today. (any) *So .... improvement in the situation today.*

3 John Cage is at a camp site. He has gone to the camp shop. He wants mineral water, salt, sugar, apples and sausages. He can see the apples, the sugar and the sausages, but he cannot see any mineral water or salt. Write his questions, using a) *Have you got ...?* or b) *Could I have ...?* and *some* or *any*.

1 .... mineral water?
2 .... apples?
3 .... salt?
4 .... sugar?
5 .... sausages?

4 Meg Jones is selling her synthesizer. She is talking to the person who is going to buy it. Complete what she says, using *some* or *any*.

It's got (1) .... fabulous sounds on it. You can get almost (2) .... orchestral instrument you want - violin, cello, trumpet, horn, harp, and so on. You can connect it to a computer too. It'll work with (3) .... computer that's got 4 megabytes of RAM. There's a 300-page manual with it that's got (4) .... really useful information. If you have (5) .... problems with it, let me know. If you've got (6) .... questions, don't hesitate to phone me at (7) .... time.

5 a) Write five sentences about the last time you went shopping. Use *some*, *any* or *no*.

Examples: *I saw some nice shoes. But they didn't have any in my size. I didn't see any interesting clothes. They had no jeans I really liked.*

b) What questions would you ask in these situations? Use *some* and *any*.
You're offering someone some coffee. There's some cake on the table; you'd like some. You're not sure if there's any petrol in the car. You want to know if there are any buses into town this evening.

Check your answers with a teacher.

65

All/everything, everybody/everyone
All/every/each Whole

Quick reference

- *Everything* (= all the things) + a singular verb. *Everything costs a lot.*
  Everybody/everyone (= all the people) + a singular verb. *Everybody has left.*
  They/them/their are used after *everybody/everyone*. *Everyone's cold. They're freezing.*

- *All* + relative clause. *All* = the only thing. *All (that) he told me was his name.*
  All + relative clause. *All* = everything. *We've done all (that) we can.*
  All + plural noun. *All the tickets are sold.*
  All (NOT Every) + uncountable noun. *All the furniture is new.*

- *Every* (OR *Each*) + a singular noun. *Every* (OR *Each*) *room has a TV.* (= all the rooms)
  Each. *Each room has its own toilet.* (= the rooms seen separately)
  Each of the rooms is different. (NOT Every of the rooms.)

- *Whole* + a singular countable noun. *They stayed the whole weekend.* (= all the weekend)
  The whole of + noun. *I slept the whole of the time.* (= the whole time)
  The whole of + a place name. *The whole of England is cold.* (NOT The whole England)

- *All* + a preposition *(about, along, over, round)*. *They come from all over the world.*
  All (NOT the whole) + an uncountable noun. *They drank all the wine.*

- *He came every day.* (= how often)
  She phoned him every two hours. (= how often)
  We stayed all day/all morning, etc. (= how long)

---

1 Read the newspaper story below and think of one word (*everyone, everything, all*) which best fits each space.

Example: Burglar Wayne Plummer thought that *everyone* in the wealthy Horfield area of Bristol must have something worth stealing.

In Westbury Avenue (1) .... had a burglar alarm - except for one house. (2) .... the lights were off in that house. It looked as though (3) .... was out. Wayne looked up and down the road. (4) .... was quiet. (5) .... was probably watching TV. He broke a window at the back of the house. He guessed that (6) .... valuable like jewellery would be upstairs. He opened all the drawers. But then he heard a car stopping outside. He watched as (7) .... in the car got out. He put (8) .... he could into his pockets. Then, just as they came in the front door, he escaped out of the back door. He climbed over a fence but then came to a three-metre high wall. (9) .... he could do was climb it and jump down the other side. Unfortunately he broke both his ankles. When he looked around he thought (10) .... looked familiar. He then realised he had jumped down into Bristol Prison. When prison guards arrested him (11) .... he could say was, '(12) .... has a bit of bad luck sometimes, but why's it always me?'

2 **George Kelly has no home and lives on the streets. Choose the right form of the verb.**

I don't eat properly because everything (1 is/are) .... so expensive nowadays, or at least everything (2 cost/costs) .... too much for me to buy. I went into hospital last week. Everybody (3 was/were) .... very kind at first. But everything (4 was/were) .... different when they found there was nothing wrong with me. Everyone (5 has/have) .... friends - except me. Everybody just (6 ignore/ignores) .... me.

3 **Complete this description of a typical suburban British street using *all*, *every* or *each*. Sometimes more than one answer is possible.**

(1) .... the houses in Mayfield Close look the same, except that (2) .... house has a different number on the front door. (3) .... morning, at about 8 o'clock, (4) .... of these front doors opens and the man or woman of the house goes off to work. This is true on (5) .... weekday morning but not at weekends. (6) .... the families in the road have a car and on Saturdays (7) .... car has to be washed and polished. (8) .... house in the road has a garden and on Sundays (9) .... the grass has to be cut. In fact (10) .... the people living in Mayfield Close do (11) .... they can to be the same as their neighbours.

4 **This is part of a letter sent by a girl on holiday on the island of Kos. Complete the sentences, using *the whole*, *a whole* or *all*.**

We spent (1) .... of the first week by the pool. Alex was in the water (2) .... the time. I spent (3) .... day reading. My book had over a thousand pages. I read (4) .... book in less than three days!

We go out every evening. We usually spend (5) .... evening choosing a restaurant and then eating dinner. Dinner usually includes drinking (6) .... bottle of wine! As a result we've spent almost (7) .... the money we brought with us already.

We've walked (8) .... round the old city three times and we've driven (9) .... over the island. In fact, we've seen (10) .... of Kos now. (It isn't very big!)

(11) .... the people in the hotel are English and (12) .... the waiters speak English so (13) .... the Greek I learnt before we came was a bit of a waste of time.

5 **Choose the correct alternative.**

We've been having problems with our neighbours (1 all/every) .... year. (2 All/Every) .... night it's the same - they have a party. And the party goes on (3 all/every) .... night. After about 5 a.m. they just sleep (4 all/every) .... the time and they keep their curtains drawn (5 all/every) .... day and we never see them. (6 Every/All) .... week we complain but it never does any good.

6 **Describe the people who live near you, using these words.**

Everybody ... Every ... Everyone ... Each ... Everything ... All ... The whole ...
Example: *Everybody knows their neighbour.*
Check your text with a teacher.

66

Quick reference

- **General**
  Most people watch TV.
  Some music is just noise.
  All children need love.
  No tickets were sold.

  Specific
  most of the people I know
  some of the music I listen to
  all (of) the children in my class
  none of the tickets I had

  With a pronoun
  most of it/you/us/them
  some of it/you/us/them
  all of it/you/us/them
  none of it/you/us/them

- *Most* means 'nearly all'. *Some* means 'a part, but not all'.

- We often leave out *of* after *all* and *half*.
  *I've read **all of** the book.* OR *I've read **all** the book.*
  *He ate **half of** the chicken.* OR *He ate **half** the chicken.*

- But before a pronoun *(it, you, us, them)* we must use *of*.
  *Where's the meat? - The dog's eaten **all of** it.* *Look at these apples. **Most of** them are bad.*

- We can use *all, most, some, a few,* etc. on their own.
  *Some people smoke and **some** don't.* *Many of my friends are here, but **a few** didn't come.*

- We can use a singular or plural verb after *none of.* *None of the players **was/were** hurt.*

- Two people or two things.
  ***Both** men are dead.* = ***Both the** men are dead.* = ***Both of the** men are dead.*
  ***Neither** computer works.* = ***Neither of** the computers works.*
  *Take **either** umbrella.* = *Take **either of** the umbrellas.*
  ***Both of** you/us/them* ***Neither of** you/us/them* ***Either of** you/us/them*

- Note the position of *all* and *both* used on their own in the sentence.
  *The people have **all** gone.* *Have you **both** finished?* *We're **all** very tired.*

1 Complete the text, using the word in brackets with or without *of*.

(1 Most) .... British people aren't very good at learning foreign languages. (2 Some)
.... them speak one language very badly and (3 many) .... them don't speak any
foreign languages at all. Nearly (4 all) .... them have studied a language at school, but only
(5 a few) .... them remember what they've learned. When they go abroad, (6 most)
.... British tourists expect all foreigners to speak English. A Greek friend of mine said that
(7 all) .... British tourists were lazy and could only say please and thank you in Greek. Last
year I went with (8 some) .... my friends to Amalfi in Italy. The weather was beautiful, so
we spent (9 most) .... the time on the beach. (10 A few) .... the people on the
beach were English. I don't think (11 any) .... them could speak a word of Italian. One
couple spent (12 half) .... the time complaining about the food and (13 half) ....
the time complaining that (14 none) .... the taxi drivers spoke English. This wasn't true,
because we found that (15 most) .... Amalfi taxi drivers spoke English. But (16 a lot)
.... them refused to speak English to (17 some) .... customers - the customers
who didn't make (18 much) .... effort to speak a word of Italian! (19 All) ....
tourists should try to remember that, (20 all) .... the time they're in a foreign country,
they're guests and not members of an invading army.

2 Read the information about these two cars.

	Car A	Car B
Power steering	✓	—
Electric windows	✓	✓
CD player	—	✓
Air-conditioning	—	—
Airbag	✓	✓
In-car phone	—	—
4-wheel drive	—	—
Sports seats	—	—
Alloy wheels	✓	✓
Automatic transmission	✓	✓

a) Say if these sentences about the two cars are true or false.

1 Both cars have got a CD player. ....

2 Both of the cars have got air-conditioning. ....

3 Neither car has got an in-car phone. ....

4 There isn't an airbag in either of the cars. ....

5 Neither car A nor car B has got electric windows. ....

6 Both the cars have got 4-wheel drive. ....

7 Neither of the cars has got power steering. ....

8 There aren't sports seats in either of them. ....

9 Neither of them has got alloy wheels. ....

10 Both of them have got automatic transmission. ....

b) Now use *both (of)*, *neither (of)* or *either (of)* to complete these sentences.

11 .... the cars have got an airbag.

12 There isn't an in-car phone in .... them.

13 .... car has got 4-wheel drive.

14 .... them have got electric windows.

15 .... cars have got alloy wheels.

3 I went with some friends to Florida last summer. Put *all* or *both* in the right position. Mark the position with a *. There is sometimes more than one possible position.

1 (all) We were tired after the journey.

2 (all) We went to bed as soon as we arrived at the hotel.

3 (both) After sleeping for three hours Sophie and I were feeling hungry.

4 (both x2) We hate airline food, so we'd eaten nothing on the plane.

5 (both) We decided to have a sandwich at the hotel bar.

6 (both) The barman asked: 'Do you want relish with the sandwich?'

7 (both) I wasn't sure what relish was, so we said no.

8 (all x2) The others were feeling energetic, so they went for a swim in the hotel pool.

4 Write ten sentences about your family. Use as many of the following expressions as possible:
All (of), most (of), some (of), none (of), both (of), neither (of), either (of).
Check your sentences with a teacher.

Quick reference

- We use *this* + a singular noun and *these* + a plural noun for things near the speaker.
  *Mmm! **This** soup tastes good.   Ouch! **These** shoes are too small for me.*

- We use *that* + a singular noun and *those* + a plural noun for things further away.
  *Who's **that** girl over there?   **Those** clothes you're wearing are dirty.*

- We use *this* and *these* when we talk about a present situation or something near in time.
  *I'm very busy **these** days.   I'll see you **this** afternoon.*

- We use *that* and *those* when we talk about something further away in time.
  ***That** film was good; I'd like to see it again.   In **those** days people didn't have cars.*

- We can also use *that* to refer back to a subject or an idea that's already been mentioned.
  *Let's go for a walk. - **That**'s a good idea.*

- Note that *this, these, that, those* can be used on their own as pronouns.
  ***This seat**'s mine.* (adjective/determiner)   ***This** is my seat.* (pronoun)

- On the telephone, in British English, we use *this* to refer to ourselves and *that* to refer to the other speaker. (In American English we use *this* for both.)
  *Hello. Who's **that**? - **This** is Andrew.*

---

1 **Complete this conversation in a clothes shop with *this, that, these* or *those*.**

'(1) .... jeans are a bit tight. What size are they?'

'They're a 32 inch waist.'

'What's (2) .... in centimetres?'

'(3) .... 81 centimetres.'

'Are (4) .... jeans over there a bigger size?'

'Yes, (5) .... are 34 inch waist.'

'Can I try them on, please?'

'Yes, (6) .... fitting room here is free.'

2 **Complete this telephone conversation with *this, these, that* or *those*.**

TIM: Hello? Who's (1) .... ?

RACHEL: (2) .... is Rachel. Um, what are you doing (3) .... evening?

TIM: I'm busy (4) .... evening.

RACHEL: You're always busy (5) .... days.

TIM: No, (6) .... not true. I'm just busy (7) .... evening, (8) ....'s all.

RACHEL: Well, how about next Tuesday?

TIM: (9) .... 's difficult. I don't know what I'm doing (10) .... evening.

RACHEL: You've changed, Tim. We used to go out together a lot. In (11) .... days you were always free to see me.

TIM: Um, (12) .... isn't easy for me Rachel, but there's something I must tell you. I met another girl (13) .... week.

RACHEL: Oh, I see.

3 Various people are eating in a restaurant. Complete the short dialogues in the speech bubbles, using *this*, *that*, *these* and *those*.

A What's (1) .... steak like?

B It's fine. But (2) .... chips are a bit cold.

D Which one?

C Who's (3) .... girl over there?

C The one who's sitting with (4) .... two men in the corner.

E (5) .... was a very good meal. But I don't understand what (6) .... £7.50 is for.

F (7) .... 's the 10% service charge, sir.

G Can we sit at (8) .... table in the window?

H No, I'm afraid (9) .... table's reserved.

G How about (10) .... two tables here?

H Yes, they're free.

I I've enjoyed myself (11) .... evening. I think (12) .... is the first time we've been out to a restaurant together (13) .... year.

J I know. You're always so busy (14) .... days.

4 Imagine you have just arrived at a party. You know most of the people there but the person you are with does not know them. Write a dialogue in which you use *this*, *that*, *these* and *those* a number of times. Check your dialogue with a teacher.

Examples: *This is Camilla. And that girl over there is Laura.*

Reflexive and emphatic pronouns:
myself, themselves, etc.

Quick reference

- We use a reflexive pronoun (*myself, themselves*, etc.) when the subject and object of the verb are the same person. The action is directed back to the person who does it.
  She hurt **herself**. (*She* and *herself* are the same person.)
  Singular: I > *myself*, you > *yourself*, he > *himself*, she > *herself*, it > *itself*
  Plural: we > *ourselves*, you > *yourselves*, they > *themselves*

- The most common reflexive verbs are: *to amuse yourself, to behave yourself, to blame yourself, to burn yourself, to control yourself, to cut yourself, to dry yourself, to enjoy yourself, to help yourself, to hurt yourself, to kill yourself, to look after yourself, to make yourself* (*a cup of tea*, etc.), *to buy yourself* (*a new sweater*, etc.)

- Note that the following verbs aren't normally reflexive in English.
  to change (your clothes), to dress, to wake up, to get up, to go to bed, to shave, to wash
  to stand up, to sit down, to lie down, to relax, to rest
  to feel tired, bored, etc.
  to complain, to concentrate, to remember, to worry

- We sometimes use a reflexive pronoun after an adjective + preposition.
  to be angry/pleased with yourself, to be ashamed/proud of yourself,
  to be sorry/responsible for yourself

- Note the expression *by myself, by themselves,* etc. meaning 'on my own, on their own', etc.
  I don't like living **by myself**. (= on my own, alone)

- Note the difference between *ourselves, yourselves, themselves* and *each other*.
  A and B blamed **themselves** *for the accident.* (= They said they were both responsible.)
  A and B blamed **each other** *for the accident.* (= A blamed B, and B blamed A.)

- We use emphatic pronouns to emphasise that someone does something without help.
  I can do it **myself**. (= I don't need any help.)   *The children made the cake* **themselves**.

- We sometimes use an emphatic pronoun to emphasise a noun or a pronoun.
  The **teacher herself** *couldn't answer the question.* (= Even the teacher couldn't answer it.)

---

1 **Alice has just come home. Her friend Jenny is looking very sorry for herself. Complete the dialogue, using *myself, yourself*, etc.**

ALICE: You look pale. Have you hurt (1) ....?

JENNY: Yes, I've cut (2) .... quite badly.

ALICE: How did it happen?

JENNY: Well, Mark and Camilla were making (3) .... some lunch. I was helping them. We were really proud of (4) ...., because for the first time we'd made some bread. But then Mark burnt (5) .... while he was getting it out of the oven, and dropped it on the floor. He was so angry with (6) .... that he broke a glass. And a piece of glass buried (7) .... in my foot!

ALICE: Mark should be ashamed of (8) ....! He should learn how to control (9) ....

2 Harvey Neilson is a successful American tennis player. He is talking about his working day. Read the text and decide which answer, A, B or C best fits each space.

Professional tennis players have to look after (1) ..... . We enjoy (2) ..... some of the time, but we also have to keep (3) ..... fit. I live by (4) ..... in a small Chicago apartment. I usually wake (5) ..... up at about 7.00 and I get (6) ..... up at 7.30. I put on a track suit and a pair of trainers and go for a three-mile run. Then I wash (7) ..... and shave (8) ..... and have (9) ..... breakfast. At 8.30 my coach and I meet (10) ..... at the gym and I train (11) ..... for two hours. If I feel (12) ..... tired during my training, I tell (13) ..... I mustn't stop (14) ..... , but it's difficult sometimes. After lunch I rest (15) ..... for an hour then I spend three hours on the tennis court. In the evening I'm usually too tired to go out. I just relax (16) ..... I worry (17) ..... a lot about injuring (18) ..... , because if I get injured, I don't earn any money.

1	A —	B themselves	C them		2	A ourselves	B —	C us
3	A us	B ourselves	C —		4	A me	B myself	C my own
5	A —	B myself	C me		6	A myself	B me	C —
7	A me	B myself	C —		8	A —	B me	C myself
9	A me	B myself	C —		10	A ourselves	B us	C —
11	A myself	B —	C me		12	A —	B myself	C me
13	A me	B myself	C —		14	A —	B myself	C me
15	A —	B myself	C me		16	A myself	B me	C —
17	A me	B —	C myself		18	A myself	B me	C —

3 Nicole Stamp has a husband and three children. She has just got a job and she is tired of doing all the work at home. Complete the sentences, using *yourself, themselves*, etc.

Example: I'm not going to do everything for the family. They must do more for ....
They must do more for themselves.

1 I'm not going to iron my husband's shirts. He must iron ....

2 I'm not going to tidy the children's rooms. They must tidy ....

3 She told her husband: I'm not going to make your breakfast. You must make ....

4 I'm not going to clean your shoes for you. You must clean ....

5 She told her children: I'm not going to help you with your homework. You must do ....

6 I'm not going to make your packed lunches every day. You must make ....

4 Complete this news story by using *themselves/ourselves* or *each other*.

Yesterday two 10-year-old children found (1) .... totally lost in a forest near Inverness. They had to spend the night there. They were found this morning by a local farmer. 'We were angry with (2) .... for getting lost,' said one of them. 'We were frightened too, so we talked to (3) .... all night. We told (4) .... stories and asked (5) .... questions about pop songs and films. We kept (6) .... warm by lighting a small fire. And we tried to make (7) .... comfortable by using our jackets as blankets. There were lots of scary noises in the forest. We could hear owls calling to (8) .... and some deer came quite close; we could hear them scratching (9) .... against the trees. When we saw the farmer coming, we were so pleased we actually hugged (10) ....!'

5 Write six things that you, your family or your friends have done on your own, without help.

Examples: *I mended the TV myself. My parents didn't buy a new boat; they built one themselves.*

Check your sentences with a teacher.

69

Someone, something, somewhere, etc.

Quick reference

- We use *someone(-body)*, *something*, *somewhere* in affirmative sentences and in polite requests, offers and suggestions.
    *There's **somebody** outside.* (affirmative) *Would you like **something** to eat?* (offer)
    *Can you tell me **something**?* (request) *Shall we go **somewhere** quieter?* (suggestion)

We use *anyone (-body)*, *anything*, *anywhere*:

- in questions and negative sentences.
    *Did you know **anybody** at the party?* *There isn't **anything** we can do to help.*
- when they mean 'it doesn't matter who, which or where.'
    *You can sit **anywhere**. We can eat **anything** we like.*
- We use *no-one(-body)*, *nothing*, *nowhere* with a verb in the affirmative.
    ***Nobody knows** we're here. **Nothing is** simple.*
- All the words above are used with a verb in the singular.
BUT we use *they, them, their* when we refer to *somebody, anybody*, etc.
    *There's someone on the phone. - Take **their** number and tell **them** I'll ring later.*
- *Someone, anything, nowhere*, etc. can be followed by an infinitive or an adjective.
    *I want **somebody to help** me. We couldn't find **anywhere cheap** to stay.*

---

1 Complete the dialogue between Simon and his sister Alice, using *somebody (someone), anybody (anyone), something, anything* or *somewhere*.

SIMON: Did (1) .... phone while I was out?

ALICE: Yes, (2) .... phoned just after you left.

SIMON: Was it (3) .... interesting?

ALICE: I don't know. It was (4) .... called Anna, I think she said.

SIMON: I don't know (5) .... called Anna. But I know (6) .... called Hannah. Did she say what she wanted?

ALICE: Yes, she said (7) .... about a party on Saturday. She said she didn't have (8) .... to go with.

SIMON: That's a pity, because I'm already going (9) .... else on Saturday night.

ALICE: Who with?

SIMON: (10) .... you don't know.

---

2 A boy is talking to a girl at a party. Complete what he says, using *someone (somebody), something, anything, somewhere* or *anywhere*.

I'm sure I've seen you (1) .... before. Or maybe you just look like (2) .... I once knew. Do you know (3) .... here? I know (4) .... in that group of people over there. But I don't know (5) .... else. You haven't got (6) .... to drink. Would you like (7) ....? Are you sure you don't want (8) ....? How about (9) .... to eat? No? Oh well, there isn't (10) .... to sit in here. Shall we go and find (11) .... in the other room? I've got (12) .... to tell you.

3 This man has been unemployed for a long time. Complete what he says, using *nobody (no-one)*, *nothing* or *nowhere*.

(1) .... understands why I don't get a job. The reason is that (2) .... ever offers me a job because I've got no address. And the reason why I've got (3) .... to live is because I can't pay a month's rent in advance. And I can't borrow the money because (4) .... I know has got any money. They're all like me - they've got (5) ....

4 Andrew and Sarah are on holiday but Sarah is determined not to enjoy herself. Complete what she says, using *anyone/anybody*, *anything* or *anywhere*.

ANDREW: Where shall we sit?

SARAH: We can sit (1) .... I don't mind.

ANDREW: What would you like to eat?

SARAH: (2) .... I don't care.

ANDREW: What do you want to drink?

SARAH: (3) .... You can choose.

ANDREW: Who shall we talk to? Those people over there?

SARAH: (4) .... I don't mind.

ANDREW: What do you want to do later?

SARAH: (5) .... I don't mind.

ANDREW: Where do you want to go tomorrow?

SARAH: (6) .... I don't care.

5 Read the dialogue below between the parents of a missing teenage girl and a detective. If a line is correct, put a tick (✓) after it. If a line has a mistake in it, underline the mistake and write the correct word in the brackets.

(1) 'She left without telling anything where she was going.   (........................)

(2) And since then we've heard nothing. We've phoned all   (........................)

(3) her friends but nothing has seen her.'   (........................)

(4) 'Can you tell me anyone else? Did you have an argument   (........................)

(5) about anything on the evening she left?'   (........................)

(6) 'No, something unusual happened at all.   (........................)

(7) She just said she was going somewhere and she wouldn't be late.'   (........................)

6 A number of students are sharing a house. Complete what each of them is saying, using *someone*, *something*, *somewhere*, *anyone*, *anything*, *anywhere*, *nobody*, *nothing*, *nowhere*.

1 I'm hungry but there's   ....   to eat.

2 A friend of mine needs   ....   to sleep tonight. Is the sofa OK?

3 The kitchen's in a mess but   ....   ever helps me to clean it.

4 I haven't got   ....   to wear and I'm going to a party.

5 There's   ....   at the door.

6 There's   ....   wrong with this video. It isn't working.

7 There's   ....   to sit. We must get some more chairs.

8 I'm not going   ....   this evening. I'm too tired.

9 Has   ....   seen my cheque book? I've lost it.

's and s'

- We add -'s to a singular noun (people and animals) to show that something belongs to someone. *the man's passport Gemma's mother the dog's collar the cat's dinner*

- With plural nouns we add an apostrophe (') after the final -s. *my parents' house*

- With plural nouns without a final -s (*men, children*, etc.) we use -'s. *the men's toilets*

- With two or more names, we put -'s after the last name. *Jenny and Mark's flat*

- We can use the -'s and -s' forms on their own when it isn't necessary to repeat a noun. *It's not my car; it's my **wife's**. It isn't the government's money; it's the **taxpayers'**.*

- We use the -'s form on its own for someone's home or shop. *I'm staying at my **aunt's**. (= my aunt's house) Go to a **chemist's**. (= a chemist's shop)*

- -'s is used with places/countries. **London's** *traffic problems* **Spain's** *tourist industry*

- -'s and -s' are used with expressions of time. **today's** *newspapers* *in three **weeks'** time*

Noun + *of* + noun OR noun + noun

- When the possessor is a thing (not a person/an animal) we usually use noun + *of* + noun. *the door **of** the house the manager **of** a record company the difficulty **of** the situation*

- We can sometimes use just noun + noun. *the kitchen window my holiday photos*

- When the possessor is a 'long' phrase or when it's followed by a descriptive phrase or clause, we use *of*, not -'s. *the problems **of unemployed workers** the brother **of the man we met in the pub***

A friend of mine, etc.

- In this construction we use a possessive pronoun (*mine, his, yours*, etc.) or the -'s/s' form. *Is Jack **a friend of yours**? - He's **a friend of Mike's**. Tess has still got **a book of mine**.*

---

1 Liz Craig is a primary school teacher. Her class is doing a project on musical instruments and she asked them to bring in any instruments they had. At the end of the lesson she is asking which instruments belong to which children. Jack brought his father's trumpet. The Taylor twins brought a concertina. Sarah brought some African drums. Sam and Zoe brought a Bolivian flute. Anna brought an accordion. The Kay sisters brought their guitars. Answer these questions.

Example: Who does the trumpet belong to? *It's Jack's.*

1 Whose are the guitars? ....

2 Who does the Bolivian flute belong to? ....

3 Whose are the African drums? ....

4 Who does the accordion belong to? ....

5 Whose is the concertina? ....

2 Read the text. Some of the lines are correct, and in some a possessive apostrophe (') or the word *of* is missing. If a line is correct, put a tick (✓). If a line has a word where the possessive apostrophe is missing, write the correct form of the word. If the word *of* is missing, write *of* in the brackets. No.1 has been completed for you.

1 Laura Lopez works at a travel agents in London. She's the manager   (*agent's*)

2 of their South American department. She's a successful manager and   (...............................)

3 her speciality is dealing with customers problems. Her parents are   (...............................)

4 Mexican, and when she travels to Mexico she stays on her grandparents   (...............................)

5 farm near Oaxaca. Laura's cousin lives in Lima, so when she goes   (...............................)

6 to Peru she stays at her cousins. Laura's got two children, but she's   (...............................)

7 divorced. Her childrens father now lives in Exeter. Once a month   (...............................)

8 the children spend a weekend at their father's. Since her divorce her   (...............................)

9 life has changed. She now has the problems being a single parent, in   (...............................)

10 addition to the demands her job. She feels that her ex-husband   (...............................)

11 doesn't understand the difficulties her situation. She reads about   (...............................)

12 the problems of other single mothers in womens magazines, and she   (...............................)

13 talks to Alice, the wife a man who works at the same travel agent's.   (...............................)

14 Alice seems to understand Lauras difficulties. She tells her to   (...............................)

15 remember that 'todays problems are tomorrow's opportunities.'   (...............................)

3 Use the noun + noun construction to rewrite the phrases in italics.

Example: Mervyn Street is a fanatical *addict of rock and roll*. (rock and roll addict)

The walls in his bedroom (1) .... are covered in *posters of Mick Jagger*

(2) .... He's got 15 *albums of the Rolling Stones.* (3) ....

He's painted 'I know it's only rock and roll, but I like it' on *the door of his garage* (4) ....

.... *The registration number of his car* (5) .... is RS 1. He

always plays rock and roll on *the radio in his car* (6) .... He even uses his

computer to contact other *fans of the Rolling Stones* (7) .... on the Internet!

4 Justin is looking for Amy Nelson, one of his sister's friends, who has got one of his CDs. He is talking to his friend, Adam. Use the construction *a friend of mine/a student of hers/a colleague of my father's*, etc. to replace the phrases in italics and to give Justin's answers.

JUSTIN: I'm looking for Amy Nelson.

ADAM: Is she *your friend* (1) ....?

JUSTIN: No, she's (2) ....

ADAM: Why do you want to talk to her?

JUSTIN: Because she's got (3) ....

ADAM: Well, my brother knows Amy. She's still got *one of his videos* (4) ....
She never gave it back to him.

5 Make sentences about your family and friends, using possessive constructions.

Examples: *My uncle Ramon is my mother's brother. Manuela is one of my parents' friends. Luis is a friend of my father's.*

Check your sentences with a teacher.

71

Possessive adjectives and pronouns:
My, mine, etc.   Whose?   My own

Quick reference

- Possessive adjectives (*my, your, his*, etc.) have the same form before a singular or a plural noun. *I've lost **my passport/my keys**.*

- We use the possessive adjective *its* when the possessor is an animal or a thing. Don't confuse this with *it's* (= *it is* OR *it has*).
  *That horse can't run very fast. There's something wrong with **its** back legs.*
  *Someone has stolen my car, but I can't remember **its** registration number.*

- Possessive pronouns (*mine, yours, his, hers*, etc.) are used on their own, without a noun.
  *This steak is good. What's **yours** like?* (= your steak)
  *Her eyes are blue. **Mine** are brown.* (= my eyes)

- We use the question word *Whose* to ask who something belongs to.
  ***Whose** is this jacket?* OR ***Whose** jacket is this?*   ***Whose** shoes are these?*

We use a possessive adjective + *own*:

- when we say that something belongs completely to someone.
  *She's got **her own** car.   It's **your own** fault.*

- when we say we did something ourselves, without any help.
  *It's all **my own** work.   He made **his own** breakfast.*

- Note the expression *on my own, on her own, on their own*, etc.
  *He lives **on his own**.* (= by himself, alone)   *They wanted to be **on their own**.*

---

1 **Choose the correct alternative.**

'What were (1) *your/yours* .... exam results like?'

'Not bad. What were (2) *your/yours* .... like?'

'(3) *My/mine* .... were terrible. I've got to take two of them again. Do you know if Rachel

passed all (4) *her/hers* .... ?'

'Yes, I think so. And Richard and Jamie passed (5) *their/theirs* .... as well.'

'Oh well, think of me. I've got to spend (6) *my/mine* .... summer holidays revising while

you all spend (7) *your/yours* .... on the beach!'

---

2 **Complete these sentences with possessive adjectives (*my, your*, etc.) and possessive pronouns (*mine, yours*, etc.).**

At the end of the summer course there was a big party at the language school. We gave

(1) .... teachers presents. I gave Juan (2) .... telephone number and he gave

me (3) .... The Italian boy, Marco, gave Steffi (4) .... fax number and she gave

him (5) .... The two Swedish sisters, Ellen and Anna, gave everybody (6) ....

address and we all gave them (7) ....

3 Complete these sentences with *it's* or *its*.

(1) .... a very old car. (2) .... got a lot of things wrong with it. One of (3) .... wheels is missing and (4) .... windscreen is broken. (5) .... got something seriously wrong with (6) .... engine - (7) .... not working and the owner admits (8) .... not been working properly for a long time. (9) .... seats are worn out and (10) .... tyres need replacing. In fact the only reason I'm interested in buying it is (11) .... price - (12) .... only £150.

4 Some people are clearing up after a party. Rewrite these sentences, using the question word *Whose* and possessive pronouns (*mine, yours, hers*, etc.).

Example: Who do these tapes belong to? *Whose are these tapes?* OR *Whose tapes are these?*
    Do they belong to you, Lucy? *Are they yours, Lucy?*

'Who does this jacket belong to? (1) ....

Does it belong to you, Justin?' (2) ....

'No, it doesn't belong to me.' (3) ....

'Who do these CDs belong to? (4) ....

Do they belong to Jessica?'

'No, they don't belong to her. (5) ....

But I think Nick likes that band so they probably belong to him.' (6) ....

5 Complete this paragraph, using *my own, his own*, etc.

My cousins live on a very isolated farm in Wales. The house is very big so when I visit them I've got (1) .... room. It's miles from anywhere so they have to produce (2) .... electricity with a generator. The house has also got (3) .... well. They grow a lot of (4) .... food and my cousin Matthew has got (5) .... shotgun so he shoots a lot of rabbits and pigeons, which they also eat. My cousin Lauren makes all (6) .... clothes. In fact they could be completely self-sufficient if they could produce (7) .... diesel oil.

6 Compare yourself with different members of your family or friends. Use the following as much as possible: *my - mine, your - yours, his - his, her - hers, our - ours, their - theirs, my own, his own, on my own, on his own*, etc.

Examples: *My eyes are blue but my sister's aren't. Hers are brown.*

Check your answers with a teacher.

Quick reference

We use *it*:

- to identify someone or something. *Who's that? - **It**'s Zoe. What's that? - **It**'s a shark.*
- to give times and dates. ***It**'s ten o'clock. **It**'s May 3rd. **It**'s time to leave.*
- to describe the weather. ***It**'s raining. **It**'s very cold.*
- to give distances. ***It**'s five kilometres to the village. **It**'s a long way to walk.*
- to comment on a situation. ***It**'s a pity he can't come. **It** isn't easy to get a job.*
- We use *it* in the following constructions.

It + **be** +	**adjective** +	**infinitive with *to***	**It** + **be** +	**adjective** +	***that* clause**
It	*'s*	*difficult*	*to find a parking place.*	*It*	*was*	*clear*	*that she was ill.*

It + **be** +	**adjective** +	**-ing**
It	*was*	*nice*	*seeing you yesterday.*

- We use *it* in question tags after *everything, something, anything, nothing.*
  *Everything was different, wasn't **it**? Something's wrong, isn't **it**?*
- We use *they* to mean people in general or unknown people, people in authority.
  ***They** say women live longer than men.* (= people in general)
  ***They**'ve found the missing girl.* (= unknown people, perhaps the police)
  ***They**'re going to build a new car park in the town.* (= the local authorities)
  *What did **they** tell you at the bank?* (= the bank officials you spoke to)
- We use *they, them, their(s)* after *everybody, nobody, somebody, anybody,* etc.
  ***Everybody** said **they** wanted to leave. **Someone**'s left **their** umbrella in the car.*

We use *you* to mean people in general, including you and me.
  ***You** can see Vesuvius from the hotel. **You** can pay for most things by credit card.*

---

1 **How will Melanie Giles spend Saturday evening? Answer the questions, using *it*.**

Example: Why is Melanie happy? (weekend) *It´s the weekend.*

1 What's the weather like? (cold/rain) .... and ....
2 Why doesn't she want to stay at home? (boring) ....
3 What would be a nice thing to do? (nice/go/cinema) ....
4 How far away is the nearest cinema? (take/35 minutes/walk to/Odeon cinema)

   ....
5 But what about public transport? (obvious/the bus/quicker) ....
6 The film starts at 14.30. What time is it now? (five to two) ....
7 What would be the best thing to do? (safer/catch/the bus) ....

---

2 **Read the text about the Eurodisney theme park near Paris. Think of the word (either *you* or *they*) which best fits each space.**

(1) .... say that it's very expensive to spend a day at Eurodisney. But now (2) .... can get in much more cheaply than (3) .... could when it first opened. (4) .... now charge a lot less so that (5) .... can increase the number of visitors. Since it opened, (6) ....'ve

built a lot more rides. (7) .... say Space Mountain is the most exciting ride in the world. I tried it last year. (8) .... really go very fast, and it's completely dark, so (9) .... can't see where (10) .... 're going. At the end of the ride I noticed that everybody was very quiet and (11) .... all looked a bit pale. But I enjoyed it. It makes (12) .... frightened, but (13) .... feel fine when it's over! The only problem is that (14) .... can't take your own food into the park. (15) .... 've got to buy food at the cafés and restaurants. I suppose (16) .... make more money like that.

3 A is telling B about her holiday in Goa in southern India. B is very interested and surprised by what A is saying. Complete the dialogue by matching B's short replies.

A	B
1 Everybody speaks English.	a) Does it?
2 Everything's very cheap.	b) Couldn't they? That's a pity!
3 Nobody slept very well.	c) Did it?
4 Because everyone was bitten by mosquitoes.	d) Did they? Did you get it back?
5 But fortunately no-one was ill.	e) Didn't they? Why not?
6 Nothing is as beautiful as a Goan sunset.	f) Is it?
7 No. As the sun goes down, everything shines like gold.	g) Do they?
8 Something bad happened on our last day.	h) Weren't they? That's good.
9 Yes, someone stole our camera.	i) Were they?
10 No. We told the police, but no-one could help us.	j) Isn't it?

1 ....   2 ....   3 ....   4 ....   5 ....   6 ....   7 ....   8 ....   9 ....   10 ....

4 Look at these signs at London airport and write sentences using either *it* or *you*.

1 Flight BA137 Madrid - Now boarding

2 Gate 36 → 50m

3 ALL PASSPORTS TO BE SHOWN

4

1 .... time to board the flight to Madrid.
2 .... to Gate 36.
3 .... your passport.
4 .... smoke.

5 Think of a tourist attraction near where you live. Describe it. Give some general details. Use *you* and *they*.

Example: *You can visit the castle any day of the week. You can get in free on Sundays. They only charge half price if you're in a group of ten or more.*

Check your text with a teacher.

Quick reference

- We use *one* to replace a singular noun and *ones* to replace a plural noun.
  *I've got **a ticket**. Have you got **one**?*
  *I'm taking these **books**. Which **ones** are you taking?*

- *One/ones* often come after an adjective.
  *We stayed in a small hotel. They stayed in a **big one**.*
  *Which shoes do you want? - The **brown ones**.*

- When we compare or select things and don't want to repeat the noun, we use *one/ones* with *the, this, that, which*?
  *'I want a melon.' '**Which one** do you want?' '**The one** in the box.'*

- We don't normally use *ones* after *these* and *those*. (But if *these* and *those* are followed by an adjective we use *ones*.)   *Which jeans do you want? **These**? - No, **those blue ones**.*

- We never use *one* to replace an uncountable noun.
  *What sort of **music** do you like? - **Music** I can dance to.* (NOT One I can dance to.)

- We don't normally use *one/ones* after possessive adjectives. We use possessive pronouns instead.   *This is **my** bed and that's **yours**.* (NOT your one)

- We don't use *one/ones* after 'number' words like *some, any, a few, many, a lot, three, fifteen*, etc. But if there's an adjective after these words, we must use *one/ones*.
  *Did you take many books with you on holiday? - I took **some**, but not **a lot**. But I bought two good **ones** while I was there.* (NOT some ones, a lot of ones, two good)

1 Rewrite this dialogue using *one/ones* where possible to avoid repetition of the noun.

'We went to the cinema last night.'
'Which cinema did you go to?'
'The cinema on Woodstock Road. We saw a good film.'
'Which film did you see?'
'The new film with Brad Pitt in it. And then we went to a pizza restaurant.'
'Which restaurant did you go to?'
'The restaurant opposite the cinema. And then we went to two clubs.'
'Which clubs did you go to?'
'The clubs in Walton Street.'

....

....

....

....

....

....

....

....

2 A hotel guest is complaining to the receptionist. Complete what he says using *one/ones* where possible + any other necessary words.

Our room is too small. We want (1) .... bigger .... And it hasn't got a balcony. We particularly asked for (2) .... with a balcony. And the beds are very uncomfortable. We'd like more comfortable (3) .... And we'd also like a shower that works. (4) .... we've got doesn't work. And we'd prefer (5) .... with hot water! And some of the towels in the bathroom are dirty. We must have (6) .... And finally, the room we're in hasn't got a sea view. We must have (7) ....

3 Look at the three cars. Answer the questions about them using *one/ones* and each of these words/phrases once:

made in Europe   white   in the middle   on the right   black

1 Which car is British? ....
2 Which one is German? ....
3 Which one is American? ....
4 Which ones are smaller? ....
5 Which one is a Rolls Royce? ....

4 Read the dialogue and decide which answer, A, B, or C best fits each space.

'I'm looking for some new sports shoes.'

'White (1) .... or black (2) .... ?'

'White.'

'Do you like these (3) .... ?'

'No, not really. I've got some (4) .... like that already. I prefer those (5) .... '

'Which (6) .... ?'

'The (7) .... in the window which cost £69.99.'

'Which window?'

'The (8) .... on the right.'

'Ah yes, those American (9) .... are new. You won't see many (10) .... like those.'

1 A–	B one	C ones		2 A–	B one	C ones		3 A–	B one	C ones
4 A–	B one	C ones		5 A–	B one	C ones		6 A–	B one	C ones
7 A–	B one	C ones		8 A–	B one	C ones		9 A–	B one	C ones
10 A–	B one	C ones								

5 Write a dialogue between two people at a football match in which you use *one/ones* as much as possible. Check your dialogue with a teacher.

Example: *Which are our seats? - The ones over there.*

Quick reference

- These adjectives aren't usually used with a noun: *afraid, alive, alone, apart, ashamed, asleep, awake, aware, glad, ill, pleased, ready, sure, unable, upset, well.*
    *She's **upset**.* (NOT an upset person)   *He's **alone**.* (NOT an alone man)

- Some adjectives aren't normally used alone after a verb. Some common ones are: *countless, eventual, existing, indoor, main, maximum, neighbouring, occasional, only, outdoor, principal.*
    *He lives in **a neighbouring town**.* (NOT The town is neighbouring.)

- Some adjectives can be used as nouns. Here are some common ones: *the disabled, the elderly, the English,* etc. *the handicapped, the homeless, the injured, the unemployed.*

    ***The unemployed** find life difficult.* (= unemployed people in general)

- 'Opinion' adjectives (*lovely, interesting, pleasant*, etc.) come before 'fact' adjectives.
    *Jenny's a **nice young** woman.* (Jenny's nice = an opinion; Jenny's young = a fact)

- 'Fact' adjectives usually go in this order.

	size	shape	age	colour	origin		material/type	
A	big	round					wooden	table.
An			old	red	American			car.

- Two colour adjectives, and two adjectives used alone after a verb, are usually joined by *and*.
    *She's wearing a **blue and green** sweater.   Claire's always **happy and friendly**.*

- With three adjectives used alone after a verb we usually put a comma after the first adjective, and *and* between the last two.   *Her parents are **kind, warm and generous**.*

- We put the adjectives *deep, high, long, old, tall, thick, wide* after measurement nouns.
    *I'm nearly two metres **tall**.   The river's three metres **deep**.   The tunnel's two kilometres **long**.*

1 Gerry Walsh is a nervous man and there are many things that worry him. Read the text and decide which sentence (A or B) is the correct one.

1   (A) The things he dislikes are countless. (B) There are countless things he dislikes. ....

2   As a child he was very afraid of people. (A) Children who are afraid become unhappy adults.
    (B) Afraid children become unhappy adults. ....

3   Gerry often feels upset himself, and (A) he feels uncomfortable with people who are upset.
    (B) he feels uncomfortable with upset people. ....

4   (A) He doesn't like visiting ill people in hospital. (B) He doesn't like visiting people who are ill in hospital. ....

5   (A) He doesn't like the idea of being alone when he's an old man. (B) He doesn't like the idea of being an alone old man. ....

6   (A) His fear of death is main. (B) His main fear is the fear of death. ....

2 Look at the sentences and, if the adjectives are in the right order, put a tick (✓). If not, rewrite the adjectives in the correct order. Sometimes you will need to add *and*.

1   The children's author Joel Pitts is *a young good-looking man*. ....

2   He's got *dark curly long hair*. ....

3　He lives in *an old 17th century farmhouse*. ....

4　It's three miles outside *an old beautiful Devon village*. ....

5　Joel's got *a well-paid interesting job*. ....

6　He's *hardworking, successful*. ....

7　His stories are *short, amusing and memorable*. ....

8　He works in *a big square stone barn* next to the farmhouse. ....

9　He drives *an American old enormous car*. ....

3 Look at the information in this holiday brochure and complete the sentences about the hotel. Put the adjectives in the correct order. Sometimes you will need to add *and*.

La Rocca Hotel: *Sicilian * charming * family*　　Walk from the town: *10-minute * short*

Beach: *sheltered * lovely * sandy*　　Atmosphere: *warm * friendly*

Cuisine: *Sicilian * traditional * first-class*　　Tennis court: *floodlit * free of charge*

Swimming pool: *palm-fringed * big * fresh-water*　　Bedrooms: *air-conditioned * spacious*

1　La Rocca is .... hotel.

2　It's a .... walk from the town.

3　The hotel stands above its own .... beach.

4　The atmosphere is ....

5　The restaurant offers .... cuisine.

6　The tennis court is ....

7　There's a .... swimming pool.

8　There are 14 .... bedrooms.

4 Look at this plan for a new swimming pool, and write the five measurements.

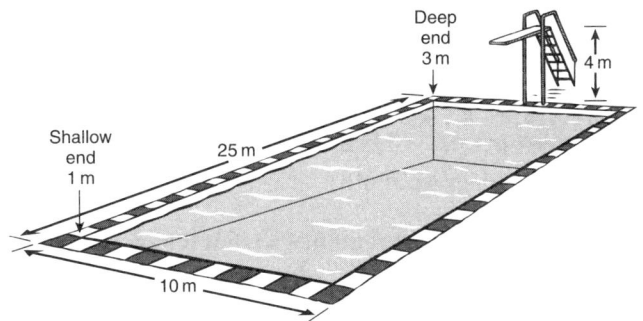

Deep
end
3 m

4 m

Shallow
end
1 m

25 m

10 m

1　*The pool will be 25 metres long.*

2　And it'll be ....

3　The water at the deep end ....

4　The water at the shallow end ....

5　The diving board ....

5 Describe your house or flat. Use more than one adjective for each sentence. Put the adjectives in the correct order.

Examples:　*I've got a small modern well-equipped kitchen. The bathroom is painted green and white.*
　　　　　　There are two big comfortable chairs in the living-room.

Check your answers with a teacher.

75

Comparatives and superlatives (1):
He's taller than me. She's the tallest

Quick reference

Comparative and superlative forms

- One-syllable adjectives
  short/shorter/(the) shortest   big/bigger/(the) biggest   dry/drier/(the) driest
- Most two-syllable adjectives ending in *-y, -le, -er, -ow*
  dirty/dirtier/(the) dirtiest   simple/simpler/(the) simplest   clever/cleverer/(the) cleverest
- Other two-syllable adjectives normally form their comparative and superlative like this.
  honest/more honest/(the) most honest
- Three syllables or more: *intelligent/more intelligent/(the) most intelligent*
- A few adjectives have irregular comparative and superlative forms.
  good/better/(the) best   bad/worse/(the) worst
  far/farther/the farthest   OR   *far/further/the furthest*
- Comparative and superlative of most adverbs: *carefully/more carefully/(the) most carefully*
- Note these irregular adverbs: *well/better/(the) best   badly/worse/(the) worst.*
- We form the comparative and superlative of the following irregular adverbs with *-er* and *-est*:
  fast, soon, hard, high, near, long, late, early. fast/faster/(the) fastest   late/ later/(the) latest

---

1 **Look at these facts and figures about two Australian cities.**

		Sydney	**Melbourne**
1	Population:	3.7 million	3.2 million
2	Founded:	1788	1835
3	Average temperature January:	25.7°	26.1°
4	Average annual rainfall:	1,216 mm	656 mm
5	Average price of a 3-bedroom house:	$122,000	$115,000
6	Latitude (degrees south):	34°	38°

Complete the second sentence so that it has a similar meaning to the first, using the word given.

Example: Melbourne's population isn't as big as Sydney's. (larger)
      Sydney's population is larger than Melbourne's.

1 Melbourne's population isn't as big as Sydney's. (smaller)
Melbourne's ....

2 Melbourne isn't as old as Sydney. (older) Sydney ....

3 In January Sydney isn't as hot as Melbourne. (hotter)
Melbourne .... in January.

4 Sydney's much wetter than Melbourne. (drier) Melbourne's ....

5 Houses in Melbourne aren't as expensive as in Sydney. (expensive)
Houses in Sydney ....

6 Sydney's further north than Melbourne. (further)
Melbourne ....

2 Read the information and use superlatives to make sentences about the Tucker family.

	Born	Height	Weight
Mark Tucker	1952	1m. 76	78 kilos
Marion Tucker	1951	1m. 72	64 kilos
Luke Tucker	1980	1m. 77	72 kilos
Katherine Tucker	1983	1m. 69	59 kilos

Example: *Marion is the oldest.*

1 (young) ....
2 (tall) ....
3 (short) ....

4 (heavy) ....
5 (light) ....

3 Write ten sentences about the USA based on this table. Use the superlative form of these adjectives: *tall, high, new, long, densely populated, big, popular, dry.*

densa espeso, compacto

1	The Mississippi	....	river.
2	Mount McKinley, Alaska	....	mountain.
3	Hawaii	....	state.
4	The Sears Tower, Chicago	....	building.
5	New York is	....	city
6	Baseball	....	sport.
7	Death Valley, California	....	place.
8	Washington, D.C.	....	state.

4 In a newspaper article people were asked about the things that really annoyed them. Complete their answers with the comparative or superlative form of the adjective/adverb in brackets.

incomodarse, enfadarse

1 For me (annoying) .... thing is sitting next to someone with a personal stereo on a train. And then, and this is even (annoying) ...., they move their head in time with the music.

2 For me (bad) .... thing is walking along the street with a boy who's constantly looking at his reflection in shop windows because he thinks he's (good-looking) .... person in the world.

3 (Irritating) .... thing is when I'm trying to sleep and there's a mosquito in the room which is getting (near) .... and (near) .... but I can never find it.

4 There's nothing (irritating) .... than trying to tie a shoe lace when one end is much (short) .... than the other.

5 Nothing makes me (angry) .... than waiting on the phone, listening to recorded music and trying to decide whether to wait (long) .... or put the phone down.

5 Write sentences in which you compare yourself as you are now with how you were five years ago. Check your answers with a teacher.

Example: *Five years ago I was thinner than I am now, and I had shorter hair.*

Quick reference

- We use *(not) as* + adjective + *as* to say that two things are or aren't the same.
  *You're **as tall as** me.   This car **isn't as powerful as** that Mercedes.*
  We can use *twice* (= two times), *three times*, etc. to state the difference more precisely.
  *The living room is **three times as big as** (OR **three times bigger than**) the kitchen.*

- We use *(not) the same … as …* to say that two things are or aren't the same.
  *She's got **the same hairstyle as** her mother.   His job **isn't the same as** mine.*

- To say that something is increasing, we can use a 'double' comparative.
  ***More and more** people are giving up smoking.   The town is getting **bigger and bigger**.*

- *the* + comparative + *the* + a different comparative, or *the more … the more …*
  ***The harder** she works, **the happier** she is.   **The more** he earns, **the more** he spends.*

- Note these constructions:

the + comparative + *the better.   I want a cheap holiday - **the cheaper the better**!*

	more/the most	+	**plural or uncountable noun**
She's got	*more*		*friends than me.*
This car uses	*the most*		*petrol. It's the least economical.*

Note that *most* can also mean *nearly all*.   ***Most** British people drink tea.*

	less/the least	+	**adjective or uncountable noun**
English is	*less*		*difficult to learn than Chinese.*
What's	*the least*		*expensive way to get to America?*
You'll spend	*less*		*money if you hitchhike to London.*

	fewer/the fewest	+	**plural noun**
There are	*fewer*		*people on the beach than there were yesterday.*
She made	*the fewest*		*mistakes in the exam. She got the best result.*

- After superlatives we often use phrases with *in* or *of*. We use *in* with the names of places and with words like *class, school, team, family, world,* etc.
  ***The highest** building **in** Paris.   **The best** player **in** the world.   **The biggest** mistake **of** all.*

---

1 **Look at the details of these four cars.**

Car A: 2,000 cc
Equipment: Standard
Top speed: 175 k.p.h.
Average fuel consumption: 8 l./100k.

Car B: 1,500 cc
Equipment: Luxury
Top speed: 175 k.p.h.
Average fuel consumption: 6 l./100k

Car C: 3,000 cc
Equipment: Luxury
Top speed: 225 k.p.h.
Average fuel consumption: 10.4 l./100k

Car D: 1,000 cc
Equipment: Standard
Top speed: 145 k.p.h.
Average fuel consumption: 5.2 l./100k

Which of these statements about the cars are true and which are false? Write *True* or *False*.

1 Car A isn't as powerful as Car B. ....

2 Car C is twice as powerful as Car B. ....

3 Car D is the least powerful car. ....

4 Car D is three times as powerful as Car C. ....

5 Car B has the same top speed as Car A. ....

6 Car A isn't as fast as Car B. ....

7 The equipment in Car D is the same as the equipment in Car A. ....

8 Car D is as well-equipped as Car C ....

9 Car A isn't as well-equipped as Car C. ....

10 Car D is less well-equipped than Car B. ....

11 Car D is the most economical. ....

12 Car C is twice as economical as Car D. ....

2 Complete the text, using 'double' comparatives (e.g. *better and better, more and more*) or two comparatives (e.g. *The bigger they are, the more expensive they'll be.*)

Global warming is increasing. We're putting (1 more/more) .... carbon dioxide into the atmosphere. (2 More/more) .... ice is melting in the Arctic and the Antarctic. Fortunately (3 more/more) .... people are becoming aware of the problem. But scientists are getting (4 worried) .... They want governments to do more. The (5 more/bad) .... time we <u>waste</u> now, the .... it will be for us later. Also, the holes in the Earth's ozone layer are getting (6 big) .... Cases of skin cancer are getting (7 common) .... The (8 long/probable) .... people lie on the beach in the sun, the .... it is that they'll get skin cancer. The (9 soon/good) .... we all realise the danger, the ....

3 A group of British people were asked what their principal form of entertainment was.

Cinema	Theatre	Television	Reading	Sport	Pubs	Clubs/discos
6%	2%	51%	3%	10%	14%	14%

Read the sentences and decide which answer, A, B or C best fits each space.

1 Television was (....) form of entertainment.
   A most common B least common C the most common

2 Going to the theatre was (....). A the most popular B the least popular C popular

3 The theatre attracted (....) people. A the least B the most C the fewest

4 (....) number of people chose going to pubs and visiting clubs and discos.
   A The same C The fewest C The most

5 (....) people did sport than read books. A Fewer B More C Less

6 Doing a sport was (....) than going to pubs. A less popular B more popular C the least popular

7 (....) people went to the theatre than to the cinema. A Less B More C Fewer

4 Match the two parts of these general knowledge facts.

1 Mount Everest is the highest mountain   a) we've known in the last 3,000 years.

2 Mont Blanc is the highest mountain   b) in the world.

3 The trip to the Moon was the longest flight   c) of all the European countries.

4 The cheetah is the fastest   d) of all the nations in the world.

5 China has the biggest population   e) in France.

6 Germany has the largest population   f) ever made in a man-made vehicle.

7 The Krakatoa volcanic eruption was the biggest   g) of all the world's land animals.

1 ....   2 ....   3 ....   4 ....   5 ....   6 ....   7 ....   8 ....

77

Adjectives ending in *-ed* and *-ing*: *I'm bored. My life is so boring*

Quick reference

- Adjectives ending in *-ing* describe what something, or someone, is like.
  This book's interesting. The teacher was boring.
- Adjectives ending in *-ed* describe how we feel.
  I was frightened and excited at the same time.
- The most common adjectives with *-ing* and *-ed* endings are:

amazed/amazing	amused/amusing	annoyed/annoying
bored/boring	confused/confusing	depressed/depressing
disappointed/disappointing	disgusted/disgusting	embarrassed/embarrassing
excited/exciting	fascinated/fascinating	frightened/frightening
horrified/horrifying	interested/interesting	shocked/shocking
surprised/surprising	tired/tiring	worried/worrying

---

1 Read the text below. Use the word(s) given in capitals at the end of each line to form a word that fits in the space in the same line.

This is a rather (1) .... story about a man called Woodrow   HORROR

W. Creekmore of Chickasha, Oklahoma. Mr Creekmore had a (2) ....   BORE

office job and he was never (3) .... at work.   SATISFY

He'd been feeling very (4) .... for a long time. His wife found   DEPRESS

his depression very (5) .... She had asked him several times to   WORRY

go to the doctor's, but each time his answer had been (6) ....   DISAPPOINT

and he got (7) .... 'Listen, honey. I'm all right. I wish you'd stop   ANNOY

worrying.' Mr Creekmore never slept very well, and after a few weeks

he was (8) ....   EXHAUST

    One morning in March 1995, on the way to work, he was so (9) ....   TIRE

he fell asleep at the wheel of his car and drove into a telegraph pole.

The police arrived and were (10) .... to find Mr Creekmore   SURPRISE

standing by the wreck of his car. It wasn't (11) ....   SURPRISE

that he was (12) .... and slightly (13) .... but   SHOCK/CONFUSE

fortunately he wasn't seriously hurt. They examined the badly (14) ....   DAMAGE

car and concluded that it was (15) .... that Mr Creekmore had got out   AMAZE

of it alive. They weren't particularly (16) .... in how the   INTEREST

accident happened but they asked him a few routine questions.

        As they were doing this, something (17) .... happened.   SHOCK

The (18) .... telegraph pole fell and hit Mr Creekmore on the head.   DAMAGE

The police were (19) .... to find it had killed him.   HORROR

2 Choose adjectives from the box to complete this description of a photographic model's job. Use each adjective once.

embarrassed	amazed	surprised	tired	exciting	excited
interesting	interested	disgusting	annoying	boring	

'People think it must be very (1) .... being a model, but it's sometimes quite

(2) .... For example, I go to bed before 10.00 most nights because I mustn't look

(3) .... the next day. But I must admit I still get (4) .... when I wear clothes

which feel and look just right on me and I go to some (5) .... places. Last week I went to

Marrakech in Morocco. The problem was I had to eat sheeps' eyes - that was really(6) ....

    I used to be a bit (7) .... when I told people I was a model. They all thought I must be

stupid and that was really (8) .... People are quite (9) .... when they find out

that I'm intelligent. A journalist I spoke to recently was (10) .... when I told him I was

(11) .... in Baroque music and that I had studied computer technology at university. He

just couldn't believe it!'

3 Rick Grant recently went on holiday. Look at the pictures and complete the sentences, using adjectives from the Quick reference box.

1 The flight was long and ....

2 The food on the plane was ....

3 Rick felt very .... The weather was awful.

4 He was .... when he saw his hotel room.

5 He was very .... and went to speak to the hotel proprietor.

4 Write a short description of an event in your life, using as many as possible of the adjectives ending in -ing and -ed in the Quick reference box.

Example: *I had a **frightening** experience when I was 15. I had to spend the night alone in a 16th century castle. I've never been so **frightened**, etc.*

Check your answers with a teacher.

Quick reference

- We use an adverb of manner to describe 'how' someone does something.
  *He walked **slowly**. She sings **beautifully**. They waited **patiently**.*

- We use an adverb of degree to talk about 'to what degree' or 'how much'.
  Verb + adverb of degree + adjective   Verb +   adverb of degree + adverb of manner
  I'm   extremely   interested.   He spoke   very   angrily.

- The sentence adverbs *unfortunately, fortunately, actually, clearly, perhaps* modify a whole clause.
  ***Unfortunately** I can't come. **Perhaps** he's gone on holiday.*

- Note the difference between *hard/hardly, late/lately, high/highly, free/freely*.
  *She worked **hard**. (= with a lot of effort) She **hardly** did any work. (= almost no work)*
  *I arrived **late**. (= the opposite of early) I haven't seen him **lately**. (= recently)*
  *He hit the ball **high** into the sky. (= a long way up) It's **highly** dangerous. (= very)*
  *I got into the park **free**. (= I didn't pay) She spoke **freely** about it. (= without restriction)*

- Note the meaning of *nearly*: *I **nearly** fell into the river. (= I didn't fall, but I almost fell.)*

- The adjectives *early, fast, first, long, low, right, straight, wrong* are also adverbs.
  *They arrived **right** in the middle of dinner. (= exactly) I went **straight** home. (= directly)*
  *I didn't stay **long** at the party. She drives **fast**.*

- Adverbs of manner normally go in mid-position, or in end position for emphasis.
  *They **quickly** changed their clothes. He spoke to me **angrily**.*
  Sentence adverbs usually go in front position, but *certainly, definitely, probably* usually go in mid-position.
  ***Fortunately** it stopped raining.*
  *I'll **probably** see you tomorrow. I'll **certainly** phone you.*
  In negative sentences, we put *certainly, definitely, probably, simply* before the auxiliary.
  *He **probably** won't arrive till 7. I **definitely** can't see you tomorrow.*
  We usually put *well* and *badly* in end position. *Did you sleep **well**?*

---

1 **Kate and Tess have just met at a French class. Read the dialogue, and use the word given in capitals at the end of each line to form a word that fits in the space in the same line.**

(1) TESS: Do you come to these classes ....?   REGULAR

(2) KATE: Yes, every week. I've studied the grammar ....,   CAREFUL

(3)   and I can write French reasonably ...., but I still   GOOD

(4)   speak it very ....   BAD

(5) TESS: I can ask questions in French quite ....,   EASY

(6)   but .... I'm not very good at understanding the reply!   FORTUNATE

(7) KATE: I'm .... going to go to France to learn to speak French   DEFINITE

(8) ....   PROPER

(9) TESS: I'll .... find myself a French boyfriend.   PROBABLE

(10)   That's the best way to learn ....   QUICK

2 Bill Yates is 65. He has just retired from the job he had all his life. Use each of the words in the box to complete what Bill says.

straight late (x2) lately hard hardly highly free freely early right first

1 I've worked .... all my life.

2 I've .... missed a day's work in 35 years.

3 I worked .... as a salesman.

4 I knew it was the right job for me .... from the beginning.

5 I was always .... motivated.

6 The sales manager always let me speak .... about any problems I had.

7 When I left, the company gave me a car. I got it .... It didn't cost me anything.

8 I used to get up .... every day, usually at about 6.30.

9 And I never arrived .... at work.

10 But I haven't been getting up early ....

11 And I don't go to bed .... now either.

12 I usually go to bed .... after the 10 o'clock news.

3 Put the adverbs in brackets into the sentences. Mark (*) their correct position. Sometimes there is more than one possible position.

1 Sarah Wright's been getting a lot of junk mail. (lately)

2 Every day she gets letters trying to sell her double-glazed windows or medical insurance. (nearly)

3 They've found her address in the telephone book. (probably)

4 Or her name and address is on a national computer database. (perhaps)

5 Sarah thinks it's a ridiculous waste of paper. (absolutely)

6 It makes her furious. (actually, really)

7 She throws all the letters into the bin. (angrily, straight)

8 She's asked the companies to stop writing to her. (politely)

9 But she won't be able to stop them. (probably)

10 It's happening more and more in Britain. (unfortunately)

11 Sarah doesn't want double glazed windows or medical insurance. (definitely)

12 She can't afford to pay for them. (simply)

4 Think of five things you do and the reaction you get from other people. Write sentences, using various adverbs.

Examples: *In the morning I often stay **too long** in the bathroom and this makes my sister **extremely** annoyed. When I come in **late** at night, I don't always come in **quietly** and my mother reacts **very angrily** when I wake her up.*

Check your sentences with a teacher.

Quick reference

- We use adverbs of frequency to say 'how often' something happens. The most common are: *always, often, frequently, usually, normally, generally, sometimes, occasionally, rarely, seldom, hardly ever, never.*
They normally come in mid-position. *She **never** smiles. He doesn't **often** come.*
*I've **rarely** smoked. Do you **normally** eat fish? - Yes, I **usually** do.*
But they come after the verb *be*. *He's **often** late. She **was always** hungry.*

- *Sometimes, often, usually, generally, normally* can go in front or end position for emphasis.
*It **sometimes** snows.* OR ***Sometimes** it snows.* OR *It snows **sometimes**.*

- Adverb phrases like *every day, every year, every evening* usually come in end position (or in front position for emphasis).
*He plays golf **every evening**.* OR ***Every evening** he plays golf.*

- Adverbs of time answer the question *When?* The most common are: *again, now, then, recently, once, nowadays, suddenly, immediately, finally, afterwards, today, tomorrow, yesterday, late, early.*
They usually go in end position, or in front position for emphasis (but NOT *early* and *late*).
*They stopped **suddenly**.* OR ***Suddenly** they stopped.*
Adverbs of definite time like *yesterday, today, tomorrow, next week,* etc. usually go in end position (or front position for emphasis) but never in mid-position.
*I went to London **today**.* OR ***Today** I went to London.* (NOT *I today went to London.*)

- Adverbs of place answer the question *Where?* They include words like *here, there, opposite, upstairs,* etc. and adverb phrases like *in Europe, at work,* etc. They normally go in end position.
*Do you work **here**? I saw him **there**. They live **opposite**.*

- If there are several adverbs in one sentence, the normal word order is:

	degree	+	manner	+	place	+	time
It rained	*very*		*heavily*		*here*		*yesterday.*

1 A Californian journalist living in London described the difference between the weather in London and Los Angeles. Mark (*) the best position for the adverbs in brackets.

1 In Los Angeles it's summer. *(always)* London has a summer. *(occasionally)*

2 In Los Angeles it rains in summer. *(hardly ever)* In London it stops raining. *(rarely)*

3 In Los Angeles the temperature falls below 25°. *(seldom)* In Britain it reaches 25°. *(occasionally)*

2 Mike has just met Jenny at a jazz club. Mark (*) the best position for the adverbs.

JENNY: How often do you come? *(here)*

MIKE: I come. *(usually/every Friday)*

JENNY: This is my first visit. I don't listen to jazz *(usually)*, but I've wanted to come to this club *(always)*. Have you liked jazz? *(always)*

MIKE: Yes, I've got my own jazz band. We play. *(often/here)* In fact, we played. *(here/yesterday)*

JENNY: Did you? What instrument do you play?

MIKE: I play the tenor sax. *(normally)* And I play the keyboard too. *(sometimes)*

3 Read the text and decide which answer, A, B, or C best fits each space.

I'm a London taxi driver. (1) .... as a taxi driver. I enjoy my job because I enjoy meeting people.

(2) .... to my passengers. But I like reading too and when I'm waiting for passengers (3) .... a book.

How many hours (4) .... ? About eight I suppose, but (5) .... I don't like working at night so (6) .... In

fact I (7) .... Ever since I started this job (8) .... I know every street in London because (9) ....

1 A Always I have worked   B I've always worked   C I always have worked

2 A I usually talk   B I talk usually   C Usually I talk

3 A I read usually   B usually I read   C I usually read

4 A normally do I work?   B do I normally work?   C do normally I work?

5 A I worked 11 hours yesterday.   B I worked yesterday   C I yesterday worked 11 hours.
                                        11 hours.

6 A I early start work.   B early I start work.   C I start work early.

7 A start work at 7.30 every day.   B every day start work   C start every day work at 7.30.
                                        at 7.30.

8 A Always I've work during the day.   B I've always worked   C I work during the day always.
      Never I work at night.   during the day. I never   I work at night never.
                                           work at night.

9 A I've always lived here.   B I've here always lived.   C here I've always lived.

4 a) Write sentences about yourself, using these adverbs of frequency in the right position: *always, usually, often, sometimes, never.*

Examples: *I'm usually good-tempered. I've never smoked.*

b) Put these adverbs of time and place in sentences: *recently, today, yesterday, in Europe, in this country, here.*

Check your sentences with a teacher.

Quick reference

- *pretty* = more than moderately   *quite* = moderately   *fairly* = a little, a bit
  *The exam was **pretty** hard.*   *The exam was **quite** hard.*   *The exam was **fairly** hard.*

- *Quite* can also mean *completely* or *absolutely* when we use it with certain adjectives. The most common are: *alone, amazing, brilliant, certain, different, extraordinary, right, sure, true, unnecessary, useless, wrong.* *I'm **quite** sure I'm right.* *I won £500,000 - it's **quite** amazing!*

- *Rather* sometimes gives a negative quality to the following adjective.
  *Those shoes are **rather** cheap.* (= Too cheap. The quality may not be good.)
  Compare: *Those shoes are **quite** cheap.* (= That's good. I might buy them.)
  We can also use *rather* to give an adjective a positive quality if the adjective is surprising.
  *I thought the exam was **rather** easy.* (= The exam was easy. It was a pleasant surprise.)
  We can use *rather* (NOT *quite, pretty* or *fairly*) before a comparative.
  *It was **rather more expensive** than I expected.*

- We can use *quite, pretty, fairly* and *rather* before an adjective + noun.
  *There's **quite a big spider** in the bath.* *He's got **rather a loud** voice, hasn't he?*
  *It's **a pretty cold day**.* *She's **a fairly lazy person**.* *I've got **a rather serious problem**.*
  (Note that we can't say: It's a quite big spider./It's pretty a cold day./She's fairly a lazy person.)

- We can use *quite* on its own with verbs like: *agree, enjoy, finish, forget, like, understand.* And *rather* with these verbs: *enjoy, hope, like, think.*
  *I **quite** enjoyed my holiday.* (= moderately) *I haven't **quite** finished.* (= completely)
  *I **rather** like this T-shirt.* (= more than moderately)

- We use *such* for emphasis before a noun or an adjective + noun.
  *He made **such a mess**. I've had **such a terrible day**. It's **such awful weather**.*

- We use *so* before an adjective without a following noun, or before an adverb.
  *I'm **so** tired. She drives **so** dangerously.*

- *Such* and *so* can be followed by a clause when we talk about a result.
  *It's **such** a big steak (that) **I can't eat it all**. It was **so** dark (that) **I turned the light on**.*

---

1 **Toby is talking about the subjects he does at school. Complete what he says, using the correct word.**

1 (fairly/quite) I .... like Maths. In fact I find it .... easy.

2 (rather/quite) I .... enjoy History, but my friends think it's .... boring.

3 (rather/quite) I'm .... good at French, but my teacher says I'm .... lazy.

4 (rather/quite) We've got a .... nice Physics teacher, so I .... like Physics.

5 (quite/rather) I .... hope I have the same teacher next year. It's .... possible.

6 (fairly/quite) I'm .... good at Geography. I got .... a good result in the exam.

7 (rather/pretty) I think I'm .... good at Chemistry, but I got .... a bad result in the summer exams.

8 (pretty/rather/quite) I didn't do well in last year's English exam, but I've improved .... a lot, so I'm .... sure I'll do .... better this year.

9 (quite/pretty) I do .... a lot of sport at school, so, physically, I'm .... fit.

10 (fairly/quite) I'm .... looking forward to leaving school next year. I'm .... sure I can find a job.

2 A woman is reporting a robbery she saw in the High Street this morning. She is telling the police about it. Sentences in the second column follow sentences in the first. Match them.

1 It was about 7.45, I think.

2 There weren't many people around.

3 I couldn't see him very well.

4 He was about 18 or 19, I think.

5 I'm not sure that he was wearing trainers.

6 He was definitely wearing jeans.

7 One minute he was standing in front of me, the next minute he'd just disappeared.

a) He looked fairly young.

b) I'm quite sure of that.

c) It was quite early.

d) But I'm pretty certain.

e) It was still pretty dark.

f) It was quite extraordinary.

g) It was fairly quiet.

1 ....   2 ....   3 ....   4 ....   5 ....   6 ....   7 ....

3 Emily Trent has just come back from her first holiday on Saint Lucia, a Caribbean island. Complete the second sentence so that it has a similar meaning to the first. Use the word(s) given in brackets.

Example: The holiday I had was so good. (such) *I had such a good holiday.*

1 Saint Lucia is so fabulous. (such) Saint Lucia .... island.

2 The climate it's got is so wonderful. (such) It's got .... climate.

3 The Saint Lucians are so friendly. (such) The Saint Lucians .... people.

4 It was such good food. (so) The food ....

5 They had such cheap fruit. (so) The fruit there ....

6 There were so many things to do. (such/a lot) There was .... to do.

7 I went snorkelling on a coral reef. The experience was so amazing. (such) It was ....
   .... experience.

8 The time I had was so good I didn't want to come home. (such) I had ....
   I didn't want to come home.

9 The only problem is, the flight is so long. (such) It's .... flight.

10 It was such an uncomfortable flight that I couldn't sleep. (so) The flight ....
   I couldn't sleep.

11 And it was such an expensive flight I won't be able to afford to go next year. (so) And the flight
   was .... I won't be able to afford to go next year.

4 a) Write ten sentences describing yourself. Use *quite, rather, fairly/pretty*.

Examples: *I'm quite tall. I've got quite a nice figure. I'm fairly good-looking. But I'm rather*
overweight and I've got rather a big nose.

b) Think of six things you do not do or did not do and give the reason. Use *such* and *so*.

Examples: *I don't eat out much, because restaurants are so expensive. I don't buy many CDs*
because they cost such a lot. I didn't go out last night because I had such a lot of work
to do. It was such terrible weather last weekend (that) I didn't go anywhere.

Check your sentences with a teacher.

81

Adverbs of degree: *a lot, a bit, much*, etc.
More, most, better, best, etc.

Quick reference

- We can use *a lot, a little, a bit, much, very much, so much, as much* on their own as adverbs. They normally come after the main verb and its object.
  *She loves you **a lot**.   I don't like him **very much**.*

- We can use *very much* in positive or negative sentences, but *much* only in negative sentences.
  *Thank you **very much**.   She **didn't** like beer **very much**.*
  *He **didn't** read **much**.   I like him **very much**.* (NOT I like him much.)

- We often use *a lot, a bit, a little, much, very much, so much* before a comparative adjective or adverb.
  *He's **a lot taller** now.   Can we walk **a bit more slowly**?*
  A bit and *a little* (but NOT *a lot, much, very much, so much*) can also be used with an adjective not in the comparative form.
  *These jeans are **a bit big**.   She's **a little jealous**.*

- The comparative forms *more, less, better, worse* and the superlative forms *most, least, best, worst* can be used on their own as adverbs of degree. We usually put them after the main verb and its object.
  *Nowadays I read **more**.   I like this colour **the most**.*

- We can use *a lot, a bit, much, very much, so much* before *more, less, better, worse*.
  *Flying costs **a lot more**.   It's **a bit less** cold today.   I'm feeling **much better**.*
  Most, least, best, worst can also be used with adjectives formed from the past participles of verbs.
  *Her age was her **best kept** secret.   He's their **worst paid** employee.*

---

1 **Read the text and decide which answer, A, B, or C best fits each space.**

Edith Sellick is 87. She lives in an old people's home. Nowadays (1) .... Instead she (2) .... There's one thing she still very much enjoys. She (3) .... The old people's home is warm and comfortable but she (4) .... Nowadays she walks and talks (5) .... In fact, when she lived on her own, (6) .... And her life (7) ....

1 A she doesn't read much.   B she doesn't much read.   C she much doesn't read.
2 A a bit watches television.   B watches television a bit.   C watches a bit television.
3 A a lot looks at old photos.   B looks at old photos a lot.   C looks at a lot old photos.
4 A doesn't like very much the food.   B very much doesn't like the food.   C doesn't like the food very much.
5 A slowly much more.   B more slowly much.   C much more slowly.
6 A she was a lot happier.   B she a lot happier was.   C she was happier a lot.
7 A was more interesting very much.   B was very much more interesting.   C very much was more interesting.

2 An Englishwoman has moved to a Greek island. Add the words in brackets to the sentences. Mark (*) their position.

1 (so much) I like living here.

2 (more) I like the summer, but I like the winter.

3 (best) I think I like February.

4 (least) And I like August.

5 (much) In summer I don't talk to my friends. They're all very busy.

6 (a lot/very much) Life in the winter is slower and quieter.

7 (a bit) I must admit I get bored sometimes.

8 (a little) I paint.

9 (a bit) And I also write.

10 (a lot) I used to write.

11 (much less) But nowadays I write.

3 Richard is in his first year at London university. Complete what he says using all the following adverbs: *very much, more* (x2), *most, less, least, better, best, worse.*

I admit, I don't work (1) .... In fact I work (2) .... than I did at school. I certainly go out (3) .... than I used to. I did badly in last year's exams and I'll probably do even (4) .... this year.

I share a house with six other students. I care (5) .... about the house than they do. They don't do any housework. One of the students is from Manchester. I get on with him (6) .... than with the others. In fact, I probably like him (7) .... because he comes from the north, like me. He's the only one in the house who's going to pass the exam. He studies (8) .... I suppose I'm the laziest. I study (9) ....

4 Write sentences about what you do on weekdays and at weekends. Use at least six of these words/phrases on their own, as adverbs: *a lot, a little, a bit, much, very much, so much, as much, more, less, better, worse, most, least, best, worst.*

Examples: *On weekdays I watch television* **a bit**. *At weekends I watch it* **a lot**. *I like Monday* **the least**. *I don't go out* **much** *during the week.*

Check your sentences with a teacher.

82 Still, yet
Any more/any longer/no longer

Quick reference

- In affirmative sentences and questions we use *still* (= 'up to now') to talk about an action or a situation which is continuing longer than we expected.
We put *still* in mid-position: after the verb *be*, before a main verb on its own, and between an auxiliary and the main verb.
    *Harry's 91. Does he **still** live on his own? - Yes. And he **still** drives a car. He's **still** very active.*

- We use *yet* in negative sentences and in questions. We use it to talk about something that hasn't happened, but that we expect to happen in the future. *Yet* usually goes at the end of a sentence or a clause.
    *Have you finished that letter **yet**? - No, I haven't finished it **yet**, but I won't be long.*

- In negative sentences, if we want to show surprise, concern or anger that something hasn't happened up to now, we use *still* for emphasis (rather than *yet*). We put *still* before an auxiliary verb.
    *Have you found your keys yet? - No, I've been looking for them for hours and I **still** haven't found them.* (NOT I haven't still found them.)

- We use *any more* or *any longer* in negative sentences. We use them to say that a past situation has now finished. We usually put them at the end of a sentence or a clause. *Any more* is more common than *any longer*.
    *She doesn't go skiing **any more**.   They don't live here **any longer**.*

- We can use *no longer* with an affirmative verb instead of *any more/any longer* with a negative verb. The meaning is the same, but *no longer* is more formal and less common. We put *no longer* in mid-position.
    *She **no longer** works at the school. She's **no longer** a teacher.*
    (She doesn't work at the school any more. She isn't a teacher any longer.)

---

1 Max Firth has got eight children. He takes them to school, but this morning they are not ready. Max is telling them to hurry up. Give their replies, using *still* or *yet*.

1 John and Joe. Hurry up! Are you still eating?

 Yes, we (not finish/our breakfast) ....

2 Laura! Are you ready?

 No, I'm (in the bathroom) ....

3 Simon! Are you still upstairs?

 Yes, I'm (get dressed) ....

4 John, where's Helen?

 She (in bed) ....

5 And where are the twins?

 They (not finish/their homework) ....

6 Carla! It's time for school!

 I (not make/my sandwiches) ....

2 Lisa is giving a talk at a conference in Italy soon. She has made a list of the things she must do before she leaves. There are still some things she has not done. Write two sentences each time, a) using *yet*; b) using *still*. (What has she not done yet? What has she still got to do?)

THINGS TO DO   (✓ = the things she's already done)

a) book plane ticket

b) book room at hotel ✓

c) prepare my talk

d) order foreign currency

e) buy new shoes ✓

f) go to the hairdresser's

g) renew passport ✓

h) buy a new suitcase

Example: *She hasn't booked her plane ticket yet. She's still got to book her plane ticket.*

1 She ....

2 She ....

3 She ....

4 She ....

3 Gerry Hardman is angry and worried. He has got money problems. He has not got a job. He has got a serious eye infection. He feels depressed. Complete what he says, using *still*.

1 My friend Simon owes me £20. He (not pay me back) ....

2 I sent him a letter two weeks ago. He (not reply) ....

3 I applied for a job three weeks ago.

I'm (wait for an interview) ....

4 I had an operation on my eyes a month ago.

I (not see very well) ....

5 I'm taking anti-depressant tablets, but I'm (not feel well) ....

4 On January 1st many people in Britain make 'New Year resolutions'. They decide to change things in their lives. The Wills family have made their resolutions. Complete the sentences, using *still, yet, any more, any longer, no longer*.

1 (Norman Wills) I .... spend too much time away from the family. I'm not going to work on Saturdays ....

2 (Sarah Wills) I .... intend to do all the cooking. I'm not going to make all the meals at the weekend ....

3 (Jenny) My brother Oliver .... makes me angry. He hasn't apologised for breaking my CD player .... But I've decided. I'm not going to get angry with him ....

4 (Oliver) I haven't made any resolutions .... I .... haven't decided what I'm going to change. Last year I said I wouldn't smoke .... , but I .... smoke. Perhaps this year I'll try to be nice to my sister, but I haven't told her ....

5 a) Write five sentences, using *yet*, about five things that are important to you and that you haven't done yet.

b) Write five sentences, using *still*, about five things that haven't happened yet and that surprise or worry you, or make you angry.

c) Make some New Year resolutions. Write five sentences about what you are not going to do any more.

Check your answers with a teacher.

83

Too and *enough:*
It's too small. It isn't big enough

Quick reference

* *Too* means 'more than is necessary'. It doesn't mean the same as *very*. It always has a negative meaning. *I can't sleep. It's **too** hot.*
Very can have a positive or negative meaning. *She's **very** rich but she's also **very** mean.*

* We often use *too* before an adjective or an adverb.
*I'm not going to buy it. It's **too** expensive. You're driving **too** fast. Slow down!*

* We often use *too* in this construction:

	too +	adjective/adverb +	(*for* + object) +	infinitive
He's	*too*	*young*		*to die.*
She spoke	*too*	*quickly*	*for us*	*to understand.*

* We can also use *too much* + uncountable noun and *too many* + countable noun.
*He eats **too much** meat and **too many** chips.*

* We can put the words *much, far, a little, a lot, a bit* before *too*.
*We arrived **a bit too** late.   These jeans are **far too** big.*

* *Enough* means 'a sufficient number or amount'. It normally goes before a noun.
*There aren't **enough** chairs.   We haven't got **enough** time.   Is that **enough** sugar?*
Enough comes after an adjective or an adverb.   *The water isn't **deep enough**.*

* We use *enough* + *of* before pronouns or words like *the, this, my*, etc. + noun.
*I've had **enough of this noise**.   You've wasted **enough of my time**.*

* *Enough* can be used on its own when the noun is understood.
*Do you want some more potatoes? - No thanks. I've got **enough**.*

* Note the use of *enough* in these constructions.   *It's **easy enough to** understand.*
*The water's **warm enough for** me to swim.   I haven't had **enough time to** do it.*

---

1 **There are some bad drivers on Britain's motorways. Read the sentences, and re-write each one, keeping a similar meaning. Use *too* or *enough* with these adjectives/adverbs:** *experienced, difficult, close to, fast, carefully.*

Example: Some drivers are too careless. *Some drivers aren't careful enough.*

1 Some people drive too slowly. ....

2 Some drivers overtake too carelessly. ....

3 Some people don't drive far enough away from the car in front.

   ....

4 Some drivers are too inexperienced. ....

5 The present driving test is too easy. ....

---

2 **Complete these facts about the Wimbledon Tennis Championships, using adjective + *enough* or *enough* + noun. Choose from these words:** *big, early, good, long, balls, money, strawberries, fine days.*

* If you get up (1) .... and if you queue for (2) .... you can get tickets.

* Alternatively, if you've got (3) .... you can buy tickets on the black market.

* The Centre Court is not (4) .... - it only has 17,000 seats.

* The organisers have to make sure they've got (5) .... They need over 22,000.
* They also have to make sure they have (6) .... Over 275,000 portions are eaten each year.
* They can never be sure that there will be (7) .... to play all the matches.
* The eyesight of line judges has to be (8) .... to see exactly where the ball lands, travelling at over 180 kph.

3 Some foreign students at a language school in London were asked 'What's wrong with Britain?' Complete their answers, using *too* + these adjectives: *expensive, interested, many, conservative, crowded, kind*.

1 'They're .... to their animals. In Greece dogs stay outside.' *Stathis Papadaki, Greece*

2 'Everything is .... Everything costs too much.' *Marco Pozzani, Italy*

3 'It's .... There are .... people on a small island.' *Annika Hedlund, Sweden*

4 'English people are .... in their royal family. There are more important things to read about.' *Dieter Schweizer, Germany*

5 'They're .... They still use miles and pints.' *François Verrier, France*

4 Annie and James are sitting on a beach. Annie is bored. James just wants to read. Complete the dialogue using *too* + adjective + (*for* + object) + infinitive.

ANNIE: Shall we walk to the end of the beach?

JAMES: No, it's .... (1 far/walk). And it's also .... (2 hot/walk)

ANNIE: Shall we go for a swim?

JAMES: No, the water's .... (3 cold/me/swim)

ANNIE: We could hire one of those sailing boats.

JAMES: No, they're .... (4 expensive/us/hire)

ANNIE: We could learn to windsurf.

JAMES: No, I'm .... (5 old/windsurf) and it's .... (6 difficult/me/learn).

5 A presenter on a radio phone-in programme has asked his listeners to say what they think is wrong with the USA. Complete each sentence so that it has a similar meaning to the previous sentences, using the word given. Do not change the word given.

Example: Children can buy drugs. It's easy. (too) *It's too easy for children to buy drugs.*

1 Many illegal immigrants get into the USA. The authorities don't make it difficult. (enough)
The authorities don't ....

2 Anybody can buy a gun. It's simple. (too)
It's ....

3 America's a rich country. It could help poorer countries more. (enough)
America's rich ....

4 Laws don't stop pollution. They aren't strict. (enough)
Laws aren't ....

5 Medical care is very expensive. Many people can't pay for it. (too)
For many people ....

Quick reference

Even means that something is surprising or unexpected.

- We can use *even* before a noun.
  He's a famous rock singer. It's amazing. **Even my grandfather** *liked him.*
  (His grandfather doesn't usually like modern music, so this was surprising.)

- We can also use *even* on its own. Note its position.

Auxiliary verb	+	***even***	+	**main verb**
He loves salt. He		*even*		*puts it on his fruit salad.*
She's crazy about animals. She has		*even*		*built a little house for her dog.*

- We can use *even* with comparatives. *His German is good, and his English is* **even better**.
  This restaurant is expensive, but the one in Broad Street is **even more expensive**.

- We sometimes use *not even* (*-n't even*).
  I didn't drink anything, **not even** *a glass of wine.   He's rude. He* **didn't even** *say hello.*

- We can use *even* before *if* and *when*.
  I won't speak to him again **even if** *he apologises.   He talks all the time,* **even when** *he's asleep.*

---

1 **Jenny Daniels does not like theme parks, but last week a friend took her to Eurodisney. She was surprised by what she did. Add *even* to these sentences. Mark (*) its position.**

1 She had her photograph taken with Mickey Mouse.
2 She went on the Space Mountain ride, although she hates being in the dark.
3 She bought herself a silly Donald Duck hat.
4 Her friend was surprised that Jenny enjoyed it so much.
5 Jenny's decided to go again next year.

2 **Luke has come to the same club for the second time. Make sentences, using *even* + a comparative.**

Example: It was expensive the first time. *Now it's even more expensive.*

1 Luke felt good when he arrived. Now after an hour's dancing ....
2 The music was loud when he came in. Now ....
3 It was hot in the club at first. Now ....
4 He was feeling thirsty after the first ten minutes. Now ....
5 He's interested in a dark-haired girl. She's just bought him a drink, so now ....
   ....

3 **Sarah met a boy she really liked at a party last week. She wants to meet him again, but there are problems. Complete the sentences, using *not even/-n't even*.**

1 She .... know his name.
2 She danced with him, but he .... talk to her.
3 She hasn't got his telephone number, so she .... phone him.
4 He didn't give her anything, ... his address.
5 .... see him leave the party.
6 No-one seems to know him, ... the person who organised the party.

85

Quick reference

- *Else* means *more* or *in addition.* *Would you like anything **else**?*
It can also mean *different.* *I don't like this suit. I must wear something **else**.*

- We often use *else* after *somebody/something/somewhere*, etc. and after *much*.
*Did she go to the party with Tom? - No, she went with **somebody else**.*
*Shall we stay here or go **somewhere else**?*
*Did **anything else** happen after that? - No, not **much else**.*

- We can use *else* after the question words *who, what, why, how, when, where*.
***What else** do you want?* ***Who else** did you meet?*

- Note the meanings of *or else*.
*We must run **or else** we'll miss the bus.* (= if not, the result will be)
*You can pay me now **or else** I can wait till Monday.* (= alternatively)

---

1 A customs officer is talking to a tourist. Rewrite the phrases in italics, using *else*.

CUSTOMS OFFICER: Have you got anything to declare?

TOURIST: Only these two cartons of cigarettes.

CUSTOMS OFFICER: Have you got (1 *any other things*) ....?

TOURIST: No, (2 *no other things*) ....

CUSTOMS OFFICER: Were you travelling with (3 *another person*) ....?

TOURIST: No, (4 *no other person*) ....

CUSTOMS OFFICER: Have you been (5 *to any other place*) .... apart from Amsterdam?

TOURIST: No, (6 *no other place*) ....

CUSTOMS OFFICER: Well, if you haven't got (7 *any other things*) .... to declare, could you just open this bag for me please?

TOURIST: Oh yes, I've just remembered. I have got (8 *one more thing*). ....

2 Ben is at a travel agent's. Rewrite the words/phrases in italics, using *else*.

BEN: I want to go to Paris for a long weekend, leaving on Friday afternoon.

AGENT: On your own, or with *another person*? (1) ....

BEN: With *another person* - my girlfriend. (2) ....

AGENT: Paris is very crowded at Easter. Why don't you go *to a different place*? (3) ....

BEN: *What other places* do you suggest? (4) ....

AGENT: Bordeaux, for example. *Alternatively*, a city in the south, like Nice. (5) ....

BEN: No, I think I'd rather go to Paris.

AGENT: The flights on Friday afternoon are already full. *At what other time* could you travel?
(6) ....

BEN: On Friday morning. *Alternatively*, on Thursday evening. (7) ....

AGENT: Well, there's a flight from Heathrow at 8.30 on Friday morning.

BEN: *What other place* could we fly from? (8) ....

AGENT: From Gatwick. But there aren't many seats left, so you must decide now. *If you don't, the result will be that* all the seats will be taken. (9) ....

Quick reference

We use *in* before periods of time.

- Parts of the day. *I'll see you **in** the morning/**in** the afternoon/**in** the evening.*
- Months, seasons. *I'm going to Spain **in** July.   She's having a holiday **in** (the) autumn.*
- Years, decades and centuries.
  *He died **in** 1995.   I lived in France **in** the 1980s.   What was life like **in** the 18th century?*
- *In* can mean a) 'during or within a period of time' OR b) 'at the end of a period of time'.
  a) *I got to London **in** three hours.*   b) *I'll be ready **in** five minutes.*

We use *on* before particular days and dates.

- Days and dates. *I'll phone you **on** Monday.   **On** my birthday I went to London.*
  *We're having a party **on** New Year's Day.   I arrive **on** April 2nd.*
- Parts of days/dates. *Come **on** Tuesday morning.   He left **on** the evening of June 6th.*

We use *at* before exact times.

- Clock times. *The bus leaves **at** 9.30.   We have lunch **at** about 12.30.*
- Words meaning a time of day. *She works **at** night.   I eat **at** midday.   Come **at** lunchtime.*
- With *beginning, start, end* and *time, moment.*
  *I'll see you **at** the beginning of the week.   I cried **at** the end of the film.*
  *I'm very busy **at** the moment.   I lived in London in 1992 - **at** that time I loved city life.*
- Public holidays/festivals. *I play squash **at** the weekend.   I'm going to Rome **at** Easter.*

We don't use *in, on* or *at* before the words *every, next, this, last* + a time word.
  *The exams start **next Monday**.   I'm not going to work **this morning**.*

---

1 **Danny Jones wants to go to the USA. He is talking to a travel agent. Read the dialogue and think of the word (*in, at* or *on*) which best fits each space.**

DANNY: I'm thinking of going to New England (1) ...... August.

TRAVEL AGENT: I wouldn't go (2) ...... the summer, if I were you. I'd go now (3) ...... spring. The
countryside's beautiful (4) ...... April and May. I can arrange flights and accommodation.

DANNY: Um, I've got a week off work (5) ...... Easter. I could go then. I finish work (6) ...... April 7th.

TRAVEL AGENT: Well, there's a flight to Boston (7) ...... Friday, April 8th.

DANNY: What time does it leave?

TRAVEL AGENT: (8) ...... 15.15.

DANNY: So it gets to Boston late (9) ...... night.

TRAVEL AGENT: No, there's a five-hour time difference. It arrives in Boston (10) ...... the early evening,
(11) ...... 17.40 local time.

DANNY: Well, it's March 24th today. Can you arrange everything (12) ...... two weeks?

TRAVEL AGENT: No problem, sir. If you tell me the kind of hotel you want, I can send you all the details
(13) ...... three days.

2 Helen is studying Spanish in Barcelona. She is writing to her mother. Complete her postcard, using *in*, *on*, *at* or no word at all.

Dear Mum,

(1) ...... the moment the weather here is beautiful. I'm sitting on a beach that was constructed (2) ......
1992 (3) ...... the time of the Olympic Games.

It's Saturday, and I don't have any classes (4) ...... Saturdays, so I thought I'd write you a card.

I have Spanish lessons (5) ...... every day and (6) ...... Wednesday evenings. (7) ...... the evenings I
usually eat at a restaurant, and (8) ...... last Thursday I went with Miguel, my Spanish boyfriend, to a
restaurant where Picasso used to eat with his friends (9) ...... the 1930s. We were still eating our first
course (10) ...... midnight! We only arrived at the restaurant (11) ...... 11.00! In Spain everybody eats
late (12) ...... the evening.

(13) ...... the weekends I often play tennis, and (14) ...... last weekend Miguel and I went to Sitges, a
lovely resort just south of Barcelona.

Well, I arrived here (15) ...... June 30th and it's already July 23rd. I'll be home (16) ...... two weeks. So
I'll see you at the airport (17) ...... midday (18) ...... August 8th.

Love,

Helen.

3 Look at the information and answer the questions, using *in*, *at* or *on*.

	James	Alison	Ryan	Chris
Born:	1981	June, 1982	Midnight/October 5th, 1982	1982/his mother's birthday

1 When was James born? ....

2 When was Alison born? ....

3 When was Ryan born? ....

4 When was Chris born? ....

4 Write sentences about yourself.

    a) Write four sentences, using the time preposition *in*.

      Example: *I was born in 1983.*

    b) Write three sentences, using the time preposition *on*.

      Example: *It´s my birthday on June 3rd.*

    c) Write three sentences, using the time preposition *at*.

      Example: *I get up at 7 o´clock.*

    d) Write three sentences using the words *every*, *last*, and *next* + a time word.

      Example: *I have a shower every morning.*

Check your answers with a teacher.

Quick reference

We use *in*:

- when we talk about an enclosed space that is surrounded on all sides.
  *There were six people **in the room**. He's got a gun **in his hand**!*
- with buildings and areas surrounded by walls, etc.
  *He lives **in a big house**. There's a lake **in the park**.*
- with larger areas like cities, states, countries, continents. *They live **in the USA, in Texas**.*
- with words that describe the relative position of something. ***in the corner of** the square*
  *He sat **in the middle of the** room. Manchester is **in the north of** England.*
- with words like *hospital, church, school. He's **in hospital**. They got married **in church**.*
- with newspapers and magazines. *I read it **in the Daily Mail**.*

We use *on*:

- when we talk about a horizontal or vertical surface.
  *The book's **on the table**. The picture's **on the wall**.*
- with any kind of line. ***on the border** between the USA and Canada **on the road** to Paris*
- with machines. *I heard it **on the radio**. She was **on TV**. Your mother's **on the phone**.*
- with *right, left. I sat **on the left** and she sat **on the right**.*

We use *at*:

- when we talk about a particular point. ***at** the bus stop **at** the bottom of the hill*
- with a building when we're talking about what normally happens there, and not the building itself: *She works **at the chemist's**. He's **at the bank** getting some money.*
- with social activities. *We met **at** a party. I see him every week **at** the football match.*
- in the expressions *at home, at work, at school. He's **at school**. She's **at work**.*
- with addresses if we give the house number: *I live **at 6, Freeland Road**.*

1 Read the text below and think of the word which best fits each space. Use only one word in each space.

Last year we read an article about house-swapping (1) ...... the *Sunday Times*. As a result we swapped houses with a Canadian family - the Montmignys. Paul Montmigny works (2) ...... the University of Quebec; his wife Anna works (3) ...... home as a freelance journalist. Both their children are (4) ...... school.

We made all the arrangements (5) ...... the phone. For three weeks they lived (6) ...... our house (7) ...... the west of England, and we lived (8) ...... their house (9) ...... Canada. They live (10) ...... the small town of St Nicholas, (11) ...... 39 Rue de l'Eglise to be exact. St Nicolas is (12) ...... the main road between Quebec and Montreal. The house itself is (13) ...... a small lake. Quebec, which is (14) ...... the middle of Canada, is (15) ...... the St Lawrence River and there are lots of mountains, rivers and lakes (16) ...... the area.

The arrangement worked perfectly - both families had a very enjoyable 'free' holiday.

2 Complete this description with the prepositions *in, on* or *at*.

Two people are sitting (1) ...... a table (2) ...... a restaurant. The woman has got a glass (3) ...... her hand. There's a wine bottle (4) ...... the middle of the table. There's very little wine left (5) ...... the bottle. (6) ...... the back of the restaurant is the door to the kitchen. (7) ...... the door there's a sign saying 'Staff Only'. (8) ...... the corner of the restaurant there's a small bar. A man is sitting (9) ...... the bar. He's (10) ...... the phone. (11) ...... his right there's a bottle of whisky and (12) ...... his left a lamp. There's an old clock (13) ...... the wall.

3 Write a description of the room you are in now or your home using the prepositions of place *in, on, at* in as many different ways as possible.

Examples: *I live in Santander, at No 7, Calle Cadiz. I'm alone in my room. There's a table in the corner. There's a computer and a printer on the table.* Etc.

Check your answers with a teacher.

Quick reference

- *I live in a small village **outside** London.   Can I sit **next to** you?*
  *There's a cinema **opposite** the bank, on the other side of the road.*
  *There's a car park **round** the corner.   They've put a flag **on top of** the castle.*
  *I couldn't see because there was a tall man sitting **in front of** me.*

- *Above* and *over* usually have the same meaning ('higher than').
  ***Above** the door/**Over** the door was a sign saying 'Private'.*
  But *over* can also mean 'covering'. *She put a scarf **over** her head.*

- We use *inside*, rather than *in*, when we want to emphasise *the interior* of a place.
  *Do you want to look **inside** the house? There are some nice paintings **in** the hall.*

- *By, beside, next to* all mean 'very close to'.
  *In the queue I stood **by** a man/**next to** a man/**beside** a man with long black hair.*
  Compare with *near*. *I sat **next to** a TV presenter.* (He was in the next seat.)
  *I sat **near** a TV presenter.* (farther away than *next to*, perhaps in the next row of seats)

- *Below* and *under* sometimes mean the same ('lower than').
  *I can see the dolphin **below** the surface/**under** the surface.*
  But we use *below* when we mean 'lower than', but not 'directly under'.
  *I stood at an upstairs window and I could see the river **below** me.*
  We use *under* when we mean 'covered by'. *Where's my pen? - It's **under** that newspaper.*

- *Among* and *between* don't mean the same. We use *among* when something/someone is
  surrounded by a group of things/people. We don't see these things or people separately.
  *I found my watch **among** some old clothes on the floor.*
  We use *between* for two or more things/people when we see them as separate objects.
  *I sat **between** Tom and Zoe.   There were flowers growing **between** the stones in the wall.*

---

1 Read this news report and decide which answer, A, B, C or D best fits each space.

GWR Radio. The news at midday. There's a blanket of snow (1) ...... the whole of the southwest of
England. 20cm of snow has fallen (2) ...... Bristol.

All traffic has stopped and, as I look out of the studio window, I can see that the street (3) ...... me is
empty. I had to walk to the studio this morning, because my car was (4) ...... a two-metre snowdrift.
All rail links have been cut (5) ...... the main towns in the region. Further heavy falls of snow are
expected tonight in hilly areas (6) ...... 600m.

Now, for some music. (7) ...... my pile of letters this morning there's one from Dave in Hotwells who
wants to hear an old 1960s hit song.

1 A above	B over	C in	D on	2 A inside	B above	C in	D under
3 A below	B outside	C under	D above	4 A below	B over	C on	D under
5 A between	B among	C in	D over	6 A on top of	B over	C above	D on
7 A Between	B Above	C Among	D Under				

2 Look at the picture and complete the description, using each of the following prepositions once.

| on top of   next to   beside   behind   near   round   opposite |

1 The family are sitting .... the kitchen table.

2 Mrs Grant is sitting .... her husband.

3 Sarah is sitting .... her mother.

4 Jack is standing .... his mother.

5 There's a pile of presents .... the table.

6 Sally is standing .... the door, ready to switch the lights off.

7 There's a big candle .... the birthday cake.

3 Look at the picture and answer the questions, using these prepositions.

| under   above   among   between   below   by |

1 Where's the man sitting in relation to the river? He's sitting ....

2 Where's he sitting in relation to the two bridges? ....

3 Where's he sitting in relation to the willow tree? ....

4 Where's the house in relation to the trees? It's ....

5 Where's the river in relation to the house? It's ....

6 Where's the bird sitting in relation to the man's head? It's sitting ....

Quick reference

- We climbed **up** the hill.
  We walked **round** the lake.
  The glass fell **off** the table.
  We went **to** the party.
  He came **towards** me.
  The cat jumped **onto** the table.
  He walked **under** the ladder.
  He jumped **over** the stream.

  The water ran **down** the hole.
  He ran **out of** the room, **into** the garden.
  I looked **through** the telescope.
  The plane **from** Palma has landed.
  Go **along** this road and then turn right.
  He walked **past** me and didn't stop.
  He sailed **across** the Atlantic to the USA.
  Come here! Don't run **away from** me.

- We can join some of these prepositions with *and*.
  He walked **round and round** the room.
  He got **in and out of** bed all night; he couldn't sleep.

---

1 A driving instructor is telling his pupil what to do. Complete these sentences, using all the prepositions in the box just once.

up	down	away from	round	into	out of	to	from	past	through	across	under

Go (1) .... this corner. Good, that's fine. Now drive slowly (2) .... this hill till you get to the bottom. OK, now stop. This is the main road. Look out for traffic coming (3) .... the right. Now I want you to go (4) .... this main road to the other side and then (5) .... the railway bridge. Fine, no problem. Now go (6) .... that cinema on the left (7) .... the traffic lights. Careful. The lights are red. OK. Now go (8) .... the tunnel in front of us and when we come (9) .... the tunnel I want you to drive (10) .... the hill to the church at the top. OK, here's the church. Now turn right into that little side street, (11) .... the traffic. Good. Now go (12) .... that car park on the right. You can practise parking the car there.

---

2 Marcel Durand is French. Last week he went to London for the first time. Choose the correct preposition for each sentence.

1	He travelled	*along*	Calais to Folkestone by train.
2	He came	*under*	the Channel Tunnel.
3	On his first day, he travelled	*up*	London on top of a sight-seeing bus.
4	Then he walked	*through*	Oxford Street, looking at the shops.
5	He walked	*round*	Westminster Bridge to the Houses of Parliament.
6	After that he went	*past*	the Post Office Tower to the restaurant at the top.
7	In the evening he got	*from*	a riverboat at Westminster.
8	He sailed	*across*	the National Theatre and the Tower of London.
9	Then he sailed	*onto*	Tower Bridge.

1 ....   2 ....   3 ....   4 ....

5 ....   6 ....   7 ....   8 ....   9 ....

3 Look at this map of part of southern England. Complete the sentences, using each of these prepositions once.

> from   out of   to   through   into   round   off   onto

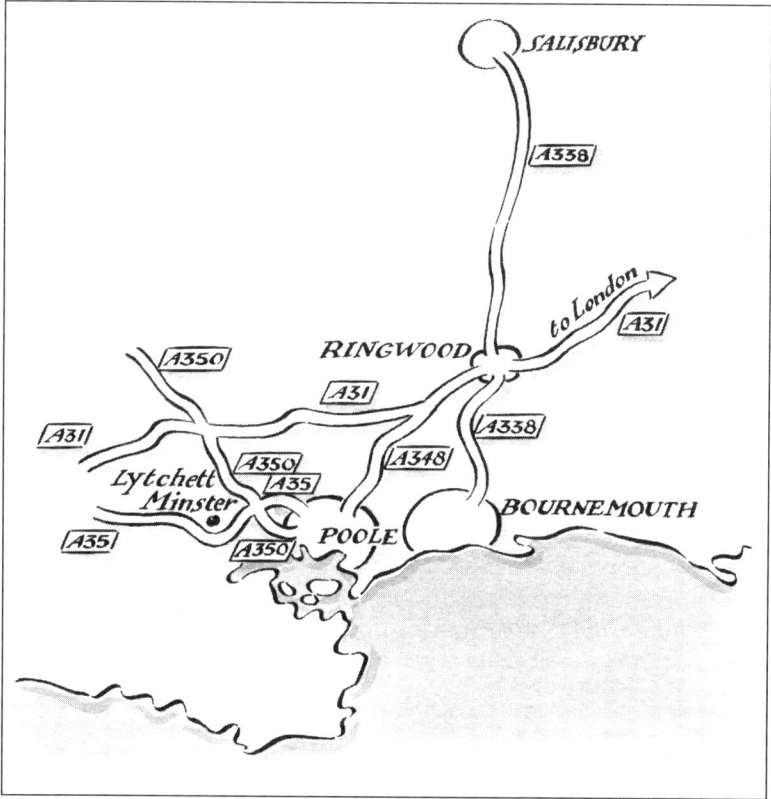

1 The A338 goes .... Bournemouth .... Salisbury.

2 On the way it goes .... Ringwood.

3 If you want to go east to London, you come .... the A338 at Ringwood and get .... the A31.

4 If you're travelling from the north, the A350 will take you .... the centre of Poole.

5 If you want to get .... Poole and go west, it's best to take the A35.

6 On the A35 you don't have to go through Lytchett Minster. A ringroad goes .... it.

4 Describe your journey to school or work using some of these prepositions: *up, down, round, into, away from, out of, off, through, down to, from, along, towards, onto, past, across, under, over.*

Example: *I go out of the flat and down to the ground floor in the lift. I go across the street to the bus-stop. The bus goes along the river and through the town centre.* Etc.

Check your answers with a teacher.

173

Quick reference

- When we talk about the means of transport, we can use *by*.
  *He travelled **by** air/**by** rail/**by** road/**by** sea.*
  OR ***by** train/**by** bus/**by** coach/**by** car/**by** plane/**by** boat/**by** taxi.*
  We can also use *on*.
  *I travelled **on** the train/**on** a plane/**on** a boat/**on** the ferry/**on** a bus/**on** a coach.*
  But with *car, truck, taxi* we use *in*. *I came **in** the car. I got a lift **in** a truck.*

- We use *out of* and *into* when we talk about buildings or rooms.
  *I went **into** the bank. She came **out of** the classroom.*
  We say *get into* (OR *in*) and *get out of* a car, a taxi, a truck.
  *I got **into** the first taxi that came. The police told me to **get out of** the car.*

- We say *get on/get off* a train, a bus, a coach, a plane, a big boat, a bike, a motorbike.
  *He **got on** his bike and rode away. We **got off** the train at Taunton.*

- We say *get to* (= reach) a town, a country or a place.
  *We **got to** Athens at 9.30. We **got to** America in four hours.*
  But we say *arrive in* a town or a country, and *arrive at* a place.
  *We **arrived in** France a week ago. What time did you **arrive at** the station?*

- We say *go to* a place, a town, a country, a continent.
  *I **go to** Spain twice a year. He's **gone to** Africa. When are you **going to** London?*

- We don't use a preposition before *home* with verbs like *go, get, come, arrive, leave*.
  *I **arrived home** at 12.30. She **left home** early. What time will you **get home**?*

---

1 **Complete the dialogue below, using *at, in, to, by, on, out of, into, off* or no word at all.**

'When did you get (1) .... home?'

'We got (2) .... the plane at five o'clock. We came (3) .... the airport at twenty-past five and we arrived (4) .... home at six.'

'Did you come (5) .... bus from the airport?'

'No, we arrived (6) .... the bus-stop just after the bus had left, so we got (7) .... the first taxi we saw. It was just six o'clock when we were getting (8) .... the taxi at home.'

'Was it the first time you'd been (9) .... France?'

'No, but it was the first time we'd been (10) .... plane. We normally go (11) .... the car. We sometimes go (12) .... the Shuttle from Folkestone (13) .... Calais, or we cross the Channel (14) .... ferry.'

'Did you have good weather?'

'Wonderful. When we left (15) .... home, it was cold and wet. But when we arrived (16) .... Nice, it was warm and sunny. As soon as we arrived (17) .... our hotel, we went for a swim in the pool. We had a great holiday!'

2 Look at this timetable and complete the questions and answers.

Hall/Mr

Thursday 29 Feb Outward

British Airways	Non-stop	Flight: BA 480
Latest reporting time:		12.55 Terminal 1
Depart: London/Heathrow		13.55 hrs
Arrive: Barcelona		16.55 hrs

Sunday 03 Mar Return

British Airways	Non-stop	Flight: BA 479
Latest reporting time:		12.20 hrs
Depart: Barcelona		13.20 hrs
Arrive: London/Heathrow		14.30 hrs

1 Is Mr Hall travelling by coach? – No, he's going .... plane from Heathrow.

2 Where's he going? ....

3 Does his flight go via Madrid? – No, it's non-stop .... Barcelona.

4 Where must he be by 12.55 on Thursday? ....

5 What time does he arrive .... ? – At 16.55 hrs.

6 When is he flying back .... ? – On March 3rd.

7 By what time must he be .... for the return flight? – By 12.20 hrs.

8 What time does his return flight arrive .... London? – At 14.30 hrs.

3 This person wants to get to South Brent, a village near Plymouth. His friend knows what to do. Match the questions with the correct answers.

1 Have you ever been to South Brent?   a) In Plymouth.

2 How do I get there?   b) By bus.

3 Isn't it worth going by car?   c) You should get to Plymouth by 11.15.

4 Where do I get off the train?   d) At the bus-station in the town centre.

5 If I get a train at about 10.00, when would I arrive in Plymouth?   e) You can get a train most of the way.

6 How do I get from Plymouth to South Brent?   f) Yes, several times.

7 Where do I get on the bus?   g) No, go on the train. It's more comfortable.

1 ....   2 ....   3 ....   4 ....   5 ....   6 ....   7 ....

4 Describe a journey you've made recently. Where did you go? How did you travel? What time did you arrive? Etc.

Use as many of the following as possible: *go by car/train*, etc. *go in the car/on the train/on the plane/on my bike*, etc. *go to Paris/England/North Africa*, etc. *go into/out of a building, get on/off the bus/the plane/the boat/my bike*, etc. *get into/out of the car, get to Paris/France*, etc. *arrive in Paris/France*, etc. *arrive at the airport/the station/the ferry terminal*, etc.

Check your story with a teacher.

91 For, since, ago

Quick reference

For

- We use *for* to answer the question *How long? For* is usually followed by a period of time, often a number of hours, days, months, years, etc. *They've had that car for ten years*.
- *For* can be used with present, present perfect, past and future tenses.
  He sleeps for nine hours every night.   He's lived in California for two years.
  She was in hospital for a month.   We'll stay for three weeks.

Since

- We use *since* + a point in time to say when something started.
  I've lived here since 1992.   They've been playing since 3 o'clock.
  OR (with a negative verb) to say when something stopped. *It hasn't rained since June.*
- *Since* is often followed by a subject + a verb to show the point in time.
  I've known him since we were at school.   We've been waiting since the plane landed.
- We usually use *since* with the present perfect (continuous).
  I've had a headache since I woke up this morning.   It's been snowing since 7 o'clock.
- We use *ever since* when we want to emphasise that something has continued without stopping for a period of time. *It's been raining ever since we arrived.*
- *Since/ever since* can be used alone. *I saw her at 3.15, but I haven't seen her since.*

Ago

- We use *ago* to say when something happened in the past. *They left five minutes ago.*
- We put *ago* after the expression of time. *The war ended two years ago.* (NOT ago two years.)
- We use *ago* with the past simple (and sometimes with the past continuous). But we don't use it with the present perfect.
  The police came an hour ago. (NOT have come an hour ago)
  She was having a bath half an hour ago.

---

1 **An old man is talking about his life. Write a second sentence which has a similar meaning to the first sentence, using the word given.**

Example: We got married 35 years ago. (been) *We've been married for 35 years.*

1 I first met my wife 40 years ago. (known) ....

2 We moved to this area 30 years ago. (lived) ....

3 We bought this house 25 years ago. (had) ....

4 I got a job at the factory 20 years ago. (worked) ....,...................

5 We became grandparents five years ago. (been) ....

2 **Two people are discussing what to do at the weekend. Complete the sentences, as in the example.**

Example: *We could go to London. We haven't been to London for ages* OR *since Easter.*

1 We could have a party. We .... months.

2 Why don't we clean the car? We .... last month.

176

3 We could buy some new clothes. We .... I bought those jeans.

4 How about seeing a film? We .... we saw 'Repulsion'.

5 Shall I phone Tom and Suzanne? I .... weeks.

6 Why don't we just do nothing? We .... a long time.

3 Young Australian men often spend a lot of time and money on their cars. Two of them are talking about their obsession. Complete what they say, using *since* or *for*.

I left school when I was 16. (1) .... then I've had five cars (and I've crashed three of them). I usually have a car (2) .... a year. Then I get bored with it and buy another one. My dad has had the same car (3) .... ten years. He hasn't bought a new one (4) .... he got married the second time. I can't understand that. But I must admit I've had this Holden Commodore (5) .... 1995 and it's still going well. I'll probably keep it (6) .... a few more months.

Greg Saradakis

I've had my own car (7) .... four years, (8) .... I passed my driving test. I've just put a new sound system in this car. I've been saving money to buy it (9) .... nine months. It's got six speakers. I've wanted this system (10) .... over a year, (11) .... I saw an advertisement for it in a car magazine.

Damian Pellati

4 Raymond Bent has worked in the Lost Property office of the London Underground for 21 years. Complete what he says about his job using *for, (ever) since* or *ago*.

I've worked in this office (1) .... over 20 years. Things have changed a lot (2) .... I started work here. 20 years (3) .... people left a lot of hats and gloves. Nowadays they leave things like personal stereos and radios. A week (4) .... someone left a computer on the train.

(5) .... I've been here, I must have had over 10,000 pairs of glasses and 5,000 sets of false teeth handed in. We keep them (6) .... three months and then, if nobody claims them, we give them to the Red Cross.

Anything really strange? Yes, a month (7) .... someone left a wooden leg on the Victoria Line. And about a year (8) .... somebody left a stuffed gorilla on the Bakerloo Line. We've had it (9) .... We've also had a human skeleton (10) .... the last six months. The Red Cross didn't want them!

5 Write at least six sentences about yourself. Say where you live, how long you have been learning English, etc. Use *for, since* or *ago* in each of your sentences.

Examples: *I've lived in this town **since** 1993. I've been learning English **for** five years. I started smoking six months **ago**.*

Check your sentences with a teacher.

Quick reference

- *For* answers the question *How long?*
  *How long did you stay in France? - I stayed **for three months**.* (NOT during three months)

- Note these common expressions with *for*. They all have the sense of 'for a long time':
  for a long time, for hours, for days, for weeks, for months, for years, for ages.
  *I sat by the phone **for ages**, but she didn't ring.*

- *During* doesn't mean the same as *for*. It answers the questions *When? In what period of time?*
  We use it before a noun, a fixed period of time (*the day, the week, the winter*, etc.).
  ***During the week** I don't get home before 6 p.m.   I was in France **during the summer**.*
  Note that we don't use *during* with a number of days, weeks, etc.
  *I went to Spain **for** two weeks.* (NOT during two weeks)

- We use *during* before an activity (*lesson, conversation, war, holiday*, etc.).
  *He went to sleep **during the lesson**.   He didn't see his father **during the war**.*

- *While* (= 'at the same time that') is a link word. It's followed by a subject + a verb.
  *He travelled a lot **while he was** in the Army.   I'll read **while you watch** television.*

- We often use *while* + the past continuous, followed by a verb in the past simple.
  *While she **was waiting**, she **had** a cup of coffee.*

- When *while* is used in a future sentence, it's followed by a verb in the present, NOT *will*.
  *I'll read a book **while I'm waiting**.   I'll have a rest **while the children are** at school.*

---

1 **This is a report of a tennis match at Wimbledon. Look at the parts of sentences in the left-hand column and match them with their second part. Add *for* or *during* to the second part.**

The match between Carter and Mendez was a real battle.

1 They were on the Centre Court

2 Carter looked much stronger than Mendez

3 But things started to change

4 Carter began to look tired and worried

5 After that, Mendez played brilliantly

6 But then Carter recovered

a) .... the tie-break and he lost the set.

b) .... the final set, and won it.

c) .... four and a half hours.

d) .... the third set.

e) .... the first and second sets.

f) .... half an hour.

So Carter finally won the match 6-4, 6-3, 6-7, 0-6, 6-4.

1 ....   2 ....   3 ....   4 ....   5 ....   6 ....

---

2 **Read the text. Some of the lines are correct, and in some there is a mistake. Put a tick (✓) after the correct lines and, in the lines where there is a mistake, underline the mistake and write the correction in the brackets.**

1 Sarah's been a student at Exeter College during 18 months. Like a lot   (.................)

2 of British students, Sarah works for the holidays to earn some extra money.   (.................)

3 During the summer last year she worked as a receptionist at the White   (.................)

4 Hart Hotel for ten weeks. And she worked in a wine bar during a month   (.................)

5 during the winter. She sometimes works in the local newsagent's   (.................)

6 for a few hours during the week. But she'll have to stop doing that   (.................)

7 during her exams, which take place for the first two weeks of June.   (.................)

3 **Lauren and Emma are talking about the party they had last night. Complete the dialogue, using *while* and the verb in brackets.**

EMMA: It was a great party, but look at all this mess!

LAUREN: I'll do the washing-up.

EMMA: OK. I'll clean the floors (1 do) .... you .... the washing-up.

LAUREN: You know, Ben asked me if I wanted to go out with him.

EMMA: When did he ask you that?

LAUREN: (2 dance) .... together.

EMMA: Did you say 'yes'?

LAUREN: No. I can't go out with Ben (3 go out) .... with Nigel, can I?

EMMA: Why don't you finish with Nigel?

LAUREN: He's got his exams at the moment. I can't do that (4 do) .... his

exams. It wouldn't be fair.

EMMA: What's he doing after his exams?

LAUREN: He's going to Barcelona for three weeks.

EMMA: Well, you could see Ben (5 Nigel/be) .... in Spain. Perhaps Nigel

will meet another girl (6 be) .... in Barcelona.

4 **Read the text and answer the questions, using *for*, *during* or *while*.**

Adam spent three weeks in Israel in the summer. He worked on a kibbutz. He picked oranges and packed them into boxes. He was picking oranges in the afternoon one day when he noticed a snake about three metres from him. He quickly climbed into a tree. He spent an hour there. He threw oranges at the snake to frighten it away. The manager came to see what was happening. He spent half an hour with Adam explaining to him which snakes were dangerous and which were harmless. As he talked, he picked up the snake and said that it was neither dangerous nor harmless. It was dead!

1 How long was Adam in Israel? ....

2 When was he there? ....

3 When did he notice the snake? ....

4 When was he picking oranges? ....

5 How long did he stay in the tree? ....

6 When did he throw oranges at the snake? ....

7 How long was the manager with Adam? ....

8 When did the manager pick up the snake? ....

5 **Write ten sentences about yourself, using the time words *for*, *during*, *while*.**

Examples: *I've lived in Barcelona for ten years. During the summer I usually go to our villa in Sitges.*
       While I'm there, I spend a lot of time water-skiing.

Check your answers with a teacher.

Quick reference

● When we talk about the future, we use either a present tense or the present perfect after the link words *when, as soon as, once, after, before, while, by the time, until (till).* We don't use the future *will.*

    I'll ring you **when** I **get** there. (NOT when I'll get there)
    As soon as it **stops** raining, we'll go out. (NOT as soon as it will stop raining)
    I won't go to bed **till** you**'ve come** home. (NOT till you'll have come home)

● It's often possible to use either the simple present or the present perfect after *when, as soon as,* etc. without changing the meaning. (But in future sentences *while* can only be followed by the present simple or continuous.)

    They're going to live in Scotland **after** they **get** married OR **after** they**'ve got** married.
    She'll get a job **as soon as** she **leaves** school OR **as soon as** she**'s left** school.

● But when it's important to make clear that one action will be finished before the second one starts, we must use the present perfect.

    I'm not going to bed **till** I**'ve listened** to the news.

---

1 In a very bad romantic film, the 'hero' makes the following promises to the girl he loves. Complete what he says, putting the verbs in the right tense.

1 I'll miss you desperately while I (be) .... away.

2 As soon as I (arrive) .... I'll ring you.

3 When I (return) .... I'll hold you in my arms.

4 We'll get married as soon as your father (give) .... his permission.

5 I'll never leave you while there (be) .... breath in my body.

6 I'll love you till the day I (die) ....

2 Jerome Palmer, a 17-year-old student, is talking about his future plans. Read what he says and decide which answer, A, B, or C best fits each space.

I'm going to leave school as soon as I (1) .... 18. I'm hoping to go to university once I (2) .... my exams. But I'll take a year out first. I'll get a temporary job once I (3) .... I've got a university place. I'll probably live in London while I (4) .... But I won't stay there all year. I'll probably travel after I (5) .... enough money. I'll go to the USA and, after I (6) .... a bit of the States, I'll go to Mexico. As soon as I (7) ...., I'll get a job as an English language teacher. Then, when I (8) .... enough money, I'll come back to England.

1 A will be	B 'm	C have been
2 A 've passed	B will pass	C will have passed
3 A have known	B will know	C know
4 A will work	B am going to work	C 'm working
5 A 've earned	B earn	C will earn
6 A see	B will see	C 've seen
7 A will arrive	B arrive	C 'm going to arrive
8 A 've saved	B save	C will save

Quick reference

By

- *By* is a preposition of time, meaning 'not later than'.
  *I'll be ready **by** 10.00.* (= at 10.00 or before, but not later)
- *By the time* is a linking phrase, always followed by a verb.
  ***By the time** he arrives, the match will be over.* (= not later than the moment he arrives)

Until

- We use *until*, or its short form *till*, to talk about an activity or a situation that continues and then stops at a particular time.
  *He slept **until/till** 10.30.* (= He was asleep before 10.30 and then woke up at 10.30.)
- *Until* and *till* can be prepositions and link words.
  *He didn't get out of bed **until/till lunchtime**.* (preposition)
  *I waited **until/till he'd eaten his lunch**.* (link word + a clause)
- *By* = not later than that time. *Until/till* = up to that time.
  *He wasn't at work **by** 2.30.* (= He wasn't at work at or before 2.30.)
  *He wasn't at work **until/till** 2.30.* (= He wasn't at work before 2.30, but he was there at 2.30.)

---

1 **Complete the text, using** *by, by the time, until/till.*

James Wright was always late. His ex-girlfriend, Joanna, had stayed with him for six months
(1) .... she got fed up. One day he'd said to her: 'I'll be home (2) .... 8.00 tonight,
so I'll phone you then.' But (3) .... he got home, it was after 9.00, and he didn't phone her
(4) .... 9.30. And (5) .... he phoned, she'd gone out. 'I waited (6) ....
nine,' said Joanna, 'and (7) .... then I was furious, so I went out.'
The other day, James was going to have dinner at a friend's flat. He thought he was supposed to get
there (8) .... 8.30, but he didn't get to the bus-stop (9) .... nine o'clock, and
(10) .... he arrived at the friend's flat it was half past nine. 'I'm sorry. I'm an hour late, but I
didn't get home from work (11) .... seven,' he said. 'You're 25 hours late,' said his friend.
'The dinner was yesterday!'

2 **It is Wednesday morning. Helen has taken her car to be repaired. She needs it again on Friday.**
She is talking to the mechanic. Read the dialogue and think of the word(s) that best fit(s) each
space. Choose between A *by,* **B** *by the time,* **C** *until.* **Write A, B or C.**

MECHANIC: When do you need the car?
HELEN: (1) .... 8.30 Friday morning. When will it be ready?
MECHANIC: Not (2) .... next week.
HELEN: Not till then?
MECHANIC: No, (3) .... we've done all the work, it'll be Tuesday at least.
HELEN: But I need it on Friday.
MECHANIC: I'm afraid it won't be ready (4) .... then.
HELEN: Can you lend me a car?
MECHANIC: Yes, I can get you one (5) .... this afternoon.
HELEN: Will all this be expensive?
MECHANIC: Yes, it will be, (6) .... you've paid for the repair and the hire car.

Quick reference

Like

- We use *like* when we compare one thing or person with another. *Like* usually means 'similar to' or 'in the same way as'.
  *She looks **like** her father.* (NOT as her father) *He swims **like** a fish.* (NOT as a fish)

- *Like* can also mean 'for example'.
  *He eats a lot of junk food, **like** crisps and hot dogs.* (NOT as crisps)

- *Like* is a preposition. We use it before a noun, a pronoun or the *-ing* form of the verb.
  *He smokes **like a chimney**.* (*like* + noun) *He looks **like me**.* (*like* + pronoun)
  *Spending £3,000 on a bicycle seems **like throwing** money away.* (*like* + *-ing*)

As

- We use *as* before a subject + a verb. We don't normally use *like* here.
  *Do **as** I say.* (NOT Do like I say.) ***As** I expected, he was late.* (NOT Like I expected)

- We can use *as* (preposition) + noun to say what someone or something really is.
  *He works **as** a dishwasher in a hotel kitchen.* (= This is his real job.)
  Note that *like* + a noun doesn't mean the same as *as* + a noun. We use *like* to compare things or people. *He works **like** a slave.* (He isn't really a slave.)

- We also use *as* when we talk about the function or role of something/someone.
  *He used the knife **as** a weapon.* *I acted **as** her manager.*

As if/as though

- We use *as if/as though* before a subject + a verb. They mean the same.
  *He behaves **as if/as though** he's the boss.* (He isn't the boss, but he behaves like him.)

- We sometimes use a past tense form after *as if/as though* when we talk about the present.
  *I treat her **as if/as though** she **was/were** my own daughter.* (She isn't his daughter).
  We use the past tense form *was* or *were* (subjunctive) here to show how unreal the idea is.

---

1 **Complete this interview with a dustman (or rubbish collector) with *like* or *as*.**

(1) .... you know, my name's Frank Rigden and I've worked (2) .... a dustman for five years now. Some people treat you (3) .... a disease, (4) .... something unclean and maybe a bit dangerous. When I get home, my wife says I smell (5) .... the rubbish I've been handling all day. But when I'm not at work, people say to me, 'You don't look (6) .... a dustman.' In fact, in the evening, when I've finished work, I do a lot of different things, (7) .... listening to Mozart and other composers, (8) .... Stravinsky and Berg.

It's not (9) .... the other jobs I've had. They've all been jobs inside, in factories. I enjoy being outside (10) .... this, in the open air. (11) .... any other job, it gets a bit routine sometimes. Some people I work with aren't (12) .... me. They use a bit of snow (13) .... an excuse to stay in bed.

I try to leave every street as neat and tidy (14) .... I like my street to be. I never leave things (15) .... egg shells or potato peel on the ground. Yes, (16) .... I told you before, I enjoy being a dustman.

2 Some students are complaining about their maths teacher. Complete what they say with *as if/as though* + subject + *was/were*.

'Sometimes he shouts at us (1) .... we .... children.'

'He talks very fast (2) .... maths .... very easy. '

'What really annoys me is when he speaks to the girls (3) .... they .... different from the boys, (4) .... they .... all stupid. And when I ask a question he looks at me (5) .... I .... some sort of trouble maker.'

'He gives us a lot of homework, (6) .... maths .... our only subject.'

3 Kate Hogarth works for a big computer company. Complete this description of her, matching the first part of the sentence on the left with the other half of the sentence on the right, adding *as*, *like* or *as if/as though*.

1 She joined the company	a)	.... a fashion model.
2 Now it looks	b)	.... they're really important.
3 Because it looks	c)	.... she'll be the next managing director.
4 Kate's 45 but she looks	d)	.... people's first names.
5 She dresses	e)	.... she predicted.
6 She treats everyone	f)	.... she's still only 35.
7 She's good at remembering things,	g)	.... a receptionist.
8 Last year the company made big profits,	h)	.... the present boss will retire early.

1 ....   2 ....   3 ....   4 ....   5 ....   6 ....   7 ....   8 ....

4 Andy Walsh likes to give the impression that he is a very important person. He is always showing off. Complete the sentences about him, using *as if/as though*.

Example: He's 55, but he acts *as if he was* (OR *as if he were*) *25.*

1 He isn't very rich, but he spends money .... millionaire.

2 He's never met his bank manager, but he talks about him .... an old friend.

3 He's got a very ordinary job at work, but he talks .... the manager.

4 He lives in a very ordinary house, but he talks .... in a castle.

5 He's got a very old Ford, but he talks .... a Mercedes and a Porsche.

6 He's married, but when he's with other women he behaves .... a wife and two children.

7 He doesn't know anything about world affairs, but he talks .... an expert.

8 He talks about the Prime Minister .... him intimately, but he's never even met him.

5 Write a description of a person you know well using *like, as, as if, as though*.

Examples: *He's 18 but he looks **as if** he's 25.   He works **as** a waiter.*

Check your description with a teacher.

Quick reference

Although, though, even though

- We use these link words to join two contrasting parts of a sentence.
  Although *it was raining, I went for a walk.* (= It was raining, BUT I went for a walk.)
  We can also say: *I went for a walk **although** it was raining.*
  We can use *though* instead of *although.* *He might come to the party, **though** I doubt it.*
  We use *even though* when the contrast is particularly strong.
  *She finished the race, **even though** she'd hurt her leg.*

- We can use *though* (NOT although) at the end of a sentence.
  *It's a good hotel. It isn't the best, **though**.* (= But it isn't the best.)

In spite of

- *In spite of* can be followed by a noun, a pronoun, or the *-ing* form of a verb.
  *I played tennis **in spite of the cold weather**.* (= although the weather was cold)
  In spite of having *very little money, he was happy.* (= although he had very little money)
  *They went swimming **in spite of the weather being** bad.* (= although the weather was bad)

Because, since, as

- We use these link words when we say why we do something or why something happens.
  We normally use *because* to give the reason. The *because* clause usually comes last.
  *I was late for work **because** I missed the bus.*
  We normally use *since* and *as* (which mean the same) when the reason is already known.
  Since (OR ***As***) *he'd forgotten his glasses, he couldn't read the menu.*

So

- We use *so* to talk about the result of an action or situation. *I couldn't sleep, **so** I got up.*

---

1 Oliver Yates is planning a holiday, but there are problems. Look at these twelve sentences. Put them together in pairs, using the link word *although.*

He'd prefer to go with a friend.   *She's recently lost her job.*

He's planning to go to India next month.   *He's quite happy to go on his own.*

He's going to sell his car.   *He wants to stay in India for six months.*

He's read a lot of books about it.   *He hasn't got enough money to go.*

He's hoping his mother will lend him some money. *He won't get much money for it.*

His mother doesn't want him to go for so long. *He's never been to India before.*

Example: *He wants to stay in India for six months, although his mother doesn't want him to go for so long.*

Now write five more sentences.

1 ....

2 ....

3 ....

4 ....

5 ....

2 **Mandy Felix loves going sailing. Complete the second sentence so that it has a similar meaning to the first, using the words given.**

Example: Mandy Felix often goes sailing, even though she can't swim. (not being able)
Mandy Felix often goes sailing, in spite of not being able to swim.

1 She usually goes alone, even though her friends tell her she shouldn't. (telling her)

She usually goes alone, ...

2 She went sailing yesterday, even though the weather was bad. (being)

She went sailing yesterday, ...

3 She went out, even though she didn't have a life-jacket. (in spite of)

She went out, ...

3 **The people in Jerry's class like some things, but not others, and they do some things but not others. Write sentences, using a final *though*.**

Example: Kate likes Art. (her Art teacher) *She doesn't like her Art teacher, though.*

1 Jerry's very good at maths. (languages) ....

2 Lauren can't sing. (a good actress) ....

3 Emily doesn't like History. (the History of Art) ....

4 Marcus plays the guitar well. (in a band) ....

5 Daniel's very popular with all the girls. (a girlfriend) ....

4 **Complete the dialogue, using *because, so* or *since*.**

ANNA: Why are you so late?

JAMES: (1) .... I missed the bus, (2) .... I had to wait for another hour.

ANNA: Why didn't you phone me?

JAMES: (3) .... I didn't have any change in my pocket.

ANNA: Why didn't you ask someone to give you some?

JAMES: (4) .... there was no-one around.

ANNA: So, what did you do?

JAMES: There was nothing I could do, (5) .... I just sat and read a book.

ANNA: Did you talk to anyone?

JAMES: No, (6) .... there was no-one around, I couldn't talk to anyone, could I?

ANNA: Well, (7) .... you're so late, there's no point going to the cinema, (8) ....
you might as well go home.

5 **a) Write five sentences about yourself. Use *although, even though* or *in spite of* + -ing.**

Example: *I was good at tennis, and, **even though** I was only ten, I could beat my father.*

b) Write three sentences, giving the reason why you did certain things. Use *because* or *since*.

Example: *I went to live in Valencia, **because** I was in love with a girl there.*

c) Write three sentences, using *so*, to talk about the result of things you did.

Example: *I failed my driving test, **so** I had to take it again.*

Ask a teacher to check your sentences.

Quick reference

- We use the relative pronoun *who* for people and the relative pronoun *which* for things.
  *She's **the girl who** always wears sunglasses.* *This is **the bus which** goes to London.*
  But we often use *that* instead of *who* or *which*.
  *She's **the girl that** always wears sunglasses.* *This is **the bus that** goes to London.*
  With people we use *who* more often than *that*. With things we use *that* more often than *which*.

- *Who, which, that* can be the subject of the relative clause.
  *I know the man **who** got the job.* (**He** got the job.)
  We can't leave out *who, which, that* here.

- *Who, which, that* can also be the object of the relative clause.
  *I read the book **which** you gave me.* (You gave me **the book**.)
  *The man **who** I spoke to is a millionaire.* (I spoke to **the man**.)
  But in informal spoken English we usually leave them out.
  I read the book you gave me. *The man I spoke to is a millionaire.*

- We can use *whom* when the object is a person, but it's very formal and rarely used in spoken English. We usually leave out the pronoun, or we use *who* instead.
  *The people **whom** we met were very interesting.* (Formal)
  We normally say: *The people (**who**) we met were very interesting.*

- When we use verbs or adjectives followed by a preposition, the preposition usually comes at the end of a relative clause.
  *I know who this umbrella belongs **to**.* *This is the car (which) I'm interested **in**.*
  In very formal English we can put the preposition at the beginning, before *whom* or *which*.
  *I met the man **for whom** you work.* *That's the job **for which** I applied.*

---

1 **In which of the following sentences is it not possible to miss out the relative pronouns *who, which* or *that*? Mark the sentences with a tick (✓).**

1 A supermarket cashier in Ashton, Bristol noticed a customer who was acting strangely. [....]
2 He also noticed the enormous hat that she was wearing. [....]
3 There were only two things in the basket that she was carrying. [....]
4 The customer paid for the things which she'd bought. [....]
5 She then suddenly fainted and fell on top of a child who was standing behind her. [....]
6 The cashier removed the hat which was still on the customer's head. [....]
7 She found a frozen chicken and a packet of frozen peas which the customer had stolen. [....]
8 It was the frozen chicken and peas that had made her faint. [....]

---

2 **Join the two sentences together using *who* or *which*.**

1 I saw a road accident today. It really upset me.

   ....

2 It was a red Ford Escort. It caused the accident.

   ....

3 It had an unusual registration number. It began with the letter X.

   ....

4 The driver was a young man. He was wearing dark glasses.

   ....

5 He hit an old woman. She was crossing the road.

   ....

6 I called an ambulance. It arrived five minutes later.

   ....

7 I took care of the old woman. She was still breathing.

   ....

8 I spoke to one of the ambulancemen. He said she was badly hurt.

   ....

9 They took her to the hospital. It's only a mile away.

   ....

10 But she died in the ambulance. It was taking her to hospital.

   ....

3 **This is part of a wedding speech given by the bridegroom. It is very formal. Make it informal. Complete the second sentence so that it has a similar meaning to the first sentence.**

1 This is a day about which my wife and I will talk for years.

   This is a day which .... about for years.

2 I must thank all the people from whom we've received presents.

   I .... from.

3 In particular, I'd like to thank all the people to whom I haven't had a chance to speak.

   In particular, ... who ....

4 You've given us some wonderful presents for which we're very grateful.

   You've given us some wonderful presents ....

5 I'd like to thank the mother of the bride, on whom we've all depended for so many things.

   I'd like to thank .... who .... for so many thngs.

6 And finally I'd like to thank my wife, to whom I owe my happiness.

   And finally .... who ....

7 There's one thing for which I must apologise.

   There's .... which ....

8 The speech to which you've just listened has been far too long.

   The speech which ....

4 **Complete these film titles with a relative clause. Make the films sound as interesting or exciting as possible. Check your answers with a teacher.**

Example: The Man ... *The Man who knew too much.*

The Man ...	The Murder ...	The Creature ...
The Woman ...	The Street ...	The Love ...
The Battle ...	The Wife ...	The Spy ...

Quick reference

- We use the relative pronoun **where** to describe places. *That's the house **where** I was born.*
We can sometimes leave out *where* and add a preposition to the verb.
    *That's the house I was born **in**.*
We can use *where* without identifying the place it describes. Here it means 'the place where/to a place where/in a place where'. *This is **where** I live. I want to go **where** it's sunny.*

- The relative pronoun **whose** for possession is always followed by a noun. It can be the subject or object of the verb.
    *She's the girl **whose dog** bit me.* (Subject) *He's the man **whose wife** we met.* (Object)
We use *whose* mostly for people, but we can also use it for things.
    *India is **a country whose culture** has influenced the whole world.*

- The relative pronoun **what** means 'the thing(s) that'.
    *He doesn't like **what** I do.* (Object) *His dishonesty is **what** worries me.* (Subject)
We can start a sentence with *what* if we want to emphasise something.
    ***What** worries me is that I can't speak any foreign languages.*
    ***What** we need is a new government.*
Note that we don't use *what* after *everything* and *all*.
    ***All you can do** is be patient.* (NOT All what you can do)
    *Have you got **everything you need**?* (NOT everything what you need)

---

1 **Rebecca is showing her holiday photos to a friend. Rewrite the sentences in brackets, using *where*.**

1 (I stayed at this hotel.) This is the hotel ....

2 (I had breakfast on this balcony.) This is the balcony ....

3 (We ate at this taverna in the evening.) ....

4 (I spent most of my time on this beach.) ....

5 (I met Angelo at this night club.) ....

2 **Amy lives near a famous singer. She is always trying to meet him. She has written down a lot of information about him. Her friend Hannah is asking about the things she has written. Read the dialogue and complete the second sentence so that it has a similar meaning to the first, using *where* each time.**

HANNAH: What's this address?

AMY: He lives there. (1) That's ....

HANNAH: Is this the name of a pub?

AMY: Yes, he often has a drink there. (2) Yes, that's ....

HANNAH: What's this place marked with an 'X' on the street plan?

AMY: He often parks his car there. (3) That's ....

HANNAH: Is this the name of the newsagent's?

AMY: Yes, he buys his newspapers there. (4) Yes, that's ....

3 A police officer is talking to newspaper reporters about a robbery at a wine store. Look at the information in the brackets, and complete what the officer says, using *whose*.

Example: (Somebody's car was parked outside the store last night) We want to identify the person
whose car was parked outside the store last night.

1 (The boot of the car is probably full of wine.)

We're looking for a red Ford Mondeo ....

2 (We found somebody's jacket in the store.)

We'd like to talk to the person ....

3 (Somebody's fingerprints are on the door of the safe.)

We're looking for the person ....

4 (We found somebody's gloves near the store entrance).

We'd like to interview the person ....

4 Sasha met Nick this evening. Carl, her boyfriend, is very jealous. Complete the dialogue, using *what, that* or no word at all.

CARL: I want to know where you went and the things (1) .... you did.

SASHA: I've told you (2) .... we did. We simply had a drink together.

CARL: What did you talk about?

SASHA: You know (3) .... we talked about. I've told you everything (4) .... we said.

CARL: Do you like Nick?

SASHA: Yes, I do, but that doesn't mean (5) .... you think it means. You don't believe

(6) .... I'm saying, do you? I've told you everything (7) .... happened.

That's all (8) .... I can do.

5 Luke Bird is complaining about public transport. Read the text and find sentences where *What* could be used to give more emphasis. Rewrite the sentences, using *What*.

It really depresses me that public transport is so poor. Yesterday I went to Plymouth by train. The cost really annoyed me. All public transport should be cheap. When I got off the train in Plymouth I had to wait two hours for a bus. It amazes me that the buses and trains aren't integrated. We badly need an integrated system of transport. I wrote a letter to the Ministry of Transport. It shocked me that they said it wasn't their problem. They didn't seem interested. They said I should write to the bus company. I really don't understand why we have a Ministry of Transport.

Example: *What really depresses me is that public transport is so poor.*

1 ....

2 ....

3 ....

4 ....

5 ....

6 Write a description of your town or area and the people who live there. Use the relative pronouns *where, whose, what*. Check your description with a teacher.

Examples: *The place where I live is very industrial. It's a town whose population is growing fast.*
I don't like what's happening here; the town's getting too big.

Quick reference

- **Defining relative clause**: *That's the woman **who's got six children**.*
(Here, the relative clause identifies the woman. It says which woman the speaker means.)
- **Non-defining relative clause**: *I met James Topolski, **who's from Chicago**.*
(Here, the person he met is already identified as 'James Topolski'. The relative clause *who's from Chicago* simply gives us extra information about James Topolski.)
We put a comma before a non-defining relative clause. If it's in the middle of a sentence, we put a comma after it as well. *His house, **which was built in 1870**, is really beautiful.*

- In a defining relative clause we can leave out *who, which, that* when they're objects.
That's the film we're going to see. (OR *that/which we're going to see*)
In a non-defining relative clause we can't leave out *who* and *which*.
*This is Louise Finch, **who** I met yesterday.*

- We never use *that* in non-defining relative clauses.
*Our hotel room, **which was on the 21st floor**, was enormous.* (NOT *that was*)

- We can use *where* and *whose* in non-defining relative clauses.
*Marilyn Monroe, **whose** real name was Norma Jean Baker, was born in 1926.*
*She went to Hollywood, **where** she starred in many films.*

- In formal English we can use *whom* and *which* after a preposition in defining and non-defining relative clauses.
*She's the girl **to whom** I sold my car. His house, **in which** he'd always lived, was in Brighton.*
But in informal English we normally say:
*She's the girl **who** I sold my car **to**. His house, **which** he'd always lived **in**, was in Brighton.*

- *Which* can refer to a whole clause. *He got married at 75, **which** surprised everyone.*

---

1 These are examples from a book of humorous definitions.

  a) Match the two parts to make correct sentences, then fill in the gaps with *who, which, whose, where* or *that*.

  b) Say how many clauses are defining and how many non-defining.

  c) Say in how many you could omit the relative pronoun.

1 A city is a place	a) .... we look at while we're waiting for the TV repairman.
2 A book is something	b) .... wife won't listen to him.
3 Home is	c) .... climbs down trees he never climbed up.
4 A parachutist is someone	d) .... is hell to live with.
5 A playboy is a man	e) .... millions of people can be lonely together.
6 A prisoner is a criminal	f) .... you can scratch any place you itch.
7 A saint is a person	g) .... comes to work from a different direction every day.
8 A politician is a man	h) .... is young enough to know everything.
9 A teenager is someone	i) .... has given up hope of becoming a capitalist.
10 A communist is a person	j) .... intelligence is so limited even the police can catch him.

a) 1 ....   2 ....   3 ....   4 ....   5 ....   6 ....   7 ....   8 ....   9 ....   10 ....

b) ....

c) ....

2 Make single sentences, using the relative pronouns *who, which, where* and *whose*. Add commas where necessary. You will sometimes need to change the word order.

1 The following incident took place in Trenton. Trenton is in New Jersey.

....

2 An elderly man drove into town. His name was Henry Kaplin.

....

3 Beside him was his neighbour. Her name was Annie Bednarska.

....

4 They got to the Riverside Shopping Mall. She wanted to go shopping.

....

5 His passenger got out. She was 79 years old.

....

6 The driver reversed. He was in a hurry.

....

7 Three pedestrians shouted at him. It wasn't enough to stop him.

....

8 He ran her over. It resulted in her breaking a leg.

....

9 Police arrived at the scene of the accident. They asked them both questions.

....

10 They spoke to the driver. They discovered he was deaf.

....

11 They also spoke to Annie Bednarska. She told them she was blind.

....

3 Read the news headlines and decide which answer, A, B, or C best fits each space.

The film star Hetty Anderson (1) .... has died at her home in Los Angeles.

Nineteen-year-old Mark Bates (2) .... was killed in a crash on the M11.

The Prime Minister (3) .... has flown to an EU conference in Brussels.

A teenage girl (4) .... has been found alive.

A Welsh shipbuilding yard (5) .... has been closed.

1 A , who was 81,
   B who was 81
   C , that was 81,
2 A who was a student at Bristol University
   B , who was a student at Bristol University,
   C that was a student at Bristol University
3 A , that is 55 today,
   B who is 55 today
   C , who is 55 today,
4 A , whose family reported her missing 2 weeks ago,
   B , who family reported her missing 2 weeks ago,
   C , which family reported her missing 2 weeks ago,
5 A where over 2,000 men were employed
   B , which over 2,000 men were employed,
   C , where over 2,000 men were employed,

Quick reference

-ing clauses

- We can use an -ing clause to say what someone is/was doing, or to describe a situation.
  *I met Tessa **coming out** of the supermarket.   He bumped into a woman **holding** a baby.*
  *She spoke to a man **wearing** dark glasses.   I lost a bag **containing** all my money.*
  An -ing clause is often used after *there is/there are/there was/there were.*
  ***There's** someone **waiting** at the bus-stop.   **There were** no trains **going** to London.*

Clauses with a past participle

- We can use a clause beginning with a past participle (*used, found, lost*, etc.) to describe something or someone. This type of clause has a passive meaning.
  *A pen **used** by Picasso has been sold for £25,000.   A woman **hurt** in the crash has died.*

With phrases

- We can use a *with* phrase to describe the physical features or possessions of someone or something.
  *I met a girl **with blue eyes and long blond hair**.*
  *A man **with a gun** rushed out of the bank.   I found a bag **with nothing in it** on the floor.*

---

1 Complete this newspaper report, using clauses with -ing or a past participle, and *with*.

When the Queen visited Barnstaple this morning, there was a big crowd (*they were waiting to see her*)

.... Half way through the visit a man (*he had long black hair - he was*

wearing jeans and a T-shirt - it had 'I ♥ Her Majesty' on it) ....

.... was arrested

by police. The man, (*he was holding a long hatpin*) ...., rushed towards

the Queen (*he was shouting 'Your Majesty!'*) .... The Queen's bodyguards,

(*they saw the danger*) ...., jumped on him. The man, (*he was badly injured in*

the attack) ...., is now in Barnstaple hospital. The Queen, (*she was*

touched by the man's efforts to reach her) ....,

has visited him in hospital. The hatpin (*it was found in the man's hand*) ....

.... was hers. She'd dropped it as she approached the Civic Centre.

---

2 Complete this sentence from a report about an election campaign by a group of Green Party activists. Put these clauses and phrases into the correct position in the sentence.

dressed as a penguin,   and driven by a woman   filled with conservationists
with green wheels,   with Green Party slogans written on them   all holding placards

A van ....

....

....

travelled round the area for a week before the election.

Key

Unit 1

1 1 go 2 weighs 3 don't read, watch 4 gets up
5 has, doesn't wash 6 drink 7 brushes
8 have 9 goes 10 live

2 1 speaks 2 doesn't speak 3 don't speak
4 speak 5 doesn't speak 6 speaks

3 1 What time does the first train leave London?
It leaves London at 08.40.
2 Does it stop in Bristol? No, it doesn't.
3 What time does it reach Exeter? It reaches
Exeter at 11.27.
4 Do the 09.15 and 10.15 trains both stop at
Bristol? Yes, they do.
5 Do they stop at Taunton? No, they don't.
6 Does the 10.30 train stop at Taunton? No, it
doesn't.
7 Does the 14.15 train from London stop at
Exeter? Yes, it does.
8 What time does the last train leave London?
It leaves London at 20.15.
9 What time does it reach Plymouth?
It reaches Plymouth at 00.22.

4 1 Are you married?
2 How often do you go shopping?
3 When do you go shopping?
4 How often does your wife go shopping?
5 How much do you spend?
6 Does your wife spend about the same?
7 How do you pay?
8 Do you go to different supermarkets?
9 Does your wife go to this supermarket?

Unit 2

1 1 What are you doing 2 I'm taking, I'm going
3 What are you doing 4 I'm not enjoying, I'm
thinking of, I'm applying for 5 I'm getting ready
6 You're always going, Where are you going
7 We're going, Alison's coming, I'm really
looking forward 8 are you going 9 We aren't
staying (We're not staying) 10 What's Alison
doing 11 She's training 12 it's getting

2 1 are ('re) 2 having 3 staying 4 belongs 5 like
6 know 7 are ('re) 8 seems 9 sitting 10 am ('m)
11 having 12 are 13 wish

3 1 are you doing 2 I'm having 3 don't believe
4 It's (is) 5 are waiting 6 you're having 7 I'm
being 8 want 9 know 10 hate 11 I'm drying
12 don't care 13 you're doing 14 want

4 1 I'm writing 2 I'm becoming 3 I remember
4 is happening 5 are going up 6 is rising
7 is getting 8 are doing 9 I know 10 I suppose

11 you are (you're) always saying 12 it isn't
13 You are (You're) always making 14 hate
15 am 16 want

Unit 3

1 1e 2d 3b 4a 5c

2 1b 2a 3a 4b 5a 6b 7a 8b 9b 10a 11a
12b 13a 14b

3 1 Is 2 I'm ringing 3 is coming 4 are having
5 they're playing 6 lives 7 has 8 ask
9 doesn't take 10 don't leave 11 don't
complain 12 it's keeping 13 you're sending
14 do I live?

4
a) (In any order)
1 He's using a computer.
2 He's wearing jeans.
3 He's listening to music.
4 He's working.
5 He plays the guitar.
6 He reads books.
7 He rides a motorbike.
8 He plays tennis.
b)
1 a) False   b) True
2 a) True   b) False
3 a) True   b) True
4 a) True   b) False

5 1c 2f 3g 4a 5b 6h 7d 8e

6 1 ✓ 2 goes is going/'s going 3 works (first
word) is working 4 ✓ 5 's travelling travels
6 sits is sitting/'s sitting 7 are thinking think
8 stands is standing/'s standing 9 start starts
10 ✓ 11 thinks is thinking/'s thinking 12 has
is having/'s having 13 's having has 14 want
wants

Unit 4

1 1 How's he travelling to Torquay? He's
travelling by train.
2 What's he doing at 8.00? He's having
breakfast with local party officials.
3 Is he doing anything at 9.15? Yes, he is.
4 Where's he meeting the mayor? He's
meeting him at the town hall.
5 Who's he having lunch with? He's having
lunch with a local family.
6 Is he free at 14.00? No, he isn't.
7 How's he returning to London? He's going by
helicopter/flying back by helicopter.

2 1g 2f 3h 4c 5a 6b 7e 8d

3 1 Where is (Where's) the concert?
  2 Which bands are playing?
  3 How much do tickets cost?
  4 How are you getting there?
  5 What time does the concert finish?

4 1 is going 2 are playing 3 is going 4 They aren't going/They're not going 5 doesn't like 6 They're going 7 leaves 8 It's 9 doesn't stop 10 arrives 11 are taking 12 starts 13 finishes 14 leaves 15 arrive

Unit 5

1 1 had 2 ate 3 sat 4 spoke 5 got on, rode

2 1 Was the flight OK? Yes, it was.
  2 Was the weather hot? No, it wasn't.
  3 Were the meetings useful? Yes, they were.
  4 Was the food good? Yes, it was.
  5 Were things expensive? No, they weren't.
  6 Was the trip successful? Yes, it was.

3 1 lost 2 got 3 rang 4 said 5 was 6 had 7 went 8 didn't know 9 understood 10 stole 11 made 12 was 13 took

4 1 lost 2 didn't do 3 slept 4 spent 5 went 6 didn't come home 7 left 8 ate

5 1 When did you go?
  2 Where did you live?
  3 Did you get a job?
  4 How did you find it?
  5 Who did you teach?
  6 Was it well paid?

6 1 works worked 2 come came 3 ✓ 4 tells told 5 was were 6 gets got 7 thinks thought 8 ✓

Unit 6

1 1 At 7.23 he was waiting for the bus.
  2 At 7.40 he was going by bus to the city centre.
  3 At 7.50 he was waiting for Andrea.
  4 At 8.10 they were having a drink in a pub.
  5 At 9.00 they were watching a film.
  6 At 10.40 they were eating a pizza.

2 1 was 2 were playing 3 were dancing 4 weren't listening 5 were 6 were eating 7 was lying 8 was 9 wasn't wearing 10 had 11 was hiding

3 2 was having had 3 were meeting met 4 shone was shining 5 went was going 6 ✓ 7 ✓ 8 was coming came 9 looked were looking

Unit 7

1 1A 2B 3C 4A 5B 6B 7A 8B 9C 10C 11A 12A 13B 14C

2 (These sentences can be in any order.)
  1 He's had breakfast.

  2 He hasn't done the washing up.
  3 He hasn't cleaned his shoes.
  4 He hasn't switched off the lights.
  5 He hasn't emptied the waste paper basket.
  6 He's forgotten his keys.
  7 He's broken a glass.

3 1 I've lost 2 I've used 3 I've left 4 I've put 5 I've paid 6 I've forgotten 7 I've had 8 I've rung 9 I've found 10 I've broken
  1d 2a 3g 4c 5b 6f 7h 8e 9j 10i

Unit 8

1 1 They've just won £5,000 in the National Lottery.
  2 Beth has just passed all her exams.
  3 Gillian Trent has just started her new job.
  4 George Trent has just bought a new car.

2 1 I've already made it.
  2 I haven't tidied it yet.
  3 I've already done it.
  4 I've already finished it.
  5 I've already had a bath.
  6 I haven't fed the dog yet.
  7 I haven't shaved yet.
  8 I haven't found it yet.

3 1 Have you ever been abroad?
  2 Have you ever worked for a travel company?
  3 Have you ever learnt German or Spanish?
  4 Have you ever been seriously ill?
  5 Have you ever used a computer?

4 1 just 2 never 3 before 4 never 5 ever 6 before 7 never 8 already 9 yet 10 just 11 just 12 already 13 yet

Unit 9

1 1 has broken out, have died 2 have arrested 3 has apologised, has reported, has worn 4 has had 5 have lost, have told

2 1 I haven't written 2 I've been 3 I've been 4 I've had 5 I've learned/learnt 6 I've made 7 I've met 8 They've taught 9 I've run out of 10 I've spent 11 I've bought 12 I've eaten 13 I haven't seen 14 I've become 15 I haven't felt 16 I've seen 17 I've stayed 18 has given 19 I've started 20 I've finished

3 1A 2B 3C 4A 5B 6A 7C

4 1 He's gone to 2 She's been to 3 has gone to 4 has been to 5 have gone to

Unit 10

1 1f 2g 3h 4i 5j 6c 7d 8b 9a 10e

2 1 was 2 was 3 didn't you come 4 had 5 I've had 6 I've been 7 Did you see 8 did 9 Did you talk 10 seemed 11 She's applied 12 was 13 they've broken up 14 haven't been

15 didn't know   16 Has Lucy found   17 told
18 didn't want

3 1 When did you start playing the guitar?
2 When did you leave school?
3 Where did you give your first concert?
4 When did you get your first recording contract?
5 How many albums have you made?
6 Who chose the name of the band?
7 How many records have you sold?
8 Have you been to the States?

4 1 ✓   2 ✓   3 I've lost   I lost   4 ✓   5 have you done   did you do   6 I've done   I did   7 ✓   8 has that happened   did that happen   9 I've let   I let   10 ✓   11 came   has come   12 ✓   13 went   have gone

Unit 11

1 1 The men have been fishing.   2 The woman has been swimming.   3 The dog's been digging a hole.   4 The girls have been collecting shells.

2 1d She's been living in it for a year.
2f She's been learning it for eight years.
3a They've been going out together since last May.
4b They've been saving money for months.
5c She's been working for a French firm for two years.
6g He's been having problems with his heart.
7e She's been thinking of moving back to France.

3 1 He's been reading it for half an hour.
2 He's been cooking for an hour.
3 She's been lying on her bed for an hour and a half.
4 He's been talking to her for three quarters of an hour.
5 He's been watching TV for two hours.
6 She's been getting ready for an hour and a quarter.

4 1 ✓   2 wait   waiting   3 felt   been feeling   4 ✓   5 had   've been having   (OR 've had)   6 ✓   7 had   've been having   8 worried   been worrying   9 ✓   10 slept   haven't been sleeping   11 are using   have been using

Unit 12

1 1a Laura's been dancing all evening.
1b She's danced with about six boys.
2a She's been drinking white wine and lemonade.
2 She's drunk about four glasses.
3a Mark Roland's been asking her to dance all evening.
3b He's asked her several times.

4a But each time Laura has said. 'No, thanks.'
4b She's never liked him very much.
5a It's late now, and Laura's been trying to phone for a taxi since 12.30.
5b She's tried three times.
6 Mark has been waiting for this moment all evening.

2 1b What has Harry been doing?   He's been playing football.
2a What has Sarah done?   She's broken her leg.
3b What has David Hall been doing?   He's been painting the bedroom.
4a What has Louise Hall done?   She's bought a new video camera.

3 1 he's been   2 he's been trying   3 He's applied   4 he's only had   5 he's been   6 he's been doing   7 he's painted   8 he's built   9 he's been getting   10 he's worked   11 he's hated   12 He hasn't been feeling (OR He hasn't felt)   13 He's seen   14 he's been taking   15 they haven't cured   16 he's decided   17 He's been watching   18 He's watched   19 he's seen   20 he's fallen   21 he's been dreaming   22 He hasn't smiled

Unit 13

1 1 She'd had   2 She'd been   3 She'd flown   4 She'd broken   5 She'd found   6 She'd made, she'd lost   7 She'd lent, they hadn't paid   8 She hadn't had, she hadn't met

2 1 When the waiter had showed them to their table, they asked to see the menu.
2 He brought them the menu after he had finished his cigarette.
3 As soon as Alexander had taken a sip of his wine, he knew it was off.
4 After they had eaten half their chicken, they suddenly lost their appetite.
5 The waiter brought their coffee before they had finished their sweet.
6 After the waiter had given them the bill, he told them that service wasn't included!

3 1 had climbed   2 jumped   3 had jumped   4 followed   5 looked   6 saw   7 saw   8 had knocked   9 realised   10 made   11 hadn't opened   12 dived   13 reached   14 put   15 pulled   16 had pulled OR pulled   17 opened   18 had checked   19 opened   20 didn't take   21 had landed

4 1 what had you been doing that evening?
2 I'd been having a good time. I'd been talking to some old friends. I'd been celebrating my birthday.
3 Had you been having a party?   4 Yes, I had.
5 Had you been drinking?   6 Yes, I had.
7 How long had you been drinking?
8 I'd been drinking since about 7 o'clock.

Unit 14

1 1 Will he be 2 he won't be 3 will he have 4 it'll be 5 He won't be able to 6 will he? 7 he won't be able to 8 He'll have to 9 He won't like 10 he'll be 11 he will 12 They'll look after 13 I won't be able to 14 I won't be 15 you'll see

2 1 Shall we look at a magazine together?
2 Shall I clean them for you?
3 Shall I make you a cup of tea?
4 Shall we go for a walk?
5 Shall I call the doctor?

3 1 I'll get it. 2 I'll feed it. 3 I'll close them.
4 I'll tell her. 5 I won't forget.

4 1 will you have 2 I won't have 3 I'll have
4 You'll write 5 won't 6 I'll write 7 will you phone 8 I won't phone 9 I won't 10 I'll phone 11 I'll send 12 will 13 I won't talk 14 Will you marry 15 I'll think 16 will you give 17 We'll talk

Unit 15

1 1 He's going to write postcards.
2 He's going to hire a car.
3 He's going to read (a lot of books).
4 He's going to play tennis.
5 He's going to go snorkelling.
6 He's going to sunbathe.
7 He's going to take photos/pictures.
8 He's going to visit churches in Barcelona.

2 1A 2C 3A 4B 5B 6C 7A 8B

3 1e 2a 3d 4b 5f 6c

4 1 I'll have 2 I'll open 3 I'm going to sit, I'll come 4 I'll answer 5 I'm going to phone, I'll give 6 I'm going to leave, I'll ring

5 1 will you eat are you going to eat 2 I'll I'm going to 3 I'm going to I'll 4 Won't you Aren't you going to 5 ✓ 6 I'm going to I'll 7 ✓

Unit 16

1 1 I'll be doing the week's shopping.
2 I'll be having a drink with Lee at the Red Lion.
3 I'll be having lunch with Emily.
4 I'll be having a Yoga lesson in town.
5 I'll be having an eye test at the optician's.
6 I'll be playing squash with Jerry.

2 1 He'll have left college.
2 He'll have moved into his new flat.
3 He'll have started work as a chef in a restaurant.
4 He'll have got his exam results.

3 1 He'll be going to work.
2 He'll have started work./He'll have arrived at work.
3 He'll be having lunch.

4 He'll have finished lunch.
5 He'll have arrived home. (OR got home)
6 He'll be having (his) dinner.
7 He'll be watching the TV news.
8 He'll have gone to bed.

4 1 Will you have slept ...?
2 Which/What train will you be catching?
3 How much luggage will you be bringing? OR Will you be bringing much luggage?
4 Will you have had lunch?/Will you have eaten?
5 What will you be wearing?

Unit 17

1 1 was put forward 2 was started was not completed 3 was begun 4 were constructed 5 were killed 6 was opened 7 were delayed 8 is used 9 is preferred, are transported

2 1 was built 2 was bought 3 has been completely modernised 4 has been installed 5 have also been added 6 was rebuilt

3 1A 2B 3A 4A 5A 6A

4 1 In which country are the most bicycles made?
2 In which country is the most oil being produced at the moment?
3 Who was dynamite invented by?
4 In which city are the next Olympics going to be held?
5 In which country will the next football World Cup be played?
6 How many times has the moon been visited by astronauts?

5 1 They want to be paid more.
2 They want to be consulted about changes.
3 They think they should have been told about the company's problems.
4 They ought to have been offered longer holidays.

Unit 18

1 1 I couldn't stand being told to make my bed.
2 I got tired of being given boring jobs to do.
3 I got fed up with being sent to the shop to buy my grandfather's tobacco.
4 I hated being treated like a servant.
5 I hated being shouted at when I did something wrong.
6 I couldn't stand being criticised all the time.

2 1 She's thought to have made a lot of money selling antique furniture.
2 She's reported to have a priceless collection of antique jewellery.
3 She was found to have £25,000 in her handbag.

4 She's said to have been a very good tennis player when she was young.

5 She's believed to have played at Wimbledon.

3 1 But you aren't supposed to drink tea/have tea.

Tea's supposed to be good for you.

2 But you aren't supposed to have sugar.

Sugar's supposed to give you energy.

3 But you aren't supposed to eat/to have fried food.

Eggs are supposed to provide protein.

4 But you're supposed to have plenty of exercise.

Too much exercise is supposed to be dangerous.

4 1 The dogs will be found new homes.

2 He's been promised compensation.

3 He was offered a gun to shoot the dogs.

4 He's been sent threatening letters.

Unit 19

1 1 has it serviced 2 has them painted 3 didn't have the software installed 4 he's going to have a new garage built/he's having a new garage built 5 he's going to have the roof of his house repaired/he's having the roof of his house repaired

2 1 I had my video camera stolen 2 I had my glasses broken 3 my wife had her passport taken 4 we had our bags searched 5 we had our car broken into

3 1 Every day she has her apartment cleaned and tidied.

2 Last month she had the whole apartment redecorated.

3 She's (has) just had new carpets laid in every room.

4 Every week she has her car washed and polished.

5 This month she's (is) having a new collection of summer clothes made.

6 Last week she had her teeth straightened.

7 That was only a week after she'd (had) had her nose remodelled.

8 Next week she's (is) going to have her portrait painted.

9 Once a month she has her fortune told.

10 And four times a year she has her poodle shampooed.

4 1 When did you last have it cut?

2 Why don't you have it repaired?

3 You should have it cleaned.

4 You should have the gas fire checked.

5 Why don't you have a telephone installed?

Unit 20

1 1 Are you doing your shopping here for the first time?

2 Do you mind answering some (a few) questions?/Do you mind if I ask you some questions?

3 Do you come often?/Do you come every week?

4 Have you bought a lot (OR much) this morning?

5 Did you come last week?

6 Is there anything you'd like to change (at the Centre?)/Would you like to change anything (at the Centre)?

2 1 Where do you come from?

2 When did you arrive in England?

3 How many times have you been to England?

4 How long have you been learning English?

5 What do you like doing?

6 What are you doing this evening?

7 Can we have dinner together?

3 1 Which model is it? 2 What type/kind of printer is it? 3 How old is it? 4 How much does it cost? OR How much is it? 5 Why are you selling it? 6 Can I see it? OR Can I come and see it?

4 1 Didn't you like it? 2 Wasn't the food very good? 3 Didn't you complain? 4 Didn't he give you another bottle?

5 1 What are you angry about?

2 What are you afraid of?

3 What are you thinking about?

4 Who were you talking to?

Unit 21

1 1b 2c 3f 4e 5i 6h 7g 8a

2 1A 2B 3C 4B 5A 6C

3 1 is it? 2 aren't they? 3 didn't I? 4 hasn't he? 5 is he? 6 doesn't he? 7 can you?

4 1 shouldn't we? 2 didn't I? 3 won't we? 4 shall we? 5 are there? 6 can we? 7 don't they? 8 will you? 9 did you? 10 can you? 11 have we? 12 should we? 13 wasn't it? 14 didn't you? 15 wasn't it? 16 was it? 17 does it? 18 haven't we?

Unit 22

1 1 What happened at 10.00?

2 What exploded?

3 Which exploded first - the television or the lamp?

4 What did Lisa do? 5 Who phoned them?

6 What time did the phone ring?

7 What did Peter disconnect?

8 Which did Peter disconnect first - the CD player or the video? 9 Who did Lisa phone?

2 1 What 2 Which 3 Which 4 Which 5 What
6 What 7 Which 8 Which 9 What 10 What
11 What

3 2 Have you any idea how far it is?
3 Do you know if I can get a train?
4 Do you know if there's (is) a bus?
5 Could you tell me what time it leaves?
6 Have you any idea how long it takes?
7 Could you tell me how much it costs?
8 Do you know if the buses run on Sundays?

Unit 23

1 1c 2e 3g 4f 5a 6d 7b

2 1 So am I. 2 So have I. 3 So do I. 4 Neither
do I. 5 Neither can I. 6 Neither have I.
7 So would I. 8 So am I.

3 1 so 2 don't 3 so 4 afraid 5 not

4 1 I think so. 2 I don't think so.
3 I don't expect so./I expect not.
4 I expect so. 5 I hope so. 6 I imagine so.
7 I'm afraid so. 8 I'm afraid not.

Unit 24

1 1 Anna and Zoe were, but Sue wasn't.
2 Sue did, but Anna and Zoe didn't.
3 Zoe has, but Sue and Anna haven't.
4 Anna and Zoe have, but Sue hasn't.
5 Sue does, but Anna and Zoe don't.
6 Anna and Zoe do, but Sue doesn't.
7 Anna and Sue won't, but Zoe will.
8 Anna and Sue can, but Zoe can't.
9 Sue and Anna have, but Zoe hasn't.
10 Zoe is, but Sue and Anna aren't.

2 1B 2C 3A 4B 5C 6A 7B 8A 9B

3 1f 2j 3e 4g 5i 6h 7d 8a 9c 10b

Unit 25

1 1 can 2 he'll be able to 3 he'll be able to 4 be
able to 5 can 6 can't 7 haven't been able to

2 1 couldn't (better than: wasn't able to) 2 was
able to 3 could (better than: was able to)
4 was able to 5 couldn't (better than: wasn't
able to) 6 couldn't (better than: wasn't able
to) 7 was able to 8 could

3 1 couldn't 2 couldn't 3 could 4 have been
able to 5 was able to 6 were able to

Unit 26

1 1b 2e 3i 4f 5g 6d 7a 8c 9h

2 1 Would you like a lift? 2 Would you like some?
3 Would you like me to show you how it works?
4 Would you like to borrow mine?
5 Would you like me to lend you some money?
6 Would you like to meet them?

7 Would you like me to invite her round for a
meal?
8 Would you like to come?

Unit 27

1 1 We had to be at Dover at 10.15.
2 We didn't have to queue.
3 I didn't have to take any seasick pills.
4 Normally you have to show your passport
when you enter a foreign country, but when
we got to Calais we didn't have to.
5 Every time I go to France I have to remind
myself to drive on the right.
6 You mustn't forget it.
7 The last ferry to Dover left at 11.00, so we
had to be at Calais by 10.30.

2 1 don't have to 2 mustn't cycle on the 3 must
be/have to be 4 don't have to pay for 5 must
take your litter 6 don't have to
7 must be/have to be, must have/have to have
8 mustn't walk on the 9 don't have to
10 must/have to, mustn't

3 1f 2e 3h 4g 5b 6a 7d 8c

4

You must/have to	You mustn't	You don't have to
A, G, H	D, F, I, K	B, C, E, J

Unit 28

1 1 She must be feeling worried.
2 She must be.
3 She can't be sleeping well.
4 She can't do.
5 She must think she's going to fail the exam.
6 Yes, that must be the problem.
7 She must know that.
8 She can't be feeling very confident, that's all
9 The exam must have been difficult.
10 She can't have done very well.

2 1 must have been 2 it can't have been 3 must
have cost 4 must have dropped 5 must have
left it 6 can't have left 7 must have damaged
8 must have been going 9 can't have been
concentrating

3 1 She must have done. 2 She must have been.
3 She can't have been. 4 She can't have done.

Unit 29

1 1 may not/might not 2 may/might/could
3 may/might/could 4 may not/might not
5 couldn't

2 1 may/could 2 may not 3 could 4 might have
5 couldn't 6 may have/might have

3 1 <u>couldn't</u> can't 2 <u>mightn't</u> couldn't 3 ✓
4 <u>might</u> could 5 <u>may</u> could 6 <u>wouldn't</u>
couldn't 7 ✓ 8 ✓

4 1 may not 2 may/could 3 couldn't 4 couldn't have 5 could 6 might have

5 1a, b, c 2a 3b 4c 5a 6a, c

Unit 30

1 1 She shouldn't (oughtn't to) work so hard.
2 She should (ought to) get home earlier.
3 She shouldn't (oughtn't to) smoke so much.
4 She shouldn't (oughtn't to) eat so much junk food.
5 She should (ought to) spend more time with her family.
6 And now she shouldn't be (oughtn't to be) driving (going) so fast.
7 She should (ought to) have both hands on the steering wheel.
8 She shouldn't be (oughtn't to be) eating a pizza when she's driving.

2 Possible answers
She should have told (ought to have told) her parents where she was going.
She should have looked (ought to have looked) at the bus timetable.
She should have (ought to have) got a taxi.
She shouldn't have walked (oughtn't to have walked) alone along the dark road.
She shouldn't have tried (oughtn't to have tried) to get into the concert without paying.
She shouldn't have behaved (oughtn't to have behaved) so stupidly.
She shouldn't have tried (oughtn't to have tried) to kiss the lead singer.
She shouldn't have refused (oughtn't to have refused) to pay the taxi driver.
He should have apologised (ought to have apologised).
She should have listened (ought to have listened) to her mother.

3 1d 2g 3f 4e 5a 6c 7b

4 1 I should have finished work by 4.15.
2 So I should be able to catch a bus at about 4.30.
3 There shouldn't be much traffic at that time.
4 So I should be able to meet you in town at 5.00.

Unit 31

1 1 has got 2 had 3 didn't have/hadn't got
4 had 5 I've got 6 It's got 7 hasn't got
8 haven't got 9 I've got 10 I'm having 11 I've only had 12 don't have 13 have 14 have
15 don't have 16 haven't got 17 have 18 are having/have 19 I've got 20 have ('ve) got
21 I've got 22 haven't had 23 had 24 didn't have/hadn't got 25 I've got 26 'll have/will have

2 1C 2A 3B 4C 5A 6B 7A 8B 9A 10B 11C 12A 13B 14A 15B 16C 17A 18C 19C

Unit 32

1 1 didn't get on with 2 get away 3 thought it over 4 get out 5 come back 6 was going out with 7 got up 8 picked up his girlfriend OR picked his girlfriend up 9 set off 10 ran out of 11 talked it over 12 went on 13 took off
14 pick them up 15 was going down 16 lay down 17 came up to 18 woke them up
19 hand them over

2 1 switches it off 2 stay in 3 puts it back
4 takes it down 5 stay up 6 takes it off
7 carries on 8 gets back 9 put up with

3 1 Turn it off. 2 You should give it up.
3 Take it off! 4 Put them away.
5 Why don't you throw them away?
6 Clear it up! 7 I can't put up with it any more.
8 You haven't paid it back yet. OR You haven't paid me back yet. 9 You haven't filled it in.
10 Why don't you ring him up?
11 Well, look it up in the telephone book!
12 I'm really looking forward to it.

Unit 33

1 1 He can still see the four walls of his cell.
2 He can still hear the sound of the prison guards shouting.
3 He can still feel the hard mattress on his bed.
4 He can still taste the awful prison food.
5 He can still smell the unwashed bodies of other prisoners.

2 1B 2C 3A 4B 5C

3 1 could hear 2 could see 3 could see 4 could see 5 couldn't hear 6 could smell 7 could taste 8 couldn't feel

4 1 could hear 2 could see 3 could smell 4 felt 5 felt 6 heard 7 couldn't hear 8 heard

5 1 slam 2 shouting 3 explode 4 burning
5 getting 6 coming 7 jump 8 approaching
9 take 10 put 11 beginning

Unit 34

1 1 I don't feel very well. 2 your face looks pale.
3 You sound terrible. 4 you seem worse today.
5 my forehead feels hot. 6 It doesn't smell very nice. 7 It tastes quite good.

2 1 What does it look like? 2 It looks like a book.
3 What does it feel like? 4 It feels like a box.
5 What does it sound like? 6 It sounds like chocolates/sweets.

3 1 of 2 of 3 of 4 like 5 like

4 1 Yes, I feel as if (as though) someone's hit me over the head.

2 I feel as if (as though) I could drink a whole
  bottle.
3 Oh, no. It doesn't look as if (as though) we've
  got any wine.
4 It looks as if (as though) we'll have to go to
  the pub.
5 I don't feel as if (as though) I could go out
  again this evening.
5 1g 2d 3h 4f 5e 6b 7a 8c

Unit 35

1 1 are there 2 There are 3 are there? 4 There's
  5 there's 6 Is there 7 there's 8 there isn't
  9 Is there 10 there isn't 11 there are 12 Is there
  13 there are 14 Are there 15 there aren't
2 1 ✓ 2 are (is) 3 's (are) 4 's (are) 5 There
  (They) 6 ✓ 7 's (are) 8 ✓

Unit 36

1 1 I used to be a history teacher.
  2 I didn't use to (OR used not to) travel much.
  3 I never used to go abroad.
  4 I didn't use to (OR used not to) have many.
  5 I never used to like getting up in the morning.
  6 I didn't use to (OR used not to) like hard work.
  7 My old pupils didn't use to (OR used not to) be
    interested in me.
2 1 used to 2 did they use to 3 used to 4 Did
  they use to 5 used to 6 used to 7 Did you use
  to 8 used to 9 didn't use to/used not to
  10 didn't use to/used not to 11 used to
  12 used to

Unit 37

1 1 He's used to seeing police officers without
    guns.
  2 He's used to getting free medical treatment.
  3 He is (He's) used to travelling by public
    transport.
  4 He still isn't used to having a small
    refrigerator.
  5 He still isn't used to living in a city centre.
2 1 Are you used to being rich yet?/Have you got
    used to being rich yet?
  2 to get used to 3 I was used to getting up
  4 I can't get used to staying
  5 Are you used to living/Have you got used to
    living
  6 I soon got used to 7 get used to living
  8 I'm not used to being/I haven't got used to
    being 9 I'll never get used to
  10 I'll ever get used to spending

Unit 38

1 1 Every year Doris Slocombe sends her sister
    Mary a birthday card.
  2 Last week she gave the card to her husband
    George.
  3 Two days later Mary sent a letter to Doris.
  4 She told her some shocking news.
  5 The postman had only given her half the card.
  6 He told Mary the reason.
2 a) 1 for 2 to 3 for 4 for 5 for 6 to 7 to
  b) 1 Make everyone some coffee.
    2 Send the producer this fax.
    3 Buy me a packet of cigarettes.
    4 Book me a table at Doyle's Bar.
    5 Order me a taxi for 6.30.
    6 Give my assistant this note.
    7 Take the editor this reel of film.

Unit 39

1 1 She doesn't need a (her) French dictionary.
  2 She needs an (her) English grammar (book).
  3 She needs her passport.
  4 She doesn't need (her/any) sun cream.
  5 She needs an (her) umbrella.
  6 She needs her (airline/plane) ticket.
  7 She doesn't need a (her) bikini.
  8 She needs her (some) English money
    (currency).
2 1 Do you need to/Will you need to 2 didn't
  need 3 just need to/'ll just need to 4 will you
  need to/do you need to 5 won't need to/don't
  need to/needn't 6 won't need to/don't need
  to/needn't 7 Do you need 8 don't need
  to/needn't 9 do you need to/will you need to
  10 don't need to/won't need to/needn't 11 just
  need/'ll just need 12 need 13 didn't need
3 1f 2e 3h 4d 5a 6c 7g 8b
4 1B 2D 3B 4B 5A 6A

Unit 40

1 1 If he leaves the window open, the mosquitoes
    will get into the room.
  2 If he closes the window, there'll be no fresh
    air in the room.
  3 If he takes off his pyjamas, he'll have
    mosquito bites all over his body.
  4 If he doesn't take off his pyjamas, he'll be too
    hot.
  5 If he tries to sleep in a cold bath, he might
    drown.
2 1 What will I do if my train's late?
  2 What will I do if I can't get a taxi?
  3 What will I do if the interviewer doesn't like
    me?
  4 What will I do if she asks difficult questions?

5 What will I do if they don't offer me the job?

3 1 I get embarrassed if people say nice things about me.

2 I don't feel good if I'm not wearing smart clothes.

3 If anyone criticises me, I feel guilty.

4 If my boyfriend doesn't listen to me, it makes me angry.

4 1 It would be better if you went on your own.

2 If you went with a group of English friends, you wouldn't speak much Spanish.

3 If you went on your own, you wouldn't be able to speak English.

4 You'd learn the language quickly if you stayed with a Spanish family.

5 If you had a Spanish boyfriend, you'd soon speak Spanish well!

5 2 <u>was</u> (would be) 3 <u>leaves</u> (left) 4 ✓
5 <u>would have</u> (had) 6 <u>will get</u> (gets)

Unit 41

1 1A 2B 3C 4A 5D 6C 7B 8D 9C 10A

2 1 If my parents hadn't been poor, I'd have had more clothes.

2 If I hadn't missed a lot of school lessons, I could have learned more.

3 If I'd been more clever, I'd have done better at school.

4 If I'd passed some exams, I might have got a well-paid job.

5 If I hadn't been shy, I'd have had more friends.

6 If I hadn't worked on a farm, I'd have fought in the war.

7 If I'd left this village, I could have got a better job.

8 If I'd got married, I might have had some children.

3 1 If I'd (had) been standing under the tree, I'd (would) have been killed. I wouldn't be here now.

2 If I hadn't been feeling ill, he wouldn't have spoken to me. And we wouldn't be living together now.

3 If I'd (had) been watching the road, I wouldn't have hit that car.

4 If I hadn't been feeling tired, they'd (would) have offered me the job. I'd (would) be in Australia now. I'd (would) be surfing on Bondi Beach.

Unit 42

1 1 unless he stops smoking.

2 unless he lets her pay for herself.

3 unless he phones her every day.

4 unless he's prepared to talk about them.

5 unless he answers her honestly.

2 1 You can go in provided/as long as/providing you've got/you have a ticket.

2 Under 7s can swim as long as/provided/ providing they're accompanied by an adult.

3 You can park in the street providing/as long as/provided you're a resident.

4 You can travel in this compartment provided/as long as/providing you don't smoke.

3 3 provided/providing/as long as
4 provided/providing/as long as   5 unless
6 provided/providing/as long as   7 unless
8 unless   9 provided/providing/as long as
10 unless   11 provided/providing/as long as

4 1 I'll pack my case now in case I don't have time tomorrow morning.

2 I'll take my hair dryer in case there isn't one at the hotel.

3 I'll take my winter coat in case it's cold in the evening.

4 I'll phone to confirm my hotel booking in case they didn't get (haven't got) my letter.

5 I'll take Andrea's phone number in case she isn't at the airport to meet me.

6 I'll book a taxi now in case there aren't any available at 8.00 tomorrow.

Unit 43

1 1 I wish my sister would turn the television down.

2 If only my brother would stop playing his music so loudly.

3 I wish my mother would stop coming up to my room. OR I wish my mother wouldn't keep coming up to my room.

4 If only she wouldn't worry so much.

5 I wish I knew what the exam questions were.

6 If only I didn't have to do the exam.

2 1 I wish I'd (had) gone to university.

2 I wish I'd (had) learned/learnt a foreign language.

3 I wish I'd (had) travelled to more foreign countries.

4 I wish I'd (had) read more books.

5 I wish I'd (had) had a more interesting job.

6 I wish I'd (had) married the first girl I fell in love with.

7 I wish I'd (had) had a son as well as three daughters.

3 2 I wish it would stop raining.

3 If only I had more money.

4 If only I lived in the country.

5 I wish I hadn't forgotten my raincoat.

6 I wish I hadn't bought so many things.

Unit 44

1 1 To protect his property.
  2 To reduce the cost of his insurance.
  3 To pay for (To buy) the alarm system.
  4 To get into the house.
  5 To stop it activating the alarm.
2 2 She wants a friend to go out with.
  3 She's only got her cat to keep her company.
  4 There's nowhere to spend it.
  5 She wants someone to share her life with.
3 1 To reduce his energy costs/In order to reduce
  2 So as not to lose any heat
  3 In order to keep fit/To keep fit
  4 so that/so he can leave his car at home.
  5 in order to reduce air pollution/to reduce air pollution 6 In order to travel less
  7 so that/so he can communicate OR in order to be able to communicate
  8 to make sure 9 So as not to waste anything
  10 so that/so it can be used on the garden
  11 so that/so they can be used again
  12 so that/so he can take it 13 to tell the world
4 1 so that/so 2 to/in order to 3 to/in order to
  4 so as not to OR so that/so she doesn't 5 so as not to OR so that/so she doesn't 6 so that/so

Unit 45

1 1 to come 2 to see 3 to pay 4 to leave 5 to be
  6 not to have 7 to admit 8 (to) tell 9 to worry
  10 to talk 11 not to understand 12 to let 13 to change 14 to leave 15 to give up 16 give it up
  17 to play 18 to earn
2 1 She doesn't know where to put her dirty clothes.
  2 She doesn't understand how to set the alarm clock.
  3 She wants to know what time to get up in the morning.
  4 She hasn't discovered how to use the dishwasher yet.
  5 They haven't discussed how much to pay her yet.
  6 She's never learned how to cook food in a microwave.
  7 She's wondering where to go to learn more English.
  8 She hasn't decided what to do on her day off.
3 1 to 2 where 3 how 4 where 5 who 6 what
  7 which 8 how

Unit 46

1 1 We don't expect students to attend all the lessons.
  2 We encourage students to choose what they want to do.

  3 We teach students to have self-respect and respect for others.
  4 We don't force students to do homework.
  5 We ask all students to help with the cooking and the cleaning.
2 1 a) She wants Amy to finish her lunch.
    b) 'I want you to finish your lunch.'
  2 a) She wants the students to listen.
    b) 'I want you to listen.'
  3 a) He wants the patient to open her mouth.
    b) 'I want you to open your mouth.'
  4 a) He wanted his student to turn right.
    b) 'I wanted you to turn right.'
3 1 (first) to 2 (first) for 3 ✓ 4 ✓ 5 that 6 I
  7 of 8 ✓
4 1 I'd like you to help
  2 What do you want me to do?
  3 I'd like you to stand 4 I want you to make
  5 I'd hate you to think 6 I'd prefer you to ask
  7 Would you prefer to go 8 wants me to post
  9 Would you like me to show
  10 I want someone to help
  11 I'd prefer you not to say
  12 Do you want me to show

Unit 47

1 1 It's cheaper to stay in a bed and breakfast.
  2 It's expensive to hire a car in July and August.
  3 It isn't easy to park in the town centres.
  4 It would be sensible to buy a map of the area.
  5 It's wonderful to walk along the cliffs.
  6 You'd be silly not to visit Land's End.
  7 It's advisable not to leave valuables in your car. OR It's not advisable to leave …
  8 You'll be disappointed to know that I won't be here in July.
2 1 It's common for young children to shout sometimes.
  2 It's rare for children to eat everything you give them.
  3 It's important for young children to have a lot of freedom.
  4 It's difficult for you to understand until you have children of your own.
3 1 It was generous of Alan (him) to give the woman (her) £20.
  2 It was dishonest of her to tell him (Alan) she was homeless. OR It was dishonest of her to say she was homeless.
  3 It was stupid of her to spend his money on things she didn't need.
  4 It was silly of Alan (him) not to ask her why she wanted the money.
  5 It was wrong of her to laugh at him.
4 1 It's good of you to come.
  2 It was nice of you to phone yesterday.

3 It isn't easy for me to walk.
4 It's difficult to say.
5 It's hard not to laugh, really.
6 I'm always happy to help.
7 Would it be possible for you to scratch my right foot?

Unit 48

1 1 They let them go to bed when they like.
2 They let them watch anything they like on television.
3 They aren't made to go to school.
4 They let them stay at home if they want to.
5 They let their eldest daughter go out with a man ten years older than her.
2 1 makes me laugh. 2 makes me happy.
3 makes me angry. 4 lets me decide 5 doesn't let me pay 6 make me wear 7 doesn't let me wear 8 makes me impatient 9 make him hurry.

Unit 49

1 1 going 2 doing 3 washing 4 filling 5 working
6 changing 7 getting 8 leaving 9 sitting
10 playing/buying 11 learning
12 brushing/cleaning
2 2 He's going windsurfing. 3 She's going swimming. 4 They're going fishing.

Unit 50

1 1 After leaving school, I studied physics at university.
2 Before starting work, I spent a year travelling in Asia. OR After spending a year travelling in Asia, I started work.
3 In India I paid for my food and accommodation by giving English lessons.
4 I got back to England last month without knowing what I was going to do.
2 1 Are you fed up with not having a girlfriend?
2 Are you keen on improving your chances?
3 Are you worried about saying the wrong thing?
4 Are you angry about losing that last girl ...?
5 Are you interested in knowing all the answers?
3 1A 2D 3C 4C 5D 6A 7C 8B
4 1 about (with) 2 do (doing) 3 ✓
4 with (for) 5 get (getting) 6 ✓ 7 ✓
8 save (saving)

Unit 51

1 1 Would you mind showing me your passport?
2 Would you mind leaving your passport with me?
3 Would you mind filling in the registration card?

4 Would you mind putting my travellers cheques in the hotel safe?
5 Would you mind ordering me a taxi?
2 1 Would/Do you mind looking after 2 won't mind/wouldn't mind you reading 3 I don't mind staying 4 would/do you mind cleaning 5 don't mind doing 6 didn't mind cooking
3 1 flying 2 being/feeling 3 sitting 4 going 5 eating

Unit 52

1 1 seeing, finding (to see + to find are possible but less natural)
2 answering, not knowing
3 waking up, going back (to wake up + to go back are possible, but less natural)
4 putting, getting (to put + to get are possible, but less natural)
5 talking (to talk is possible, but less natural)
2 1 writing, to write 2 to revise 3 talking, to phone 4 to keep 5 asking
3 1 I'd like to go on 2 I'd hate to give up 3 I'd like to move 4 I wouldn't like to live 5 I'd hate to lose touch 6 I'd love to go 7 I wouldn't like to spend 8 I'd like to leave 9 I wouldn't like to have won 10 I'd hate to have been 11 He'd love to have gone

Unit 53

1 1 crying 2 bleeding 3 holding 4 screaming 5 sending 6 treating 7 trying
2 1 In May she had a car accident coming home from work.
2 In June her father had a heart attack playing tennis.
3 In August she broke her arm falling down the stairs.
4 In October she nearly electrocuted herself trying to mend her guitar amplifier.
3 1d 2e 3a 4c 5b
4 1 Having beaten the eggs, add a little salt and pepper to them.
2 Having chopped the mushrooms, add them to the eggs.
3 Having melted the butter in the frying pan, pour in the mixture.
4 Having cooked the omelette for three minutes, serve it with a little fresh parsley.
5 1 Now, not being able (OR being unable) to find a job, he spends most of his time at home.
2 One day last month, having nothing to do (OR not having anything to do), he bought some juggling balls.
3 After two weeks, having practised three hours a day, he could juggle five balls.

4 Feeling that this might be his career, he practises regularly every day.

5 His friends, having seen him juggle, think that he could earn some money as an entertainer.

6 This week, having done three performances, he's earned over £150.

7 Being a very cautious person, Tim has put half the money in the bank.

8 Having found something he can do well, Tim's now a lot happier than he was.

Unit 54

1 1 Jerry Griggs prefers reading to watching television OR Jerry Griggs prefers to read rather than watch television.

2 Katherine Griggs prefers riding a bike to driving a car. OR Katherine Griggs prefers to ride a bike rather than drive a car.

3 Tim prefers playing football to watching it (on TV). OR Tim prefers to play football rather than watch it (on TV).

4 Jessica prefers playing computer games to studying. OR Jessica prefers to play computer games rather than study.

2 1 I'd rather not live in this flat. OR I'd prefer not to live in this flat.

2 I'd prefer to be in a ground-floor flat rather than this one.

3 I'd rather not have to do that. OR I'd prefer not to have to do that.

4 I'd rather be married. OR I'd prefer to be married.

5 I'd rather have some children. OR I'd prefer to have some children.

6 I'd rather talk to people than watch television.

3 1 Gabby, I'd prefer you not to pull Beth's hair.

2 Jessica, I'd rather you didn't eat your lunch on the floor.

3 Jack, I'd rather your feet were on the floor, not on Matthew's head.

4 Alice, I'd prefer you to talk quietly rather than shout like that.

5 Nicola, I'd rather you ate your sandwiches than threw them at Amy.

6 Carla, I'd prefer you to sit on your chair rather than stand on the table.

7 Neil, I'd rather your coat was in the cloakroom than on my desk.

8 Charles, I'd rather you didn't pour your orange juice over Zoe.

4 1B 2B 3D 4A 5A 6C

Unit 55

1 1 to stay 2 to enjoy 3 to get 4 to put/putting 5 to have/having

2 1 to have 2 repairing 3 talking 4 talking 5 working 6 to go 7 to make 8 to light 9 leaving 10 to revive 11 shaking 12 deceiving 13 seeing

3 1 I regret leaving school when I was only 16.

2 I didn't even try to go to university.

3 I regret not working hard when I was at school.

4 I forgot to go to the last class reunion.

5 I went on working in a (the) supermarket till I had a baby.

6 He went on to become a professional player.

7 I'll never forget meeting him a year ago in a London night club.

8 I've stopped smoking now.

Unit 56

1 1 She said she could see a man. She said he was my uncle Walter who died/had died in 1994.

2 I told her I'd never had an uncle Walter.

3 She said I often went/I'd often been to see him in Manchester.

4 I told her I'd never been to Manchester. I said I didn't know anyone in Manchester.

5 She said I must/had to try to remember. She told me he had given me/gave me the necklace I was wearing.

6 I told her that nobody had given/gave me the necklace. I said I'd bought/I bought it myself.

7 She said the man looked sad because I hadn't gone to his funeral. She said he was trying to give me a message. But he couldn't speak.

8 I told her I was sorry, but she'd made a mistake.

9 She said the man would come to see me again in a dream.

2 1 You said you couldn't live without me.

2 You said you'd never leave me.

3 You said I was the only one for you.

4 You said you felt fine when you were with me.

5 You said you wouldn't ever be untrue.

6 You said you'd never felt that way before.

3 1 you said you couldn't give me the money then, but you'd pay me back the next day or the following week.

2 You said you'd (had) done (OR you did) some temporary work for a travel agency the week before (OR the previous week), and you thought they were going to pay you that day.

3 You said you'd (would) certainly be able to give me £50, and you hoped that would be all right.

4 You told me you were really sorry you hadn't paid me back yet.

5 You said I could phone you that night if I wanted to talk about it.

6 You said you wouldn't go out till I'd (had) phoned.

Unit 57

1 Robert asked if he could speak to Tess. Jill said she was sorry but Tess wasn't in. She asked him who was speaking. He told her/said his name was Robert and asked her what time Tess would be back. Jill told him/said she wouldn't be back till ten. Robert asked if/whether she could give Tess a message, and ask her to ring him. Jill asked him what his number was. He told her it was 9298465. Jill asked him what time he went to bed and he said he wouldn't be in bed before midnight.

2 1 He asked to see my driving licence.
2 He told me to start the engine.
3 He reminded me that there was a 30 mph speed limit in town.
4 He suggested (that) I drove a little more slowly.
5 He told me not to drive so fast.
6 He threatened to get out and walk if I didn't drive more slowly.

3 He asked her if/whether she had any beds free (for) that night. She said (that) she had. She offered him a bed in a room with four other people. He said that was OK. She then asked (him) how many nights he wanted to stay. He replied (that) he only wanted to stay for one night. She told him that breakfast was at 8.00 and added that he must (OR had to) make his own bed. She warned him that alcohol wasn't allowed in the hostel. He promised (that) he wouldn't be late for breakfast. (OR He promised not to be late for breakfast.) She offered to look after his passport and valuables if he wanted. She explained that it was a bit risky leaving them in his room. She reminded him to collect them before he left.

Unit 58

1 1 The River Nile is the longest river in the world.
2 The Volga is the longest river in Europe.
3 Mount Kilimanjaro is the highest mountain in Africa.
4 Downing Street is the residence of Britain's Prime Minister.
5 The White House is where the President of the USA lives.
6 The rich and the famous stay at the Ritz Hotel in London.

7 Trafalgar Square is the most famous square in London.
8 The English, the French and the Spanish colonised the West Indies.
1h 2d 3f 4e 5b 6g 7c 8a

2 1 (the last year) 2 (the last April) 3 (the Leicester Square) 4 (After the lunch) 5 ✓
6 (The last month) 7 (the Russian) 8 ✓ 9 (by the bus) 10 (The next summer)

3 1a 2 the 3 the 4 the 5a 6 The 7a 8a 9a 10 the 11a 12a 13a 14a 15 the 16a 17 the 18 the

4 5 the 8 the 9 the 14 the

Unit 59

1 1 General 2 Particular 3 Particular 4 General 5 General 6 Particular 7 General 8 Particular 9 General 10 Particular (used in a general sense)

2 1 (the wine) 2 ✓ 3 (the diesel) 4 (The unemployment) 5 (the sex) 6 (the British television) 7 ✓

3 1 The ozone layer that protects the Earth from radiation has been damaged by (the) CFC gases coming from aerosols and refrigerators.
2 Scientists believe that emissions of carbon dioxide are causing global warming, and that temperatures will continue to rise worldwide.
3 Water is being polluted. Fertilisers and pesticides are killing (the) fish and insect life in the world's rivers. The oceans of the world are full of industrial waste.
4 Acid rain caused by air pollution is damaging forest trees and plant growth.
5 The world's rain forests are disappearing because of the demand for hardwoods, and millions of hectares are burnt every year to provide farming land.
6 Energy resources, like oil and coal, are being rapidly exhausted, and the burning of these fuels adds to atmospheric pollution.
7 (The) Air pollution in big cities is mainly caused by cars.

Unit 60

1 1 An hour and a half. 2 A one-way ticket.
3 A European. 4 An American. 5 A university.
6 It's an easy job. 7 A hotel. 8 An uncomfortable bed. 9 An orchestra. 10 An honest person. 11 A used car. 12 A history teacher.

2 2 an 5 an 7 a 8 Some 10 a 11 a 14 Some 17 some 19 a 20 Some

3 'I'm (a) Russian. I'm an architect. But I haven't got a job at the moment. Getting a job is a problem for me, because jobs for architects aren't easy to find in Russia at the moment. I haven't got rich parents, so I must find work soon. Some Russian architects go abroad to find jobs. I've got an American friend in California who has offered me a job with his company that builds swimming pools. I want to speak good English before I go to the USA. My friend is very successful. He makes a lot of money. He's got an enormous house near the beach at Malibu. I hope I'll be rich like him in a few years.'

Unit 61

1 1 two American wives 2 three children 3 two electronics factories 4 two computer companies 5 two large houses 6 two parties 7 three men, two women, six gorillas 8 two people, twelve pet monkeys

2 1 men 2 wives 3 women 4 children 5 babies 6 cities 7 churches 8 thousand 9 coaches 10 mountains 11 valleys 12 tomatoes 13 loaves 14 tomato sandwiches 15 bottles 16 hundred 17 flies 18 mosquitoes 19 feet 20 crashes 21 ladies 22 teeth 23 people 24 lives 25 addresses

3 1 ✓ 2 were (was) 3 (first) were (was) 4 aren't (isn't) 5 ✓ 6 was (were) 7 was (were) 8 weren't (wasn't) 9 ✓ 10 was (were) 11 ✓

Unit 62

1 1 children (countable) 2 freedom (uncountable) 3 problem (countable) 4 furniture (uncountable) 5 doctor (countable) 6 satisfaction (uncountable) 7 sleep (uncountable) 8 love (uncountable) 9 egg (countable)

2 1B 2B 3A 4C 5A 6C 7A
Uncountable

advice	warmth
money	love
happiness	knowledge
progress	travel
work	independence
furniture	tolerance

3 1 some 2 – 3 a 4 is 5 a 6 is 7 a 8 – 9 a 10 –

Unit 63

1

1 much	a lot
2 much	not much
3 many	a lot/a few
4 many/a lot	very few
5 many/a lot of	a lot
6 many/a lot	a few
7 many	A lot
8 many	Very few

2 1 ✓ 2 ✓ 3 little (few) 4 much (many) 5 many (a few/a lot) 6 ✓ 7 Much (A lot) 8 much (many) 9 little (few) 10 ✓ 11 much (many) 12 ✓ 13 many (much) 14 few (little) 15 ✓ 16 few (little)

3 1b 2f 3d 4c 5e 6a

4 1 There's plenty of fruit 2 There's plenty of wood. 3 there's plenty of fresh water 4 There are plenty of fish 5 There are plenty of ships

Unit 64

1 1 any 2 some 3 any 4 any 5 any 6 none 7 some 8 no 9 some 10 any 11 some 12 none 13 some 14 no 15 no 16 no 17 some 18 any

2 1 There weren't any buses or trains.
2 There aren't any flights out of Bristol Airport today.
3 And there'll be no trains to London.
4 There aren't any places left in the city car parks.
5 And there's no movement on the M5 at Junction 19.
6 Union officials see no chance of a breakthrough in negotiations.
7 So there won't be any improvement in the situation today.

3 1 Have you got any mineral water?
2 Could I have some apples?
3 Have you got any salt?
4 Could I have some sugar?
5 Could I have some sausages?

4 1 some 2 any 3 any 4 some 5 any 6 any 7 any

Unit 65

1 1 everybody/everyone 2 All 3 everybody/everyone 4 Everything (All) 5 Everybody/Everyone 6 everything 7 everybody/everyone 8 everything 9 All 10 everything 11 all 12 Everybody/Everyone

2 1 is 2 costs 3 was 4 was 5 has 6 ignores

3 1 All 2 each (every) 3 Every (Each) 4 each 5 every 6 All 7 every (each) 8 Every (Each) 9 all 10 all 11 all

4 1 the whole/all 2 all 3 the whole/all 4 the whole 5 the whole/all 6 a whole 7 all 8 all 9 all 10 the whole/all 11 All 12 all 13 all

5 1 all 2 Every 3 all 4 all 5 all 6 Every

Unit 66

1 1 Most British people 2 Some of them 3 many of them 4 all of them 5 a few of them 6 most British tourists 7 all British tourists 8 some of my friends 9 most of the time 10 A few of the people 11 any of them 12 half (of) the time 13 half (of) the time 14 none of the taxi drivers 15 most Amalfi taxi drivers 16 a lot of them 17 some customers 18 much effort 19 All tourists 20 all (of) the time

2 1 False 2 False 3 True 4 False 5 False 6 False 7 False 8 True 9 False 10 True 11 Both/Both of 12 either of 13 Neither 14 Both of 15 Both

3 1 We were all tired after the journey.
2 We all went to bed as soon as we arrived at the hotel.
3 After sleeping for three hours both Sophie and I were feeling hungry. OR After sleeping for three hours Sophie and I were both feeling hungry.
4 We both hate airline food, so we'd both eaten nothing on the plane.
5 We both decided to have a sandwich at the hotel bar.
6 'Do you both want relish with the sandwich?'
7 I wasn't sure what relish was, so we both said no.
8 The others were all feeling energetic, so they all went for a swim in the hotel pool. OR All the others were feeling energetic, so ...

Unit 67

1 1 These 2 that 3 That's 4 those 5 those 6 this

2 1 that 2 This 3 this 4 this 5 these 6 that's 7 this 8 that 9 That 10 that 11 those 12 this 13 this

3 1 that 2 these 3 that 4 those 5 That 6 this 7 That 8 that 9 that 10 these 11 this 12 this 13 this 14 these

Unit 68

1 1 yourself 2 myself 3 themselves 4 ourselves 5 himself 6 himself 7 itself 8 himself 9 himself

2 1B 2A 3B or C 4B 5A 6C 7C 8A 9C 10C 11B 12 A 13B 14A 15A 16C 17B 18A

3 1 He must iron them himself.
2 They must tidy them themselves.
3 You must make it yourself.
4 You must clean them yourself.
5 You must do it yourselves.
6 You must make them yourselves.

4 1 themselves 2 ourselves 3 each other 4 each other 5 each other 6 ourselves

7 ourselves 8 each other 9 themselves 10 each other

Unit 69

1 1 anyone/anybody 2 someone/somebody 3 anyone/anybody 4 someone/somebody 5 anyone/anybody 6 someone/somebody 7 something 8 anyone/anybody 9 somewhere 10 someone/somebody

2 1 somewhere 2 someone/somebody 3 anyone/anybody 4 someone/somebody 5 anyone/anybody 6 anything 7 something 8 anything 9 something 10 anywhere 11 somewhere 12 something

3 1 No-one/Nobody 2 no-one/nobody 3 nowhere 4 no-one/nobody 5 nothing

4 1 anywhere 2 Anything 3 Anything 4 Anyone/Anybody 5 Anything 6 Anywhere

5 1 anything anyone/anybody 2 ✓ 3 nothing no-one/nobody 4 anyone anything 5 ✓ 6 something nothing 7 ✓

6 1 nothing 2 somewhere 3 nobody 4 anything 5 someone 6 something 7 nowhere 8 anywhere 9 anyone

Unit 70

1 1 They're the Kay sisters'. 2 It's Sam and Zoe's. 3 They're Sarah's. 4 It's Anna's. 5 It's the Taylor twins'.

2 2 ✓ 3 customers' 4 grandparents' 5 ✓ 6 cousin's 7 children's 8 ✓ 9 of (being a single parent) 10 of (her job) 11 of (her situation) 12 women's 13 of (a man) 14 Laura's 15 today's

3 1 His bedroom walls 2 Mick Jagger posters 3 Rolling Stones albums 4 his garage door 5 His car registration number 6 his car radio 7 Rolling Stones fans

4 1 a friend of yours 2 a friend of my sister's 3 a CD of mine 4 a video of his

Unit 71

1 1 your 2 yours 3 Mine 4 hers 5 theirs 6 my 7 yours

2 1 our 2 my 3 his 4 his 5 hers 6 their 7 ours

3 1 It's 2 It's 3 its 4 its 5 It's 6 its 7 it's 8 it's 9 Its 10 its 11 its 12 it's

4 1 Whose is this jacket? OR Whose jacket is this? 2 Is it yours, Justin? 3 No, it isn't mine. 4 Whose are these CDs? OR Whose CDs are these? 5 No, they aren't hers. 6 They're probably his.

5 1 my own 2 their own 3 its own 4 their own 5 his own 6 her own 7 their own

Unit 72

1 1 It's cold and it's raining. 2 It's boring.
3 It would be nice to go to the cinema.
4 It takes 35 minutes to walk to the Odeon
cinema. 5 It's obvious that the bus is (would
be) quicker. 6 It's five to two. 7 It would be
safer to catch the bus.
2 1 They 2 you 3 you 4 They 5 they 6 they
7 They 8 You 9 you 10 you 11 they 12 you
13 you 14 you 15 You 16 they
3 1g 2f 3e 4i 5h 6j 7a 8c 9d 10b
4 1 It's time to board the flight to Madrid.
2 It's 50 metres to Gate 36.
3 You must (have to) show your passport.
4 You mustn't smoke.

Unit 73

1 'Which one did you go to?'
'The one on Woodstock Road.'
'Which one did you see?'
'The new one with Brad Pitt in it.'
'Which one did you go to?'
'The one opposite the cinema.'
'Which ones did you go to?'
'The ones in Walton Street.'
2 1 a bigger one 2 one 3 ones 4 The one 5 one
6 (some) clean ones 7 one with a sea view
3 1 The one in the middle. OR The black one.
2 The one on the right. 3 The white one.
4 The ones made in Europe. 5 The black one.
OR The one in the middle.
4 1C (A) 2C (A) 3A 4A 5A 6C
7C 8B 9C 10A

Unit 74

1 1B 2A 3A 4B 5A 6B
2 1 a good-looking young man
2 long dark curly hair
3 ✓ 4 a beautiful old Devon village
5 an interesting well-paid job
6 hard-working and successful 7 ✓ 8 ✓
9 an enormous old American car
3 1 La Rocca is a charming Sicilian family hotel.
2 It's a short ten-minute walk from the town.
3 The hotel stands above its own lovely
sheltered sandy beach.
4 The atmosphere is warm and friendly.
5 The restaurant offers first-class traditional
Sicilian cuisine.
6 The tennis court is floodlit and free of charge.
7 There's a big palm-fringed fresh-water
swimming pool.
8 There are 14 spacious air-conditioned
bedrooms.

4 2 And it'll be ten metres wide.
3 The water at the deep end will be three
metres deep.
4 The water at the shallow end will be one
metre deep.
5 The diving board will be four metres high.

Unit 75

1 1 Melbourne's population is smaller than
Sydney's.
2 Sydney is older than Melbourne.
3 Melbourne is hotter than Sydney in January.
4 Melbourne's much drier than Sydney.
5 Houses in Sydney are more expensive than in
Melbourne.
6 Melbourne is further south than Sydney.
2 1 Katherine is the youngest.
2 Luke is the tallest.
3 Katherine is the shortest.
4 Mark is the heaviest.
5 Katherine is the lightest.
3 1 The Mississippi is the longest river.
2 Mount McKinley, Alaska, is the highest
mountain.
3 Hawaii is the newest state.
4 The Sears Tower, Chicago, is the tallest
building.
5 New York is the biggest city.
6 Baseball is the most popular sport.
7 Death Valley, California is the driest place.
8 Washington, D.C. is the most densely
populated state.
4 1 the most annoying, more annoying 2 the
worst thing, the best-looking 3 The most
irritating, nearer and nearer 4 more irritating,
shorter 5 more angry/angrier, longer

Unit 76

1 1 False 2 True 3 True 4 False 5 True 6 False
7 True 8 False 9 True 10 True 11 True
12 False
2 1 more and more carbon dioxide 2 More and
more ice 3 more and more people 4 more and
more worried 5 The more time we waste, the
worse it will be 6 bigger and bigger 7 more
and more common 8 The longer people lie, the
more probable it is 9 The sooner we all realise,
the better.
3 1C 2B 3C 4A 5B 6A 7C
4 1b 2e 3f 4g 5d 6c 7a

Unit 77

1 1 horrifying 2 boring 3 satisfied 4 depressed
5 worrying 6 disappointing 7 annoyed
8 exhausted 9 tired 10 surprised
11 surprising 12 shocked 13 confused
14 damaged 15 amazing 16 interested
17 shocking 18 damaged 19 horrified
2 1 exciting OR interesting 2 boring 3 tired
4 excited 5 interesting OR exciting
6 disgusting 7 embarrassed 8 annoying
9 surprised 10 amazed 11 interested
3 1 tiring OR boring 2 disgusting 3 depressed
4 shocked OR amazed 5 annoyed

Unit 78

1 1 regularly 2 carefully 3 well 4 badly 5 easily
6 unfortunately 7 definitely 8 properly
9 probably 10 quickly
2 1 hard 2 hardly 3 first 4 right 5 highly
6 freely 7 free 8 early 9 late 10 lately 11 late
12 straight
3 1 Sarah Wright's been getting a lot of junk mail
lately. (OR *Lately* Sarah Wright's been getting
a lot of junk mail.)
2 *Nearly* every day she gets letters trying to
sell her double-glazed windows or medical
insurance.
3 They've *probably* found her address in the
telephone book.
4 Or *perhaps* her name and address is on a
national computer database.
5 Sarah thinks it's an *absolutely* ridiculous
waste of paper.
6 *Actually* it *really* makes her furious.
(OR *Actually* it makes her *really* furious.)
7 She *angrily* throws all the letters *straight* into
the bin.
8 She's *politely* asked the companies to stop
writing to her.
9 But she *probably* won't be able to stop them.
10 *Unfortunately* it's happening more and more
in Britain. (OR It's happening more and more
in Britain, *unfortunately.)*
11 Sarah *definitely* doesn't want double glazed
windows or medical insurance.
12 She *simply* can't afford to pay for them.

Unit 79

1 1 In Los Angeles it's *always* summer. London
occasionally has a summer.
2 In Los Angeles it *hardly ever* rains in summer.
In London it *rarely* stops raining.
3 In Los Angeles the temperature *seldom* falls
below 25°. In Britain it *occasionally* reaches
25°.

2
JENNY: How often do you come *here*?
MIKE: I *usually* come *every Friday*.
JENNY: This is my first visit. I don't *usually* listen to
jazz, but I've *always* wanted to come to this
club. Have you *always* liked jazz?
MIKE: Yes, I've got my own jazz band. We *often*
play *here*. In fact, we played *here yesterday*.
JENNY: Did you? What instrument do you play?
MIKE: I *normally* play the tenor sax. And I
sometimes play the keyboard too.
3 1B 2A 3C 4B 5A 6C 7A 8B 9A

Unit 80

1 1 quite fairly 2 quite rather 3 quite rather
4 rather quite 5 rather quite 6 fairly quite
7 pretty rather 8 quite pretty rather
9 quite pretty 10 quite fairly
2 1c 2g 3e 4a 5d 6b 7f
3 1 Saint Lucia is such a fabulous island.
2 It's got such a wonderful climate.
3 The Saint Lucians are such friendly people.
4 The food was so good.
5 The fruit there was so cheap.
6 There was such a lot to do.
7 It was such an amazing experience.
8 I had such a good time (that) I didn't want to
come home.
9 It's such a long flight.
10 The flight was so uncomfortable (that) I
couldn't sleep.
11 And the flight was so expensive (that) I won't
be able to afford to go next year.

Unit 81

1 1A 2B 3B 4C 5C 6A 7B
2 1 I like living here *so much.*
2 I like the summer, but I like the winter *more.*
3 I think I like February *best.*
4 And I like August *least.*
5 In summer I don't talk to my friends *much.*
6 Life in the winter is *a lot* OR *very much* slower
and *very much* OR *a lot* quieter.
7 I get *a bit* bored sometimes. 8 I paint *a little.*
9 I also write *a bit.* 10 I used to write *a lot.*
11 But nowadays I write *much less.*
3 1 very much 2 less 3 more 4 worse 5 more
6 better 7 best 8 most 9 least

Unit 82

1 1 Yes, we haven't finished our breakfast yet.
2 No, I'm still in the bathroom.
3 Yes, I'm still getting dressed.
4 She's still in bed.
5 They haven't finished their homework yet.

6 I haven't made my sandwiches yet.

2 1 She hasn't prepared her talk yet. She's still got to prepare her talk.
2 She hasn't ordered her foreign currency yet. She's still got to order her foreign currency.
3 She hasn't been to the hairdresser's yet. She's still got to go to the hairdresser's.
4 She hasn't bought a new suitcase yet. She's still got to buy a new suitcase.

3 1 He still hasn't paid me back.
2 He still hasn't replied.
3 I'm still waiting for an interview.
4 I still can't see very well.
5 I'm still not feeling well.

4 1 still, any more 2 no longer, any more/any longer 3 still, yet, any more 4 yet, still, any more, still, yet

Unit 83

1 1 Some drivers don't drive fast enough.
2 Some drivers don't overtake carefully enough.
3 Some people drive too close to the car in front.
4 Some drivers aren't experienced enough.
5 The present driving test isn't difficult enough.

2 1 early enough 2 long enough 3 enough money 4 big enough 5 enough balls 6 enough strawberries 7 enough fine days 8 good enough

3 1 too kind 2 too expensive 3 too crowded, too many 4 too interested 5 too conservative

4 1 too far to walk 2 too hot to walk 3 too cold for me to swim 4 too expensive for us to hire 5 too old to windsurf 6 too difficult for me to learn

5 1 The authorities don't make it difficult enough for illegal immigrants to get into the USA.
2 It's too simple (for anyone) to buy a gun.
3 America's rich enough to help poorer countries more.
4 Laws aren't strict enough to stop pollution.
5 For many people medical care is too expensive (to pay for).

Unit 84

1 1 She *even* had her photograph taken with Mickey Mouse.
2 She *even* went on the Space Mountain ride,
3 She *even* bought herself a silly Donald Duck hat.
4 *Even* her friend was surprised that Jenny enjoyed it so much.
5 Jenny's *even* decided to go again next year.

2 1 he feels (OR he's feeling) even better 2 it's even louder 3 it's even hotter 4 he's feeling even thirstier 5 he's even more interested

3 1 She doesn't even know his name.
2 but he didn't even talk to her.
3 so she can't even phone him.
4 not even his address.
5 She didn't even see him leave the party.
6 not even the person who organised the party.

Unit 85

1 1 anything else 2 nothing else
3 anyone/anybody else 4 nobody/no-one else
5 anywhere else 6 nowhere else 7 anything else 8 something else

2 1 someone else 2 someone else
3 somewhere else 4 Where else 5 Or else
6 When else 7 Or else 8 Where else 9 Or else

Unit 86

1 1 in 2 in 3 in 4 in 5 at 6 on 7 on 8 At 9 at 10 in 11 at 12 in 13 in

2 1 At 2 in 3 at 4 on 6 on 7 In 9 in 10 at 11 at 12 in 13 At 15 on 16 in 17 at 18 on

3 1 In 1981. 2 In June, 1982. 3 At midnight, on October 5th, 1982. 4 In 1982, on his mother's birthday.

Unit 87

1 1 in 2 at 3 at 4 at 5 on 6 in 7 in 8 in 9 in 10 in 11 at 12 on 13 on 14 in 15 on 16 in

2 1 at 2 in 3 in 4 in 5 in 6 At 7 On 8 In 9 at 10 on 11 On 12 on 13 on

Unit 88

1 1B 2C 3A 4D 5A 6B OR C 7C

2 1 round 2 next to 3 opposite 4 behind 5 beside 6 near 7 on top of

3 1 by the river. 2 He's sitting between the two bridges. 3 He's sitting under the willow tree. 4 among the trees. 5 below the house. 6 above his head.

Unit 89

1 1 round 2 down 3 from 4 across 5 under 6 past 7 to 8 through 9 out of 10 up 11 away from 12 into

2 1 from 2 through 3 round 4 along 5 across 6 up 7 onto 8 past 9 under

3 1 from, to 2 through 3 off, onto 4 into 5 out of 6 round

Unit 90

1 1 – 2 off 3 out of 4 – 5 by 6 at 7 into
8 out of 9 to 10 by 11 in 12 on 13 to
14 by 15 – 16 in 17 at

2 1 No, he's going by plane. 2 To Barcelona.
3 No, it's non-stop to Barcelona.
4 At Heathrow airport./At the airport./At Terminal 1.
5 What time does he arrive in Barcelona?
6 When is he flying back to London?
7 At Barcelona airport./At the airport.
8 What time does his return flight arrive in London?

3 1f 2e 3g 4a 5c 6b 7d

Unit 91

1 1 I've known my wife (We've known each other) for 40 years.
2 We've lived in this area for 30 years.
3 We've had this house for 25 years.
4 I've worked at the factory for 20 years.
5 We've been grandparents for five years.

2 1 We haven't had a party (OR one) for months.
2 We haven't cleaned it since last month.
3 We haven't bought any (new clothes) since I bought those jeans.
4 We haven't seen a film (OR one) since we saw 'Repulsion'.
5 I haven't phoned them for weeks.
6 We haven't just done nothing for a long time.

3 1 Since 2 for 3 for 4 since 5 since 6 for
7 for 8 since 9 for 10 for 11 since

4 1 for 2 since 3 ago 4 ago 5 Since 6 for
7 ago 8 ago 9 ever since 10 for

Unit 92

1 1c for four and a half hours 2e during the first and second sets 3d during the third set
4a during the tie-break and he lost the set
5f for half an hour 6b during the final set, and won it

2 1 during for 2 for during 3 ✓ 4 during for
5 ✓ 6 ✓ 7 for during

3 1 while you do the washing-up. 2 While we were dancing together. 3 while I'm going out with Nigel 4 while he's doing his exams.
5 while Nigel's in Spain. 6 while he's in Barcelona.

4 1 For three weeks. 2 During the summer.
3 While he was picking oranges. 4 During the afternoon. 5 For an hour. 6 While he was in the tree. 7 For half an hour. 8 While he was talking to Adam.

Unit 93

1 1 I'll miss you desperately while I'm away.
2 As soon as I arrive, I'll ring you. (Less probable: As soon as I've arrived, I'll ring you.)
3 When I return, I'll hold you in my arms.
4 We'll get married as soon as your father gives his permission. (Alternative: We'll get married as soon as your father has given his permission.)
5 I'll never leave you while there is breath in my body.
6 I'll love you till the day I die.

2 1B 2A 3C 4C 5A 6C 7B 8A

Unit 94

1 1 until/till 2 by 3 by the time 4 until/till
5 by the time 6 until/till 7 by 8 by 9 until/till
10 by the time 11 until/till

2 1A 2C 3B 4A 5A 6B

Unit 95

1 1 As 2 as 3 like 4 like 5 like 6 like 7 like
8 like 9 like 10 like 11 Like 12 like 13 as
14 as 15 like 16 as

2 1 as if/as though we were 2 as if/as though maths was/were 3 as if/as though they were
4 as if/as though they were 5 as if/as though I was/were 6 as if/as though maths was/were

3 1g She joined the company as a receptionist.
2c Now it looks as if/as though she'll be the next managing director.
3h Because it looks as if/as though the present boss will retire early.
4f Kate's 45 but she looks as if/as though she's still only 35.
5a She dresses like a fashion model.
6b She treats everyone as if/ as though they're really important.
7d She's good at remembering things, like people's first names.
8e Last year the company made big profits, as she predicted.

4 1 as if /as though he was (OR were) a millionaire.
2 as if/as though he was (OR were) an old friend.
3 as if/as though he was (OR were) the manager.
4 as if/as though he lived in a castle.
5 as if he had a Mercedes and a Porsche.
6 as if he didn't have a wife and two children.
7 as if/as though he was (OR were) an expert.
8 as if/as though he knew him intimately

Unit 96

1 (The sentences don't have to be in this order.)
1 He's planning to go to India next month, although he hasn't got enough money to go.
2 He's never been to India before, although he's read a lot of books about it.
3 He's going to sell his car, although he won't get much money for it.
4 He's hoping his mother will lend him some money, although she's recently lost her job.
5 He's quite happy to go on his own, although he'd prefer to go with a friend.

2 1 She usually goes alone, in spite of her friends telling her she shouldn't.
2 She went sailing yesterday, in spite of the weather being bad.
3 She went out, in spite of not having a life-jacket.

3 1 He isn't very good at languages, though.
2 She's a good actress, though.
3 She likes the History of Art, though.
4 He doesn't play in a band though./He isn't in a band, though.
5 He hasn't got a girlfriend, though.

4 1 Because 2 so 3 Because 4 Because
5 so 6 since 7 since 8 so

Unit 97

1 1✓ 5✓ 6✓ 8✓
2 1 I saw a road accident today, which really upset me.
2 It was a red Ford Escort which caused the accident.
3 It had an unusual registration number which began with the letter X.
4 The driver was a young man who was wearing dark glasses.
5 He hit an old woman who was crossing the road.
6 I called an ambulance, which arrived five minutes later.
7 I took care of the old woman, who was still breathing.
8 I spoke to one of the ambulancemen, who said she was badly hurt.
9 They took her to the hospital, which is only a mile away.
10 But she died in the ambulance which was taking her to hospital.

3 1 This is a day which my wife and I will talk about for years.
2 I must thank all the people we've received presents from.
3 In particular, I'd like to thank all the people who I haven't had a chance to speak to.
4 You've given us some wonderful presents which we're very grateful for.
5 I'd like to thank the mother of the bride, who we've all depended on for so many things.
6 And finally I'd like to thank my wife, who I owe my happiness to.
7 There's one thing which I must apologise for.
8 The speech which you've just listened to has been far too long.

Unit 98

1 1 This is the hotel where I stayed.
2 This is the balcony where I had breakfast.
3 This is the taverna where we ate in the evening.
4 This is the beach where I spent most of my time.
5 This is the night club where I met Angelo.

2 1 That's where he lives.
2 Yes, that's where he often has a drink.
3 That's where he often parks his car.
4 Yes, that's where he buys his newspapers.

3 1 We're looking for a red Ford Mondeo whose boot is probably full of wine.
2 We'd like to talk to the person whose jacket we found in the store.
3 We're looking for the person whose fingerprints are on the door of the safe.
4 We'd like to interview the person whose gloves we found near the store entrance.

4 1 - 2 what 3 what 4 - 5 what 6 what
7 that 8 -

5 (These sentences could be in any order)
1 What really annoyed me was the cost.
2 What amazes me is that the buses and trains aren't integrated.
3 What we badly need is an integrated system of transport.
4 What shocked me was that they said it wasn't their problem.
5 What I really don't understand is why we have a Ministry of Transport.

Unit 99

1 a) 1e where 2a which/that 3f where 4c who
5g who 6j whose 7d who 8b whose
9h who 10i who
b) All are defining.
c) You can't omit the relative pronoun in any of the sentences, except 2a.

2 1 The following incident took place in Trenton, which is in New Jersey.
2 An elderly man, whose name was Henry Kaplin, drove into town.
3 Beside him was his neighbour, whose name was Annie Bednarska.

4 They got to the Riverside Shopping Mall, where she wanted to go shopping.

5 His passenger, who was 79 years old, got out.

6 The driver, who was in a hurry, reversed.

7 Three pedestrians shouted at him, which wasn't enough to stop him.

8 He ran her over, which resulted in her breaking a leg.

9 Police arrived at the scene of the accident, where they asked them both questions.

10 They spoke to the driver, who they discovered was deaf.

11 They also spoke to Annie Bednarska, who told them she was blind.

3 1A 2B 3C 4A 5C

Unit 100

1 When the Queen visited Barnstaple this morning, there was a big crowd waiting to see her. Half way through the visit a man with long black hair, wearing jeans and a T-shirt with 'I ♥ Her Majesty' on it, was arrested by police. The man, holding a long hatpin, rushed towards the Queen shouting 'Your Majesty!' The Queen's bodyguards, seeing the danger, jumped on him. The man, badly injured in the attack, is now in Barnstaple hospital. The Queen, touched by the man's efforts to reach her, has visited him in hospital. The hatpin found in the man's hand was hers. She'd dropped it as she approached the Civic Centre.

2 A van with green wheels, filled with conservationists all holding placards with Green Party slogans written on them and driven by a woman dressed as a penguin, travelled round the area for a week before the election.